Cognitive Styles and Classroom Learning

COGNITIVE STYLES AND CLASSROOM LEARNING

Harry Morgan

PRAEGER

Westport, Connecticut
London

Library of Congress Cataloging-in-Publication Data

Morgan, Harry, 1926–
Cognitive styles and classroom learning / Harry Morgan.
p. cm.
Includes bibliographical references and index.
ISBN 0–275–95684–9 (alk. paper)
1. Learning, Psychology of. 2. Cognitive styles in children—United States. 3. Personality and cognition—United States. 4. Individual differences in children—United States. 5. Classroom environment—United States. I. Title.
LB1060.M674 1997
370.15'23—DC20 96–36357

British Library Cataloguing in Publication Data is available.

Library of Congress Catalog Card Number: 96–36357
ISBN: 0–275–95684–9

First published in 1997

Praeger Publishers, 88 Post Road West, Westport, CT 06881
An imprint of Greenwood Publishing Group, Inc.

Printed in the United States of America

The paper used in this book complies with the Permanent Paper Standard issued by the National Information Standards Organization (Z39.48–1984).

10 9 8 7 6 5 4 3 2

This book is dedicated to the many scholars who prepared the way for this academic document. It is through their persistent endeavors that the academic community has had access to a continuous flow of research reports, philosophical monographs, and theoretical treatises that have advanced a systematic examination of cognitive style theory. This group includes, but is not limited to, Gordon Allport, Katherine C. Briggs, Jeanne S. Chall, David R. Goodenough, Maxine Greene, Jerome Kagan, Nathan Kogan, Manuel Ramirez, Samuel Messick, Allan F. Mirsky, Isabel Briggs Myers, Philip K. Oltman, Stephanie L. Shipman, Virginia C. Shipman, and Herman A. Witkin.

Contents

Acknowledgments

I am indebted to friends, colleagues and students for their assistance in assuring the quality and quantity of this work. I gratefully acknowledge the contributions of the many people who provided their knowledge, their wisdom and labor in various ways. This group includes, but is not limited to Janet Baty, Ellen J. Gruber, Paul L. Phillips, Gwen C. McAlpine, Anne C. Richards, Elaine P. Roberts, and Tyrone Smith.

Illustrations

Cognitive Styles and Classroom Learning

Introduction

> He seemed to know the soft, hard, and bumpy places in the field and just how high a ball would bounce on them. From the flags on the stadium roof he noted the way the wind would blow the ball, and he was quick at fishing it out of the tricky undercurrents on the ground. Not sun, not shadow, nor smoke-haze bothered him, and when a ball was knocked against the wall he estimated the angle of the rebound and speared it as if its course had been plotted on a chart. He was good at gauging slices and knew when to charge the pill to save on the throw. Once he put his head down and ran ahead of the shot. Though the crowd rose with a thunderous warning, he caught it with his back to the wall and did a little jig to show he was alive. Everyone laughed with relief. . . . He was a natural.
>
> —Bernard Malamud

There are many examples of higher-level thinking in the processing of information by children who under traditional circumstances appear unable to perform classroom tasks to the satisfaction of their teachers. For example, in various cities where major sports teams occasionally play through final play-off games, many children who are not particularly successful in school mathematics or classroom reading assignments seem to have little trouble figuring out the meaning of batting averages or how to spell the names of their favorite athletes. It is also true that many children who do not read well in school have almost no trouble understanding and writing the words of songs that have swept their neighborhood in popularity. Knowledge acquired by these learners through out-of-school experiences have been self-selected through their own cognitive preferences for solving the problems of difficult word sounds and math skills that they have acquired—frequently on their own.

Because of various individual cognitive preferences, learners appear to have skills available to them under some circumstances, and in some situations, that are not necessarily available to them at other times. Some skills seem available to them during out-of-school experiences (those that are more under their control) that might not be available to them in the quiet settings of the classroom. Adults are often surprised when young children expand beyond adult's expectations.

Gordon Allport, in his book *Personality: A Psychological Interpretation,* published in 1937, was among the first to refer to particularized modes of processing information utilized by individuals as styles. Since that time thousands of articles have been written about differentiated patterns of perceiving, thinking, and problem solving in various situations under different conditions. Cognitive style studies have entered the scholarly domains of education, psychology, anthropology, social work, counseling, and many others.

This book will select the most commonly known cognitive styles that have been systematically studied by psychologists and educators and describe how this knowledge can enable classroom teachers to expand the number of ways in which children can experience teaching and learning activities. This writing also intends to create an awareness of the possibilities for youth experiences among college and university educators, grade school teachers, counselors, psychologists, social workers, administrators of educational programs, and the informed public. Within the context of the aforementioned, it strives to provide a useful body of knowledge and critical perspective for policy makers, behavioral scientists, and all human service professionals who provide group and individual services to children and young adults. This book will also bring attention to the importance of valuing learners, educators, and others involved in the teaching/learning process as individuals important in their own right, and not merely a human aggregate whose presence contributes solely toward constituting a school or a classroom.

The attentive teacher learns very early that children bring a variety of personal capabilities to each classroom experience. Ideas put forth in this book are intended to encourage all educators to be receptive to various ways in which children process information—not limited to those "authorized" in this book. To the contrary, all educators with the time and inclination have the potential to become their own "authority" on being able to recognize the personalized variations employed by pupils in their processing of information.

There are personalized characteristics that emerge from various experiences that each child has had prior to—and continually outside of—the school experience. Such experiences will contribute to the formation of values, interests, and even become personality traits. And there will be an intermix of these acquisitions with elements that are common to the growth and development of all children. Cognitive style theorist and researcher Samuel Messick stressed that individual differences make a difference.

Each individual has preferred ways of organizing what he sees and remembers and thinks about. Consistent individual differences in these ways of organizing and processing information and experience have come to be called cognitive styles. These styles represent consistencies in the manner or form of cognition, as distinct from the content or the level of skill displayed in the cognitive performance. They are conceptualized as stable attitudes, preferences, or habitual strategies determining a person's typical modes of perceiving, remembering, thinking, and problem solving. As such, their influence extends to almost all human activities that implicate cognition, including social and interpersonal functioning. (1976, p 4-5)

As discussed in Chapter 3, the two most common cognitive styles that have been defined and tested by psychologists are field dependent and field independent. These two styles are linked in descriptions because they have somewhat opposite meanings along a bipolar plane. Persons who are more field independent are able to pick out objects that have surroundings that might hide them from view. For example, they can easily see fruit on a vine or tree even though the colors might not be very different from the leaves and branches.

In other words, field independent persons are able to view objects in a manner as if such objects are independent from other parts of the scene. On the other hand, field dependent learners are less able to view things as separate from the overall environment and would have greater difficulty viewing fruit as standing apart from the tree or surrounding foliage. Therefore, field dependent learners prefer that things remain in their total context to enable them to better understand the meaning of their individual parts. In social settings, the field dependent style person prefers group interaction, while the field independent style person would prefer to interact with individuals or act independently.

From the perspective of children's educative processes, this book makes substantial contributions toward an understanding of philosophies and theories concerned with how youth make meaning from their experiences. It is designed to create an awareness among parents and educators of the diversification of cognitive preferences among learners as they acquire new information. This writing will describe classroom practices that can provide self-valuing opportunities for our youth within friendship groups in their schools and neighborhoods, during their dinner table conversations with parents and other family members, and during their varieties of simple daily rituals.

Chapter 1 deals with the philosophical foundations of cognitive style theories. Every professional endeavor of substance is influenced by philosophies that have been previously developed. This is probably more true for those who provide human services than for any other group. Educators, psychologists, social workers, and those in the medical profession, to name a few, are all guided by philosophical approaches to work. Some have missions guided primarily by a single philosophical context, while others are eclectic having created their own variation by combining several philosophies with which they are impressed. The discussion of various philosophies that have influenced cognitive styles places Chapter 1 in an important strategic position to set the stage for readers who are seeking a deeper understanding of cognitive style theories.

Chapter 2 is a discussion of the theoretical basis for cognitive styles and how various ideas have contributed to the foundations of knowledge acquisition and human performance as influenced through cognitive preferences. The role of the brain and its central nervous system is discussed in light of what we now know about neuronal theory and the processing of information from our experiences. It is rather remarkable that one hundred years ago Sigmund Freud theorized the roles of the central nervous system and neurons in our acquisition of information. The state of what was known at that time, and a lack of interest from colleagues, led Freud to abandon his "Project for a Scientific Psychology." Since the time of Freud's frustrations with his quest for a scientific theory of psychology, scholars in anatomy, biochemistry, cognitive science, neurology, neurobiology, and physiology have conducted studies to unravel the mysteries of how we process new information—and the work is still in progress

Some theorists have attempted to describe the brain in terms of how computers function. Hard-wired information processing models have been deemed to be too unlike the human information system and have been abandoned by many theorists. Because cognitive preferences imply significant variations in how individuals come to know things, the ways in which information is processed by the organism is therefore critical to an understanding of cognitive style theory. Chapter 2 attempts to provide that understanding from general theories of learning.

Chapter 3 explores field independent/field dependent perception. This construct of cognitive styles is usually presented in a bipolar plane between two extremes. This matched pair of cognitive styles has been investigated and described more than any other set of cognitive preferences. When they first appeared almost fifty years ago, field independent individuals were defined as the preferred student because their analytical approach to academic work and problem solving tended to match classroom expectations of the times. It is also true that field independent learners preferred academic experiences that were primarily of a didactic nature and therefore more compatible with how classroom teachers of that period were trained.

It was a natural outgrowth of traditional classroom expectations during these early years when cognitive preferences were emerging in personality and learning theory that the cognitive styles of field dependent learners were negatively valued. They demonstrated difficulty in differentiating elements of an experience, whether it involved a social event or a task of problem solving. Field dependent learners also preferred to interact in groups, while their field independent agemates preferred to work independently in problem solving while more often than not avoiding social interaction. Classrooms of the times were steeped in the etiquette of quietude, a style that appeared to favor field independent learners.

Within the past decade, as classroom teachers have become less likely to define differences of information processing among students as academic deficits, the social and global approach to processing information that field dependent students bring to the classroom, has been creatively integrated into various classroom formats. Cooperative learning, individual and small group assignments, and whole language approaches to teaching language arts and reading are but a few. Field independence/field dependence preferences continue to attract the research interests of psychologists and educators and remain the most popular cognitive styles in literature today.

In a sense, the theoretical foundations inherent in the work of practitioners can be viewed as a steady stream of influences from generation to generation. From this linear process, it is reasonable to expect that the systems of teaching and learning will improve as our philosophies and theories are examined in light of the quality of our practice. It is therefore essential that an examination of teaching practice and school curriculum be studied from the perspectives of their underlying philosophy, theory, and practice.

Following the chapters that explore philosophical and theoretical foundations relevant to cognitive styles, each of the remaining chapters will define a cognitive style construct and describe human characteristics that are associated with these styles. These descriptions are aimed at the practice of teaching and where appropriate, research and evaluating instruments associated with particular styles will be discussed.

As educators assimilated the basic concepts of cognitive styles into their scholarly activities, they started to investigate other personalized qualities that individual learners bring to the classroom and the extent to which matching the teacher's cognitive style to the learner's cognitive style might yield more productive classrooms. These general themes were pursued in relationship to gender, culture, social class, and racial differences between the environment and the learner. Here, the environment is considered everything within the learner's purview including the teacher and peers.

Comparisons were also made among many significant variables like music, linguistics, creativity, analytical reasoning, mathematics, reading skills, and social adjustment in the school environment. And, more recently, studies have begun to examine the relationship between cognitive style and success in computer studies.

An examination of classroom learning, by necessity, calls for an informed perspective of the experiences of classroom teachers, students, and their supporting school personnel. Practicum assignments like student teaching, conducting case studies, and other classroom observational activities, provide teachers-in-training, and their university-based professors, the content for an analysis of the meaning of what was observed during classroom experiences. Essential factors for consideration would include philosophies and theories that influenced the teacher's approach to work (practice), and the benefits that were derived by children who experienced these school activities.

Cognitive style theory suggests that individuals utilize different patterns in acquiring knowledge. Cognitive refers to the processes involved in the overall act of processing information in becoming knowledgeable. It includes perception, judgment, values, and memory. Style is used here in very much the same manner as in everyday speaking terms, in that, we often do things in a different manner than someone else might in carrying out the same act. As a part of the term cognitive style, *style* implies that as individuals, we employ personal characteristics in the acquisition of knowledge, and more often than not, approach a learning experience in ways that differ from other individuals.

Cognitive style is not an indication of one's level of intelligence, but a description of the unique ways employed by learners in acquiring new information. Information is presented to us in various ways, sometimes through experiences that we initiate, such as when we select a hobby or read a book; at other times through experiences provided by significant adults during child rearing; or by other persons, such as during classroom activities when we are students.

Classroom experiences are intended to increase the knowledge of learners, and successful teachers vary the ways in which information is presented. Part of the time, teachers are lecturing to the entire class, and learners are expected to remain quiet and relatively inactive. There are other times when children are engaged in group activities or individual assignments where they are expected to be active. We now know that some children demonstrate a greater potential for processing information in an active setting than in a quiet one. And, there are learners who prefer to work alone rather than in groups.

Classroom teaching sessions are sometimes followed by written or oral responses to questions or problems posed by the teacher. This enables children to demonstrate what new information they have acquired. The teacher will evaluate the pupil's response, and imply from the student's performance that a certain amount of learning has taken place. The word imply is important here because the teacher does not know for certain how much the student has learned from a particular lesson solely by how well the student performs on an oral or written test, because we do not know the extent to which performance matches capacity. It is also true that tests are written in various styles and some styles are more complex to fully decipher for some children than others. So, instead of measuring the knowledge that the tests purport to measure, in reality, the teacher might be measuring how well particular students perform on different types of tests.

Research in psychology has informed us that our various styles of processing information have been influenced by the environment in which we spent our childhood. There are differences, for example, in the way children who were confined to a play pen process information compared to those who were allowed, under the watchful eyes of adults, to explore the entire house and learn to walk by climbing stairs and holding on to furniture during critical years of early development. The time during which children are learning to use their muscles for sitting up, crawling, standing, and walking is a period in which they are giving a great deal of thought about how these skills are being accomplished. Child development experts have also suggested that this important learning period, from birth to the age of twenty-four months, is the time frame within which we develop foundations for a later understanding of how things work in logical and mathematical terms. The different experiences that children are encouraged to have during this early period of growth will influence their capacity to process information later in life.

Today a common resolution for problems that emerge between active youth and school authorities is a referral to a physician that culminates in a prescription for Ritalin. This is done primarily to ease the frustrations that parents, teachers, and administrators encounter with children who cannot or will not conform to the etiquette of family and/or the institution. A conservative estimate suggests that approximately one million U.S. school children are taking Ritalin, or some other mind-altering prescribed drugs designed to modify their behavior. Many other students obtain Ritalin from their classmates illegally and use it as something to get them through the day. More discussion of this phenomenon appears in Chapter 4 on cognitive preferences associated with reflectivity and impulsivity. Here as in the case of field independent/field dependent cognitive styles, one dimension has been identified as more desirable than the other. Scholars involved in cognitive style research have made serious attempts to resurrect impulsivity/reflectivity from negative/positive paradigms.

Chapter 4 also introduces a modern trend in teacher education sometimes called *the reflective teacher* that involves journal writing, professional discourse, and action research. Theoretical foundations for this approach to professional training originated in models employed in psychiatry, social work, psychotherapy, counseling, and allied fields.

Chapter 5 explores historical perspectives and what is now known about the cognitive style conceptualization. Theories of perception, personality development, and self-concept are central to an understanding of the work associated with this cognitive preference. Themes, categories, and organizing associated with sorting tasks are important elements in measuring the nature of conceptualizing as a cognitive preference.

Chapter 6 is concerned with the work of Katherine C. Briggs and her daughter Isabel Briggs Myers in developing a psychological instrument of great value to practitioners. Since the early 1970s, the Myers-Briggs Type Indicator (MBTI) has been used by psychologists, educators, and other human service providers to describe selected types of personalities and cognitive style preferences. The unique history of the MBTI, with its roots in the work of Carl Gustav Jung, is blended into an understanding of one of today's most widely used measures of normal attitudes and behavior as they contribute to assessments of cognitive styles. Jung's work also contributed considerably to the broader philosophical foundations of cognitive style theory in general, and this is discussed in Chapter l.

Leveling versus Sharpening as cognitive preferences is described in Chapter 7. This paradigm was first introduced in the 1950s and gained considerable attention through the 1980s along with a related construct called Scanning. Psychoanalytic foundations associated with these domains are also explored.

The final chapter offers conclusions from various perspectives concerning the current state of the art and the many ways in which cognitive style theory has expanded our views of the influence that experience can exert on educators, learners, and the learning environment. These conclusions are framed within the general context of the philosophy, theory, and practice of what has been identified by others as the field of critical theory.

REFERENCES

Allport, Gordon. (1937). *Personality: A Psychological Interpretation.* New York: Henry Holt and Company.

Malamud, Bernard. (1980). *The Natural.* Avon Books.

Messick, Samuel. (1976). *Individuality in Learning.* San Francisco: Jossey-Bass.

1

Philosophical Foundations of Cognitive Style

> Life is largely a process of adaptation to the circumstances in which we exist. A perennial give-and-take has been going on between living matter and its inanimate surroundings, between one living being and another, ever since the dawn of life in the prehistoric oceans. The secret of health and happiness lies in successful adjustment to the ever-changing conditions on this globe; the penalties for failure in this great process of adaptation are disease and unhappiness.
>
> —Hans Selye

Professional knowledge that is brought to the classroom by teachers has been influenced by *their* experiences as students in university-based teacher education programs. Professors in university settings, who served as their teachers, were in turn, also influenced by thinkers and scholars who came before them. Philosophical beliefs, more often than not, form the values that direct classroom practice, research interests, and ultimate discoveries by scholars who are active in various fields of study. The work of scholars and thinkers in various fields of study is represented in the university-based curriculum and those active in promoting it. Information derived from this process will ultimately influence the relationship between teachers who take courses in these programs and children in classrooms where they teach.

Cognitive style theory describes relationships between the learner and the environment. Central to this relationship is the role of the individual in various experiences. In human experiences there are investments of self with various intensities.

From the philosophical perspective of phenomenology, experience has two dimensions. Objects of consciousness is one dimension of human experience, and it prevails at the level of our ordinary awareness. Acts of consciousness is the other dimension, and it involves perceptions, values, and the conscious processing of information. These two dimensions are related in significant ways, and this relationship is labeled intentionality by phenomenologists. In *Landscapes of Learning*, Maxine Greene captures the pragmatic nature of this theme.

> Consciousness is always *of* something; it is characterized by intentionality. To say that I am conscious of someone approaching me is to say that I am perceiving a figure down the street as a man coming closer and closer to my space. As he comes nearer to me, I may intuit a threatening quality in his stance . . . or I may suddenly remember that he was once a coworker of mine. Who he turns out to be, for me, depends upon the way I finally become conscious of him. At best I can only come in touch with certain aspects of the man, because my understanding of him depends upon my vantage point and previous experiences. I know that there are sides to him that are hidden from me; there are profiles of his personality, of his character, that are out of my reach. . . . Consciousness as perspective grasping is our way of encountering the natural and human world. (1978, 14-15)

Phenomenology is a philosophy that has been a subject of scholarly pursuit in various fields of study like education, psychology, psychiatry, social work, theology, anthropology, and other social sciences. Phenomenology focuses primarily on individual experiences as a basis for analysis. It is theorized that as individuals we process new information derived from our experiences, and the act of experiencing is influenced by knowledge acquired from previous experiences. The knowledge that is retained from various experiences—formal and informal—can be limited by our life circumstances and what we bring to the experience. Therefore, individuals are involved in a natural process of attempting to expand upon the conscious awareness that results from experiences. This effort is limited by previous experiences that have influenced our ideas, beliefs, and wishes and limits to a degree how we think about certain phenomena.

Phenomenologists theorize that individuals attempt to deal with these limitations through creative imagination. These acts of imagining enable individuals to expand upon the meanings derived from an experience by increasing the possibility for variations through thought. This method of expansion is called fantasy variations. It is not possible to remove limiting factors completely, and what remains from the experience and fantasy variations is called the essence. Fundamental to phenomenological thought is the belief that individual interpretations of experiences cannot be invalidated by the emergence of a proposed objective truth. Philosophers and other scholars with major interests in phenomenology have established common interests with existential philosophers and scholars.

Founded by German philosophers Immanuel Kant and Georg

Wilhelm Fredrich Hegel, existentialism rejected the prevailing scholarly thought that dominated European philosophy during the 1800s. European philosophers of great influence during that time defined philosophy as an objective science with the capacity to report universal truths. Kant, Hegel, and their followers insisted that the scientific methods prevailing at that time were inappropriate for the study of philosophical issues. Objective methods seeking certainties, they argued, would obscure a study of experiences as the basic principles of individual existence.

G.W.F. Hegel (1770-1831) remains as one of the most influential German philosophers of his time. It was his philosophy that was related to his dialectic for which he is most remembered. Here he theorized three phases of dialectic emergence: thesis, antithesis, and synthesis. Even though the area of Hegel's dialectic development gained great attention, as well as his interpretations of social, political, and historical issues, it is his ideas related to the inner self that are significant for existential phenomenologists. In this regard, he extended dialectic thought to all areas of the human experience. Hegel argued that we all strive for an inner tranquility. When individuals attempt to achieve inner harmony and tranquility through external wealth, influence, and power, whatever conflict might emerge is usually resolved in favor of inner states. Such conflicts can be avoided, Hegel theorized, if one's external activity emerged from an inner state that is tranquil and harmonious.

Long before Edmund Husserl's interest in psychology, Hegel studied forms of consciousness, ethics, social organization, and human maturation and discussed these complex issues in his book *Phenomenology of Spirit,* published in 1807. Approximately five years later he published *Science of Logic;* and in 1821—almost forty years before Husserl's birth—he published *Philosophy of Right,* in which he analyzed some of the same ethical issues.

Nonetheless, it was Edmund Husserl, born of Jewish merchant parents and later baptized as a Protestant, who many credit as the founder of phenomenology. He pursued recognition for phenomenology as a serious scientific approach to an understanding of individuality. For Husserl, the most natural setting for an understanding of individuality is experience.

Focusing our experiencing gaze on our own psychic life necessarily takes place as reflection, as a turning about of a glance which had previously been directed elsewhere. Every experience can be subject to such reflection, as can indeed every manner in which we occupy ourselves with any real or ideal objects—for instance, thinking or in the modes of feeling and will, valuing and striving. So when we are fully engaged in conscious activity, we focus exclusively on the specific thing, thoughts, values, goals or means involved, but not on the psychical

> experience as such, in which these things are known as such. Only reflection reveals this to us. . . . Through reflection instead of grasping simply the matter straight-out—the values, the goals, the instrumentalities—we grasp the corresponding subjective experiences in which we become "conscious" of them. . . . For this reason they become "phenomena," and their most general essential character is to exist as . . . perception *of* something, recalling *of* something, thinking *of* something, hoping *for* something, fearing something, striving *for* something, deciding *on* something, and so on. If this realm of what we call "phenomena" proves to be the possible field for a pure psychological discipline related exclusively to phenomena, we can understand the designation of it as *phenomenological psychology.* The terminological expression . . . for designating the basic character of being as consciousness of something, is *intentionality.* (Zaner and Ihde, 1973, 50)

During the late 1800s, philosophers in England and Germany were looking to psychology as the area of discourse from which a coherent theory of knowledge and logic could emerge. It was a period when philosophers, psychologists, and scholars of scientific thought were attempting to apply the rigors of scientific methods to complex problems of logic. This period of advanced thought in philosophy and psychology has been identified by various scholars as the emergence of a new psychology for that time called *psychologism.*

As in any new theoretical emergence of thought in a discipline, not all scholars who explored psychologism had common agreement about its value as a scientific approach to a study of knowledge and thought. And some scientists of that time, whose work was embraced by this group, rejected this new "scientific" pathway.

Ivan Petrovich Pavlov (1849-1936) was among the critics who was disdainful of psychology as a science. Pavlov received the Nobel Prize in 1904 for his laboratory work on the digestive system. Pavlov rejected the idea of psychology as an area of study that could be "scientific." He identified physiology as the empirical science of the human condition and rejected any attempts to identify himself as a psychologist. He was reported to have fired any laboratory assistant who referred to his or her work as psychology or psychologism.

Ironically, Pavlov is credited with being a major influence on John Broadus Watson (1878-1958), a psychologist who many considered the founder of behaviorism in the United States. After graduating from the University of Chicago, Watson became a research professor at Johns Hopkins University. The influence of Pavlov's work on Watson's theories was pervasive. He argued that all theories that emerged from philosophies that proposed innate individual differences, concepts of the self, and emotional behavior in general were variations of behaviorism, or they were nonexistent. He reduced human behavior to a few simple reflexes; reactions to fear (loud noises, sudden loss of support), love (fondling and stroking), and rage (evoked by such conditions as tight confinement).

Human behaviors, proposed Watson, were the result of classical conditioning in the Pavlovian tradition. In an experiment that brought much criticism to him from the professional community, Watson demonstrated how a negative emotion could come from a negative stimuli. Here, Watson's subject was a boy, less than a year old, who was shown a white rat at the same time a loud noise was made by hitting a steel bar with a hammer. After seven trials, "Little Albert" started crying and attempted to avoid the rat. Little Albert could have been conditioned to pair a positive experience (feeling) with the rat, or two different positive experiences could have been paired, but conditioning does not constitute the whole of human information processing as proposed by Watson.

Watson ended his career after colleagues became highly critical of his writing for various magazines like *Cosmopolitan, Harper's, and McCall's.* It is interesting to note, that two decades after J. B. Watson's fall from grace, a popular psychology magazine—*Psychology Today*—became successful in the general public and in the academic community.

From the late 1890s through the 1920s, Husserl wrote extensively on the topic of psychological studies in logic, and it was within this context that he sought methods to systematically study and apply knowledge as content and integrate that knowledge with the meaning of human experience. Within the same time frame, Watson wrote "Psychology as a Behaviorist Views It" (1913), and "Conditioned Emotional Reactions" (1920), the latter being the "Little Albert" study.

Husserl was influenced by Franz Brentano, a philosopher who emerged as Husserl's mentor, with whom he frequently confided during their lifetime.

> In Brentano's view the true method of philosophy is the method of the natural sciences. He accordingly regarded philosophy as being scientific in character, and he thought that the possibility of basing knowledge upon immediate evidence would provide a presuppositionless beginning in philosophy. The following five propositions may serve to characterize Brentano's philosophy: (1) The basic structure of human existence or of subjectivity is intentionality. (2) Every intentional act refers to something real, "real" meaning everything that comes from concrete intuition or that which can be presented. (3) Every cognition refers to an existing thing. (4) Every existent is a single individual thing. (5) Every cognition apprehends the existent as something general. (Farber, 1943, 11)

The influence of Brentano can be recognized in Husserl's proposal that perception was not the same as thoughts and images created by individuals. In his efforts to describe imagination as an essential element in phenomenology, he was confronted by empirical scholars who thought that imagination and thoughts existed as matter embedded in consciousness. Husserl argued that the essence of an experience rested on a consciousness that had an awareness of its own imagination—and at the same time transcended this knowing as an intentional act.

The theme of intent that flowed through the writings of Husserl can be recognized in the work on brain theory fifty years later. In *The Working Brain: An Introduction to Neuropsychology* (1973) by Alexander Luria, the human brain is described as *intentionally* selecting, transforming and organizing information. It has also been reported that individuals actively construct their own meaning from experiences and are not solely passive recipients of observed events.

The general set of ideas associated with neurological aspects of Husserl's work, will be identified later in Chapter 2 as they relate to evolution and the brain from the work of Gerald Edelman. Edelman proposes an intriguing set of ideas that imply preexisting brain structures that are not restricted to sensory experiences.

Born in Czechoslovakia, Edmund Husserl (1859-1938) has had more written about his philosophical ideas than many commonly known philosophers. After a traditional classical education in Vienna, he studied science and mathematics at the University of Leipzig. He followed these studies with a graduate assistantship at the University of Berlin.

It was during his return for additional graduate work at the University of Vienna that he became fascinated with psychology from the lectures of Franz Brentano. The redirection of his career to philosophy, however, could not supplant his earlier studies in mathematics and physical science. From the beginning, Husserl's search for a coherent theory of phenomenology was often an integration of his form of philosophy with scientific methods of exploration from his mathematics and science beginnings. As a professor at Freiburg in Breisgau, Husserl devoted his career to various themes of phenomenology and attracted hundreds of students and followers who have since become important in their own right.

Immanuel Kant (1724-1804), one of the original founders of the existential movement, argued that individual mental processes are actively involved in objects and events that are experienced. Beyond this, he believed that individuals can have knowledge of what they haven't experienced only if there remains a *possibility* of it becoming an experience. In essence, Kant was supporting the concept of intuition. This philosophical belief was important for its time because views held by scholars prior to Kant's popularity argued that our minds generalized knowledge gained from experiences and, therefore, our knowledge could extend beyond actual experiences. David Hume, a philosopher who Kant studied and respected, argued that individuals were limited by actual experiences because we cannot be certain about phenomena beyond our experiences. The prevailing thought among European philosophers of the time was at variance with Hume's arguments because it interfered with the prevailing theological belief in God. Hume argued that such beliefs must be articles of faith because, in the absence of a direct experience, a belief in God could not be proved or disproved. Nevertheless, the role of experience in the interpretation of a shared reality was central to practically all of the philosophical arguments of that time.

When professionals associated with educational systems approach their work with formalized objective truths about the role of teacher and learner, a restrictive environment emerges for those who cannot fulfill the expectations of the system because they bring a personalized or creative spirit to the environment. Teachers and learners in such a system are often discouraged from expanding upon the system's expectations.

Early in the 1970s, following an annual meeting of the Philosophy of Education Society, a group of scholars called a meeting to discuss the relationship between phenomenology, existentialism, and education. In an atmosphere where historical connections are often too complex to analyze, and one in which present day communication among scholars creates an illusive common ground, philosophers still persist in creating compatibleness between phenomenological and existential thought.

Existentialism is a philosophy with major concerns about individual experience in society. Basic to existential thought is the belief that all human choices are ultimately embedded in our experiences, which make these choices subjective. According to existentialists, laws, rules, folkways, and traditions are external standards and not particularly helpful because individuals must make their own choices and are ultimately responsible for their choices.

Existentialists believe that individuals are fully free to choose their own pathways, therefore, they are also fully responsible for their choices. For existentialists, freedom is always accompanied by responsibility. Many existentialists consider freedom the pleasant side of the equation, and responsibility is often the unpleasant side. Individuals are committed to both sides, and this bipolar situation can be the cause of human discomfort. Individual unpleasantness can emerge with the awareness that we are responsible for our expressions of beliefs and behaviors associated with personal decisions. Existentialists believe that the burden of personal responsibility for one's own beliefs and behaviors has the potential for creating anxiety in the minds of individuals who wish to avoid this aspect of the equation.

Jean-Paul Sartre (1905-1980), existentialist scholar, philosopher, activist, and writer, has been credited with popularizing existentialist thought. He studied phenomenology in Berlin and taught philosophy at the Lycee Condorcet. Among his many interpretations of existential thought, he sought to define imagination in existential terms as compatible with Husserl's arguments for phenomenologists.

Sartre thus sets out to develop Husserl's contention that imagining is to be distinguished from perceiving not by reference to the objects it intends, but by reference to the act of intending. The mental image is not just a thing existing along side other things; it is a unique orientation of consciousness towards things. . . . What defines the imaginary world, and also the world of the real, is an attitude of mind. The image and the percept are not therefore different *objects* of consciousness; they are different ways of being *conscious* of objects. (Kearney, 1991, 49)

In other scholarly works, Sartre argued against Freud's approach to psychoanalysis. He agreed with Jung, that Freud's emphasis on sexual forces obscured a greater meaning that was necessary for a deeper understanding of individual experience as a basis for psychoanalysis. Eventually he developed what he called *existential psychoanalysis*. Sartre's most well-read works include, *Being and Nothingness* (1943), *No Exit* (1944), and *Sketch for a Theory of the Emotions* (1948). There is clear evidence of his existential thought in these writings; however, his approach to psychoanalysis is more evident in a series of biographies that he wrote that included *Baudelaire, Saint Genet,* and *Flaubert.*

Sartre was also read by psychologists, educators, sociologists, and political scientists. His theories associated with these disciplines appeared in, *Critique of Dialectic Reason* (1964). Sartre's belief in existential philosophy, and its fundamental meaning for him, was expressed in these thoughts:

The first effects of existentialism is that it puts every man in possession of himself as he is, and places the entire responsibility for his existence squarely upon his own shoulders. And, when we say that man is responsible for himself, we do not mean that he is responsible for his own individuality, but he is responsible for all men. (Kaufmann, 1965, 291)

Existential philosophers believe that the individual must fully accept freedom and the responsibility that emerges from any experience, and this acceptance will enable individuals to live more meaningful lives. Individuals who are frightened by this freedom, possibly because of the responsibility it requires, will be victims of anxiety which, according to existentialists, can cause a flight from freedom. Further, in an effort to reduce the symptoms of anxiety (caused by rejecting freedom because one does not want to accept responsibility), the individual engages in what existentialists call self-deception. Existentialists with a psychoanalytic orientation would discuss these issues in terms of neurosis.

The message of existential thought has been expressed in scholarly writings as well as in novels, plays, and motion pictures. The Japanese motion picture of the 1950s, *Rashomon;* Richard Wright's novel *The Outsider;* and Alan Paton's novel in the 1950s depicting relationships between Blacks and Whites in Southern Africa, titled *Cry the Beloved Country,* are examples of existentialism expressed in public media.

Messages of existential thought in the literary world are often designed to interpret and display the philosophy from its more unpleasant sides. Existential thought, which is central to unfolding patterns in novels and dramatizations by playwrights, depicts life's futile consequences, suicidal tendencies evoked by dread and disappointments from life's experiences, difficulties individuals encounter in maintaining lasting relationships with significant others, anxiety, and brooding that can emerge from individual day-to-day experiences.

The selection of extreme experiences from life, and variations in the interpretation of those experiences as existential and phenomenological themes, was central to the plot of the Japanese movie *Rashomon.* The movie starts with three men—a woodcutter, a priest, and a commoner—who just happen to congregate in an old abandoned temple as shelter from a severe rain storm. The woodcutter, whose work involved roaming through the forest seeking trees to cut, starts to utter comments of personal disgust because of his observations of human cruelty and experiences with the dishonesty of individuals which seem to him to be a general pattern of life. When the woodcutter is pressed by individuals in the group to be more specific about his observations, he starts to describe the details of an experience that he had in the forest. As the woodcutter's story unfolds, the film cuts to a Japanese nobleman, dressed in Samurai regalia, holding a sword strapped to his side, leading a horse by its reins while walking along a tranquil path in the forest. His attractive wife, wearing a long, white flowing seductive garment and a wide brimmed hat that shaded her face from the occasional rays of sun that filtered through the tree leaves, was riding astride the horse. Eventually they were attacked, robbed, and the woman was raped.

The woodcutter described how he became suspicious after finding several personal articles in various places in the forest. He then describes how he overheard the details of the attack and rape as told to the magistrate by a bandit who was arrested for the crime.

The bandit told the magistrate that he approached this striking couple and tricked the husband, then tied him to a tree. He said that he had intended to rape the wife, but to his surprise she gave in to him. As he was about to leave the woman with her husband still tied to the tree, the wife goaded the two men into a fight over her permanent affection. In this fight, the bandit boasted that he had killed the husband with a sword, and the wife ran away.

The priest, who had been speaking about the sinfulness of humanity in general, revealed that he had overheard the wife tell the magistrate a different version. In her story, she admitted giving herself to the bandit, and after the sexual act, her husband rejected her with stares of silent hatred. She was so distraught by her husband's hatred that she killed him with the dagger.

A third version was told to the magistrate through the words of a medium who contacted the spirit of the slain Samurai. The version of the slain man came through the lip-sync of the medium, sounding like words spoken out of a deep chamber. Through the mouth of the medium, he told the magistrate that after his wife had given herself to the bandit, she tried to get the bandit to murder him. The bandit refused and walked off in disgust. Also through the spirit voice, he said that in the face of the personal humiliation, he took his dagger and killed himself in the noble Samurai tradition.

Finally the woodcutter admits that he did not tell all of what he had witnessed. He said that after the rape the husband did express disgust with his wife's actions, and in her anger she goaded the two men into a fight. In the fight, the bandit killed the husband with a sword, and the wife fled from the scene.

The dagger that was a possible murder weapon (the wife's version), and the suicide weapon (the spirit's version), was not found. The bandit said that he sold the sword that he used in the battle that ended in the husband's death, and he rode off on the husband's horse. He also said that their "swords crossed" so many times that fatigue overcame him and he was caught while taking a nap on the beach.

The woodcutter said that the bandit did steal the horse, but having such a poor knowledge of riding, he was thrown into the water by the horse. Authorities recognized the stolen horse, and the bandit's injuries from the fall made it easy for the police to arrest him.

As these various versions are shared, the cries of an infant are overheard in the corner of the old temple where the men are talking. They discover an abandoned infant crying because of exposure to the cold and rain as the commoner is stealing the blankets in which the infant is wrapped. The woodcutter attacks the commoner for this lowly act and suggested that this was another example of the depths to which humanity has fallen.

The commoner, in his own defense, suggests that if he did not take these wrappings for his own use, they would only be left for the next person to take. He also attacked the woodcutter for not revealing the whole story in his first telling and suggested that his reason for not doing so was that he had stolen the missing dagger and probably benefited from its sale, and there is a veiled suspicion that he might have been the murderer. A sense of shame overcame the woodcutter as the commoner ran off into the rainy night with the baby's blanket.

Only the priest and the woodcutter are now left in the old temple as the rain stops. The saddened and guilt-laden woodcutter picks up the baby. The priest, who is suspicious of the woodcutter's motives, attempts to remove the infant from his arms. The woodcutter assures the priest that his intentions are to care for the infant along with his other children, because caring for one more child would not be a difficult matter.

In expected symbolic fashion, the rain stops, the sun begins to shine, and the woodcutter and the priest leave their shelter from the rain and enter the brightness of the new day. The symbolism of bright sunshine following the gloom of darkness and rain, to bring closure to *Rashomon,* was a common metaphor in motion pictures of the times. The recognition that each version of the experience, as told by different characters, was given equal credibility, however, was uncommon for the 1940s and 1950s. More often than not, popular motion pictures and stage plays of the times sought to provide their audiences with an objective truth. This motion picture also went to deeper psychological depths than any contemporary film. *Rashomon* created a popular discussion and brought media attention to this knew dramatic approach to describing an experience.

To the phenomenologist, even if there were a perfectly objective version of the attack and rape as they actually occurred, such a version would not be a model for the interpretation of this experience, by those who experienced it. In phenomenology, phenomena are dealt with in terms of the experiencer's perceptions and interpretations; and objective empiricism is suspended. This does not mean that one must suspend one's belief in *reality;* but rather, *reality* should not be objectified or offered as a model to supplant the individual's *perceptions of experience.*

Existentialists and phenomenologists have been criticized for dwelling on the dark sides of human experiences in order to describe the basic elements of their philosophies. Philosophers have pointed out that, despite the fact that their examples frequently dwell on the dark sides of human experiences, real life experiences match—and often surpass—the dread and brooding that are central to fictional depictions of existentialism and phenomenology. For example, during the military conflict between the United States and Vietnam, one of the strategies employed by U.S. military forces was to remove friendly South Vietnam noncombatants from the country side, to safety in relocation centers in Quang Ngai Province. The policy was based upon the assumption that persons remaining in the country side would be enemy guerrillas, and the U.S. troops would be able to mount "seek and destroy" missions and inflict high casualties on the enemy and practically no casualties would occur among innocent villagers. Toward this goal, Vietnam noncombatants were ordered to leave their home whether there was proof of enemy guerrillas in their community or not.

The inhabitants were first warned to leave, then their homes and villages were destroyed by intensive air and ground bombardment. As this policy achieved greater implementation, the "safe" relocation centers became overcrowded with South Vietnamese noncombatants who had been forcibly removed from their homes for safety. Because of mounting serious problems caused by overcrowding, the United States military policy was changed, and units were requested to cease sending any more Vietnamese civilians to the relocation centers. But the seek and destroy policy remained unchanged.

By mid-1967, villagers were no longer notified of impending air and ground bombardments of their homes, nor were they relocated to safe centers. It is believed that this policy of disregard for the lives of noncombatants helped set the stage for the devastation in the village of My Lai.

In mid-March of 1968 a company of U.S. servicemen experienced an event that resulted in hundreds of media stories, which would later escalate to a memorable experience for almost every U.S. citizen who could read, hear, or witness pictures associated with this experience—it was labeled *The My Lai Massacre.*

As detailed in news stories and other written reports, United States soldiers entered the village of Son My and rounded up four hundred residents, who offered no resistance, and shot them. At the same time, another company of United States soldiers was killing approximately one hundred non-combatants in a smaller village, also near My Lai.

The My Lai experience, at various levels of intensity, entered the consciousness of perpetrators and surviving inhabitants, as well as citizens of the world who read about it in print media or witnessed television news footage and commentary. And, as Edward M. Optom, Jr., of the Wright Institute observed, "The American war in Indochina radically changed the perspective of many Americans."

For some, it was an experience common to military conflict. For others, a crime against humanity, as well as variations along a continuum between these two extremes. A U.S. general stationed in Vietnam at the time remarked that he was not bothered by the killing of Vietnamese civilians because that "deprives the enemy of a population."

From the perspective of the experience of existence, Henry and Sanford, in their important book, *Sanctions for Evil: Sources of Social Destructiveness,* paired various human phenomena to demonstrate evil as experiences of existence.

> While taking issue with critics who argue that the United States purpose in Vietnam has been genocidal or that our society is now fascistic, we do find certain disturbing similarities between mass victimization of another people in Vietnam and the way black people in our country have been treated as if they were things or even the way the Nazi regime set out to eliminate "inferior races." . . . In each of these situations members of one culture hold the power of death or grievous harm over a people regarded as inferior and sometimes as subhuman, as material to be acted upon. Most of the large-scale destructiveness is done by people who feel they have received some kind of permission for what they do—as we call it, a sanction for evil. (1971, 1-2)

Robert Jay Lifton paired the My Lia Massacre with the U.S. invasion of Cambodia, and the killing of college students at Kent State, Augusta, and Jackson State in the 1960s as existential evil.

The dark sides of human experiences as displayed in *Rashomon* and The My Lai Massacre provided opportunities for individual observers and participants to interpret these events in the context of their own lives and knowledge placed in their memory from previous experiences. Their interpretation of these experiences, in turn, assisted in shaping experiences that are yet to emerge in their lives.

A normative global view commonly emerges from events and issues that become a part of generally shared information. Such views provide staging points for the sharing of ideas and for creating human values. For the existentialist and phenomenologist, however, there is no objective truth of what occurred that can invalidate the "story" that might be told by any of the participants in Rashomon or The My Lai Massacre.

Despite the prevalence of themes depicting the dark sides of humanity by existential writers, and the presence of equally dreadful experiences in ordinary society, Jean-Paul Sartre, thought it necessary to respond to frequent criticism from various scholars who suggested that existentialist writers were preoccupied with human despair, at the expense of more humane characteristics equally worthy of note. Sartre responded:

> My purpose here is to offer a defense of existentialism against several reproaches that have been laid against it. First, it has been reproached as an invitation to people to dwell in quietism and despair. . . . We are reproached for having underlined all that is ignominious in the human situation, for depicting what is mean, sordid or base to the neglect of certain things that possess charm and beauty and belong to the brighter side of human nature. . . . It is to these various reproaches . . . that I reply. . . . Existentialism is a Humanism. (Kaufmann, 1965, 287-288)

The role of experience in the process of human development and learning, and a focus on the individual as the experiencer, establishes existentialism and phenomenology as important philosophical foundations for cognitive style theory. In his book, *Existentialism and Phenomenology in Education,* David Denton provided classroom teachers with this thoughtful contribution:

> We attempt order with schedules and outlines. We try to explain it all. We set forth role descriptions. We operationalize our terms in an effort to quantify that which is going on. Out of these attempts come formulas . . . for teaching, methods for researching teaching, and numerous conceptual analyses of the talk about teaching. That person who wishes to be called teacher soon develops a facility for differentiating among the arguments for and against the competing formulas. According to the formulas, teaching is communication, modifying behavior, classroom management, serving as a resource person, guiding youth, influencing society's tomorrow, establishing I Thou relationships. . . . Our new teacher walks into the classroom and quickly discovers that coercion is necessary to make the situation conform to the method . . . that chronic fatigue is his reward at the end of the day. One day, early in his life, he looks on himself as though he were standing outside that window, looking at himself through a closed window. From that new and sudden perspective, his own movements seem absurd, his gestures meaningless, and his prior communication sheer folly. The shock of awareness—the experience of nothingness, of no-thing-ness, the moment of degree zero—explodes from the emptiness of his depths, reverberating against the walls of the classroom, creating dissonance among the students. And in that moment, our teacher confronts the necessity of choice. Many possibilities are open to him. . . . He may leave the profession, acquire from older teachers and behavioristic psychologists necessary coping mechanisms, or he may define himself as a being who, in teaching, transcends the limits of . . . functionality. That choice, however, does not provide a definition; it merely opens possibilities for a new understanding of what it is to be a teacher. (Denton, 1974, 99-100)

In the late 1800s philosophers and theorists in psychology and related fields began to focus on the self as fundamental to their scholarly discourse and therapies. William James (1842-1910) in his two volume book, *Principles of Psychology,* devoted an unusually large section to consciousness of the self. The James book was published in 1890 at the height of a very important period in the field of psychology in the United States. Psychologists who were influenced by Freud were concentrating on the ego as a critical focus for constructs of self. The Freudian concentration was primarily psychoanalytic, rather than normative, as described by James in "The Unconscious Self," a major chapter in *Principles of Psychology.*

For a limited period of time, psychologists (and educators who were influenced by them) focused on the self as important for research and other scholarly activity that would ultimately influence practice in these fields. It was a reasonable outgrowth of the philosophical atmosphere that was created by scholars of phenomenology and existentialism. In this scholarly environment, theories that focused on the individual and experience emerged, and will be discussed in

Chapter 2.

It was not long before philosophies related to structuralism would provide the foundation for behaviorism to emerge, and James Broadus Watson was the leading researcher in this movement. He led an important line of thought that tended to ignore practically all human characteristics that were not observable. Philosophical ideas and psychological constructs related to self-esteem for example, were critically rejected by Watson and his followers. Their studies of human phenomena were empirically focused on the control of individual behavior related to objectified performance. Theories that recognized self-esteem would be cited by behaviorists as lacking in observable human characteristics that could be measured by quantitative empirical methods.

Watson was influenced by the work of the Russian physiologist Ivan Petrovich Pavlov, who was granted the Nobel Prize in 1904 for his work on human digestive processes. Despite Pavlov's dislike of psychologists, his work with classical conditioning and the study of observable behavior in animals identifies him as one of the original founders of the behaviorist movement in psychology. From the early 1920s through the late 1940s, Watson's followers and many psychologists who had earned their degrees under his guidance dominated the field of psychology, and theories of learning in education.

PHILOSOPHICAL AND THEORETICAL FOUNDATIONS OF THE SELF

By the 1940s educators and psychologists were taking note of the self as central to personality development and academic performance. This attention emerged, in part, from the work of Kurt Lewin, Kurt Koffka and Wolfgang Köhler, who started to interest the psychology community in the mid-1930s in studies of individual experiences. The contributions of these three theorists will be discussed in Chapter 3.

The Self Concept: A Critical Survey of Pertinent Research Literature, a major study by Wylie that appeared in 1961, helped to set off a wave of studies investigating *self-concept* and academic performance. By 1970, psychologists had developed several instruments designed to measure *self-esteem.* This work, and many studies that followed, reported an unequivocal relationship between academic achievement and *self-esteem.*

Psychologists of the 1940s who had been influenced by the work of Husserl were disdainful of the manner in which studies of the *self* were being poorly integrated with *perception.* It was their view that too often individuality was ignored in the effort to objectify self-esteem as something to measure.

Few of us regard the perceptual system as self contained and autonomous. . . . In the careful research on seeing, hearing, feeling; the seeer, the hearer, the feeler are somehow obscured or lost. The person himself, the pivot of all of these sensations, the source and root of motives whose influences are sought, is ignored as a determinate of his own perceptual behavior. (Klein and Schlesinger, 1948, 32)

This infusion of ideas associated with self-concept and self-esteem brought the academic community closer to rejecting behavioristic psychology as a major theory of knowledge acquisition.

With a philosophical and theoretical recognition of self as a critical factor in the learning environment, and in therapeutic settings, scholarly activity moved toward studying the critical nature of individual differences more than ever before. It was within this shift of academic interests that studies of cognitive styles emerged as a major area of investigation for educators and psychologists.

Cognitive style theorists examine the particularized ways in which individuals perceive and conceptualize their experiences. Studies of cognitive styles suggest that there are idiosyncratic differences in the ways that individuals organize and process information. Experimental work in that regard is built upon the foundations of philosophical thought from the works of Husserl, Hegel, Sartre, and their many followers.

CONCEPTS OF SELF AMONG BLACK SCHOLARS: PHILOSOPHICAL FOUNDATIONS

Cognitive style theory suggests that in the processing of information, individuals employ a relatively stable tendency to respond in a particular manner. The various modes of interaction that are called for in an experience—whether in a social situation or a classroom teaching/learning environment—will reflect stable tendencies in how an individual acquires new information.

With this perspective in mind, cognitive style can be defined as a construct that identifies the individual, and individual behavior as its primary foci. A construct in this context implies a complex set of concepts that form a commonly agreed upon label, that when examined, does not necessarily conform to the strict expectations of empirical objectivity. Examples of a construct could include such things as self-esteem, intelligence, and personality.

Between the scholarly interests created by the work of William James on the concept of self (1890), and the domination of psychological thought by behaviorists in the 1950s, significant lines of thought related to self-esteem were emerging among Black scholars. William Edward Burghardt Du Bois (1868-1963) was a major voice in the movement promoting self-esteem among Black youth. While many

Black leaders called for vocational training toward a career for African Americans, Du Bois emphasized scholarly endeavors as equally important. In that view, he was way ahead of his time. By the 1950s Du Bois was an elder statesman and scholar in the African American community and was called upon frequently to espouse a role for Black scholars in study and performance in the arts, education, and sciences at their highest levels.

Throughout the early 1900s, Du Bois' s philosophy was ridiculed by academics who believed that Blacks lacked the intellectual capacity for scholarly pursuits. His critics—both Black and White—insisted that Black youth could not benefit from what they termed "mere book learning," but would be better served with vocational training that would lead to jobs in industry. Du Bois suggested that a talented tenth of the Black academic community should be identified to become leaders of scholarly thought and culture in the academy.

Joining these critics was Booker T. Washington, another African American scholar of the time, who had founded the successful Tuskegee Institute in Alabama, a training ground for many Black artisans, and suggested a more pragmatic agenda for the education of Black youth. Du Bois responded to Washington by pointing out that the teachers at Tuskegee were products of a classical education, and at least a tenth of the Black population at that time should devote their scholarship to this endeavor. Washington was not impressed. With Washington an elderly statesman and Du Bois an active research scholar, writer, and social critic, Alain Locke, a Black philosopher, supported the ideas of Du Bois.

From a philosophical perspective, Locke identified three elements that he thought were essential to the education of all children, and Du Bois's and Washington's philosophies were represented in the equation. Locke suggested that in keeping with traditional philosophical thought, there existed (1) the need to provide experiences that served to expand the learner's values and social context, (2) the need to provide experiences that extend the learner's understanding to the practical visions of living, and (3) the need to provide learning experiences that enable learners to become critical thinkers.

Alain Locke (1886-1954) was inspired by his Black students at Howard University to write articles and eventually a book, *The New Negro* (1925), that highlighted the work of Black scholars, writers, poets, and performing artists as contributors to American culture. Other Black scholars like E. Franklin Frazier, Carter G. Woodson, and James Weldon Johnson supported the movement. As Black college youth were joined by some of their Black professors, the movement widened among Black poets, writers, performers, and scholars and became known as the Harlem Renaissance.

Alain Locke, then a philosophy professor at Howard University in Washington D.C., brought the significance of self-esteem among Black students to the attention of the academic community. Prior to his appointment at Howard, he earned a Ph.D. graduating with honors from Harvard University in 1907. Because of his exemplary scholarship, Locke was nominated for a Rhodes Scholarship, the first time in history that an African American had been awarded this honor.

With nominated documents in hand, Locke's request for admission was refused by several highly respected Oxford Colleges, for which the Rhodes Scholarship made him eligible. Some time later, he was admitted to one of Oxford's less prestigious colleges; however, faculty and fellow students seldom accepted him as a scholar or colleague.

This was not a new experience for Locke. Black intellectuals of that time were accustomed to rejection and overt racial discrimination at home in the United States, but they were seldom prepared for the subtle covert undercurrents in European circles that ignored their presence in the higher domains of social stratifications. Such positions were presumed for Whites only.

Ironically, his namesake, John Locke, the renowned White philosopher, had sewn the seeds of racism among British intellectuals a century before Alain Locke's arrival. Because of his wealthy friends among English planters in the American colonies during slavery, John Locke supported the slavery of Africans and the genocide of Native Americans as justified in the wake of more "civilized" English bringing Christianity and organized productive land-use to "heathens."

Alain Locke, during his three years of study in Oxford's Hertford College, England could be characterized as a living example of Ralph Ellison's *Invisible Man*. The idea that a Black intellectual could qualify for a Rhodes Scholarship had not been contemplated by the authorities at Oxford. Their response was to ignore, as much as possible, the presence of an African American scholar. This could be defined as an existential experience for this young African American scholar.

After the completion of his work in one of Oxford's less prestigious colleges—followed by two years of advanced study at the University of Berlin—Locke returned to the United States. It was during this time in Berlin that he studied the work of Brentano, Husserl, Kant, and Ehrenfels. During his studies, Locke pursued his own value theory. In a general sense, he theorized that one's interpretation of an experience is embedded in the values that are brought to the experience. In 1912 he was appointed professor of education at Howard University, and in 1917 he became professor of philosophy, and later chairman of the department of philosophy.

As a professor at Howard University, Locke supported students and other Black professors in their efforts to design and implement courses aimed at uplifting the self-esteem of students. In 1915 Locke designed a course on interracial relations and social problems related to the Black experience in the United States.

Carter G. Woodson, professor and dean at Howard who had founded *The Journal of Negro History* and *Black History Month,* both surviving to this present day, also designed a course in African American history. Woodson, like Locke, had earned a Ph.D. from Harvard. Proposals for the new courses by Locke and Woodson were rejected by Howard's predominately White board of trustees, and the president of Howard University, who was also White. After continued pressure from Black students, Locke, and other Black professors, a course in African American history was approved five years later.

Leo Hansberry, outstanding scholar and teacher, was appointed associate professor to teach the approved course. This proved to be a poor career choice for Hansberry, because after more than ten years the course was viewed as frivolous by Howard's trustees. As a reflection of this attitude, Professor Hansberry was never given a promotion or tenure in his more than twenty years at Howard.

It was Locke's view that in the absence of an academic content on self-esteem through a study of their culture, Black youth, without an awareness of major contributions made by their elders, would have too little information to repel the negative images of Blacks in literature and in general society. This missing ingredient of positive valuing in the experiences of Black youth, thought Locke, would eventually lead them to despise their heritage.

College and university studies at that time identified African Americans as the race problem, which had to be resolved by intellectually superior Whites. Locke feared that Black university students, lacking in knowledge of African American history, would choose not to identify with their precollege Black community, but become concerned solely with their own personal career for economic advancement. He thought an intellectual awareness of African American contributions to civilization, past and present, would foster positive self-esteem among college graduates by giving them a sense that studies about African Americans had a rightful place in academia.

Locke emphasized the need for educators to start early in elementary school to integrate pedagogy and curriculum with the practical aspects of living, to create an intelligent population that is knowledgeable enough to participate in the social and political life of the country. Locke was not convinced that educators of the times had an understanding of the need for critical changes or how such changes could be brought about. Too many educators, he believed, thought that necessary changes in how we educate children could come about through a mere tinkering with the content in the teaching/learning environment. In this regard he was in agreement with John Dewey, a philosopher, who was considered a radical thinker for his time.

It was Dewey who suggested fundamental changes in the physical environment, teaching strategies, teacher training, and curriculum for grade schools in the early 1900s. It was also Dewey who worked with Du Bois in forming a group called The Niagara Movement in upstate New York. The Niagara Movement founded what is now known as The National Association for the Advancement of Colored People (NAACP).

Alain Locke and John Dewey believed that the experience of schooling at that time was too restrictive to enable young learners to become critical thinkers with a capacity for intellectual inquiry into questions about their beliefs and those of others.

Alain Locke pursued this line of thought because he viewed the opportunities of learners to experience free and open inquiry as the key to an appreciation of cultural and racial diversity. While White liberals, in an effort to create racial equity, were offering "tolerance" of Blacks by Whites as a solution, Locke believed that intellectual inquiry provided a more likely solution to Black/White racial disparity, because it would lead to a common ground where Black opportunities would be on par with those of whites. Tolerance, he thought, still fed the concept of White superiority.

As a philosopher, he was aware that language, phrases, slogans, word choices, and public discourse had a major influence on the agendas of philanthropic institutions, the structure of education, and public policy in general. He viewed the policies of government, and public and private institutions as responsible, in large part, for the isolation of Black and White children in separate schools—Whites in superior facilities and Blacks in inferior ones.

It was also Locke's view that starting in the early grades, children should be students of the various cultures in order to understand those elements that create a common bond among all people. With this understanding, Locke thought that learners would come to appreciate the contributions and values that are inherent in the heritage of all people. This he thought was also critical to eliminating racial prejudices.

From Locke's philosophical perspective, the various styles that learners bring to the learning experience should be viewed as important differences in their own right, and not deficits to be negatively valued.

An assessment of the status of education today after it has undergone various changes brought about through such experiences as the public turmoil of the 1960s, the emergence of school desegregation, and programs like Head Start would receive mixed reviews from John

Dewey's and Alain Locke's 1920s vision for educational change. Dewey's progressive education has brought a change in the school environment from strict regimentation and seating that segregated children by gender. It also introduced us to flexabilities in the study of mathematics, reading, science, and social studies. From Alain Locke's vision, the courts have eliminated restrictions by race (even though de facto ones remain), African American studies has become an academic unit in most institutions of higher learning, and Howard University has emerged as a center for innovative change. Locke would not approve of the pragmatic single vision for employment that is becoming popular in many predominantly Black institutions of higher education.

As late as the 1990s, for example, some divisions in Black colleges and universities were reduced to a fundamentally vocational mission. Administrators and deans in these institutions approach businesses and institutions that were hiring to seek a description of the qualifications desired in the workers they wish to employ. Administrators and deans return to their Black institutions, and more often than not, design a curriculum to match industry's needs and relieve these industries of job training costs.

For example, a nursing school dean might inquire at insurance companies and hospitals to learn their hiring needs, then redesign their academic program to virtual job training in order to satisfy industry employment needs. In this approach, thoughtful scholarship that has been refined over a period of time is sacrificed for the short-run placement of graduates in positions that might have limited value in an ever changing society.

Philosophical thought along the lines of Black academic scholarship and performance in the arts and literature, which survived through the late 1930s, has been lost in several predominantly Black institutions of higher education in the 1990s. Philosopher, activist Peter McLaren, writing on issues in teacher education, has identified this phenomenon as an emerging problem in all institutions.

> When teachers in their acceptance of the role of technician, fail to challenge the ways in which educational curricula corresponds to the demands of industry or the means by which schooling reproduces existing class, race and gender relations in our society, they run the risk of transmitting to disadvantaged students the message that their subordinate roles in the social order are justified and inviolable. We are unable, then, to assist students in determining how certain individuals, because of their race, class, gender, or social status, come to be positioned favorably or unfavorably within larger sociopolitical relations. (1989, 2)

This remarkable period in the late 1920s and early 1930s was influenced by Alain Locke, who started a movement that focused on self-esteem in institutions of higher education that served Black youth and among the informed Black public. By the mid-1920s, Locke's work marked the first efforts toward an inclusion of African American studies at the highest levels of scholarship. It has been wrongly assumed that the quest for Black and African American studies in colleges and universities originated during the Civil Rights Movement in the 1960s.

Black colleges and universities were founded by religious groups and missionaries and supported by state and federal grants. These institutions were designed primarily to foster religion and the work ethic in Black youth. By the 1920s Black youth wanted more of what was available to White scholars in colleges and universities. They were rebelling against the heavy emphasis on religious worship and strict moral codes of behavior that prevailed in Black institutions to a greater degree than in White ones. Many Black scholars who obtained their Ph.D.'s in White institutions supported these new aspirations of Black youth. A major force in this movement was W.E.B. Du Bois.

As a major force in the African American cultural renaissance, Locke's interests in education went beyond the hallowed walls of academia and led to his founding of the Associates in Negro Folk Education. He also edited a series of monographs for adult education that became known as "Bronze Booklets."

Locke identified the positive valuing of self as a critical mission of education in Black institutions. He was a prolific writer on educational issues, and participated with various educational organizations in planning and promoting institutes and workshops dealing with his philosophy of race relations and education. Among these works is *The Negro in America, Frederick Douglass, A Decade of Negro Self Expression,* and co-editor of When *People Meet: A Study in Race and Culture Contacts.*

The Great Depression that griped the nation in the late 1920s started to effect the southern states in the mid 1920s. Black institutions of higher learning were controlled by White presidents and their predominantly white boards. Locke was espousing the need for courses in African American and African studies as being essential for the building of positive self-esteem among Black college students.

In an atmosphere of separate and unequal education in the U. S., Locke suggested to his colleagues that they should grasp the opportunity to develop courses that did not mimic White institutions that promoted the Aryan model as academically superior. Carter G. Woodson, Locke's colleague at Howard University, was among those who agreed. Locke wrote and gave speeches expressing emphatically that the primary goal of Black institutions should be to develop a racially inspired Black professional class devoted to Black community service.

During this period, ideas about Black self-esteem, African American studies, and other fundamental changes in Black institutions of higher education, became the major focus of discontent among Black students and supporting Black faculty. By the mid 1920s Black college students and alumni at Howard University, Fiske University, Lincoln University in Missouri and Florida A & M University in Tallahassee mounted demonstrations and strikes that ousted several conservative Black and White faculty and administrators.

In June 1925 philosopher Alain Locke was fired by the board of trustees at Howard University because of his stand on student issues and equitable salaries for Black and White professors.

Locke returned to Howard in 1928 and expanded his interests to include an active role in writing and lecturing about what by then was termed the Harlem Renaissance. This was a period that lasted until the late 1930s during which time Black writers, actors, poets, and culturally inspired artists became active participants in their crafts. It was an inspirational period for Black youth with no shortage of role models; and it was a time when the Black community supported artistic endeavors with their attendance.

Locke had agreed with Du Bois that the Black community needed a talented tenth, at least 10 percent of educated youth devoted to inspiring other young scholars to participate in classical educational pursuits at the highest levels of scholarship. Locke did not, however, ignore the needs of those who followed vocational pursuits. His desire was to inspire all African Americans toward a positive sense of self-worth.

Locke became active in the adult education movement to help promote a system that might provide guidance and support for the other 90 percent of the African American population, as well as occupational workers in general. He was elected president of the American Association for Adult Education (AAAE). Prior to his presidency, he was invited to give an address to a meeting of the AAAE titled, "The First Annual Conference on Adult Education and the Negro." At a time when U.S. industries were interested in cheap labor and generally opposed to a more literate labor source that might demand greater benefits and salaries. Locke's remarks at the conference noted that adult education should not be viewed as an appendage to mainstream education, but rather, educators should pursue this area of service with enthusiasm and verve. It should not be assumed, according to Locke, that adult education is merely a second chance for academically handicapped students, but teaching and learning opportunities beyond the level of minimal literacy.

At Howard University, Alain Locke remained chairman of the philosophy department for forty years. His philosophy of positive self-actualization among Black college students through the study and appreciation of their artistic performance and scholarship remains as a legacy in many majority Black institutions of today. Locke never lost sight of the importance of self-esteem as an essential ingredient in academic success among Black youth.

During the 1970s and 1980s a large number of studies were designed to investigate gender and racial variations in self-esteem. The great preponderance of studies utilizing self-report methodology revealed more often than not that Black males reported the highest self-esteem and White females reported the lowest self-esteem. In some studies Black females were second and White males were third, while in other studies this trend was reversed. However, there was seldom any doubt about Black males being the highest and White females reporting the lowest (Simmons, 1978; Taylor and Walsh, 1979; Morgan 1995).

The apparent disparity between Black male self-reports of high self-esteem, and their modest academic achievement when compared to their White age-mates, was cause for some investigators to reexamine their methodologies. These concerns were laid to rest following a compelling analysis of the then current literature by Adam (1978) that tended to support the aforementioned gender/racial split in self-esteem findings.

With the poor academic success rates among low-income African American children in mind, academicians started to utilize various constructs of cognitive style to address these deficits.

> Cognitive style is a psychological construct, which has been of concern to psychologists and educators for more than five decades and continues to be a focus of research by psychologists working in the interface between cognition and personality. This interest has resulted from a number of factors. One has been a concern for improving the academic performance of low income children who have experienced lower rates of success than their middle-class counterparts. Another has been the interest that has developed in the area of cognitive development in young children. (Saracho, 1989, iii)

The theoretical and philosophical backdrop for these trends was driven by the belief that educators needed to expand the number of opportunities that children have to experience learning. Educators realized that the traditional didactic teacher/learner settings worked well for some pupils, but were inappropriate for others. The basis for this re-evaluation of their approach to work rested in part on a rediscovery of the philosophy of John Dewey and the theories of Jean Piaget. Classroom practices utilizing open classroom structures, whole language studies, cooperative learning, small group assignments and individualized instruction, and a variety of other innovative approaches, started to emerge in grade schools in the United States.

REFERENCES

Adam, B.D. (1978). "Inferiorization and Self-Esteem." *Social Psychology* 41, 47-53.

Aronowitz, S., and Giroux, H. A. (1985). *Education Under Siege: The Conservative, Liberal and Radical Debate Over Schooling*. South Hadley, MA: Bergin & Garvey.

Burnett, J. R. (1988). "Dewey's Educational Thought and His Mature Philosophy." *Educational Theory* 38, 203-211.

Dewey, J. (1933). *How We Think*. Boston: Heath.

Denton, D. (1974). *Existentialism and Phenomenology in Education*. New York: Teachers College.

Dreyfus, H. L. and Hall, H., eds. (1982). *Husserl: Intentionality and Cognitive Science*. Cambridge, MA: MIT Press.

Du Bois, W.E.B. (1970). *The Souls of Black Folk*. New York: Simon and Schuster.

Du Bois, W.E.B. (1971). *The Autobiography of W.E.B. Du Bois*. New York: International Publishers.

Farber, M. (1943). *The Foundations of Phenomenology: Edmund Husserl and the Quest for a Rigorous Science of Philosophy*. Albany, NY: Research Foundation of the State University of New York.

Greene, M. (1978). *Landscapes of Learning*. New York: Teachers College Press.

Greene, M. (1986). "In Search of a Critical Pedagogy." *Harvard Educational Review* 56, 424-441.

Greene, M. (1988). *The Dialectic of Freedom*. New York: Teachers College Press.

Hammer, R. (1970). *One Morning in the War: The Tragedy at Son My*. New York: Coward-McCann.

Harris, L., ed. (1989). *The Philosophy of Alain Locke*. Philadelphia, PA: Temple University Press.

Henry, W. H., and Sandford, N. (1971). *Sanctions for Evil: Sources of Social Destruction*. San Francisco: Jossey-Bass.

Hersh, S. M. (1970). *My Lai 4: A Report on the Massacre and Its Aftermath*. New York, NY: Random House.

Kagan, J. (1967). "On the Need for Relativism." *American Psychologist* 22, 131-142.

Kant, I. (1959). *Critique of Pure Reason*. New York: Anchor Books.

Kaufmann, W. (1965). *Existentialism from Dostoevsky to Sartre*. New York: Meridian Books.

Kearney, R. (1991). *Poetics of Imagining: From Husserl to Lyotard*. New York: Harper Collins.

Kelly, G. A. (1969). *Idealism, Politics and History: Sources of Hegelian Thought*. London: Cambridge University Press.

Klein, G. S. & Schlesinger, H. (September, 1949). "Where is the Perceiver in Perceptual Theory?" *Journal of Personality* 18, 32-47.

Laird, S. (1988). "Women and Gender in John Dewey's Philosophy of Education." *Educational Theory* 38, 111-129.

Lawler, P. A. (1980). "Pragmatism, Existentialism, and the Crisis in American Political Thought." *International Philosophical Quarterly* 20, 327-338.

Lifton, R. J. (1970). *History and Human Survival.* New York: Random House.

Lifton, R. J. (1971). "Existential Evil." In W. H. Henry and N. Sanford, eds., *Sanctions for Evil: Sources of Social Destructiveness.* San Francisco: Jossey-Bass.

Locke, A. (1936). *The Negro and His Music.* Washington, DC: Associates in Negro Folk Education.

Luria, A. (1973). *The Working Brain: An Introduction to Neuropsychology.* New York: Basic Books.

McLaren, P. (1989). *Life in Schools: An Introduction to Critical Pedagogy in the Foundations of Education.* White Plains, NY: Longman.

Moore, G. E. (1959). *Philosophical Papers.* London: Allen & Unwin.

Morgan, H. (1995). "Drug Use in High School: Race and Gender Issues." *Journal of Educational Research* 88 (5), 301-308.

Natanson, M. (1973). *Edmund Husserl: Philosopher of Infinite Tasks.* Evanston, IL: Northwestern University Press.

Proefriedt, W. (1980). "Socialist Criticism of Education in the United States: Problems and Possibilities." Harvard Educational Review 50, 467-480.

Saracho, O. (1989). "Preface." *Early Childhood and Care* 50, iii.

Selye, H. (1956). *The Stress of Life.* New York: McGraw-Hill.

Simmons, R. G. (1978). "Blacks and High Self-Esteem: A Puzzle." *Social Psychology* 41, 54-57.

Taylor, M. C. and Walsh, E. J. (1979). "Explanations of Black Self-Esteem: Some Empirical Tests." *Social Psychology Quarterly* 42, 242-253.

Walters. R. (1975). *The New Negro on Campus: Black College Rebellions of the 1920s.* Princeton, NJ: Princeton University Press.

Watson, J. B. and Rayner, R. (1920). "Conditional Emotional Reactions." *Journal of Experimental Psychology* 3, 1-114.

Watson, J. B. (1913). "Psychology as the Behaviorist Views It." *Psychological Review* 20, 157-158.

West, C. (1989). *The American Evasion of Philosophy.* Madison, WI: University of Wisconsin Press.

Zaner, R. and Ihde, D. (1973). *Phenomenology and Existentialism.* New York: G. P. Putnam.

2

Theoretical Foundations of Cognitive Style

> Psychological type as *style* is analogous to differences among batters in a baseball game. Cursory observation during a baseball game reveals a variety of batting styles—left or right handed, open or closed stance, bat held high or low, body crouched or erect, and others. These characteristic preferences represent style differences among hitters. However, these differences all occur against a background of commonality. All batters regardless of individual style, have much in common. Batters stand within the limits of the batter's box, watch the ball, use the bat, etc. In other words, styles of hitting differ across the common process according to certain typical differences. Each style has its advantages; none is inherently superior to the others.
>
> —Barger and Hoover

Several theories have emerged in education and psychology suggesting that individual learners employ various strategies in processing information during classroom experiences. Beginning in the 1950s reports concerning this individual variability have had various labels. Psychological differentiation seems to be the earliest label and it inferred a broad-based set of principles that expanded to include the relationship between individuals and their environment encompassing all human experience. Various disciplines approached this concept from the perspective of their individual professional practices. University professors and the teachers of children who were influenced by the theories of B. F. Skinner, for example, will in all likelihood bring a different perspective to the practice of teaching than those who were primarily influenced by the theories of Jean Piaget. It is therefore important for professionals to be knowledgeable about those philosophies and theories that are fundamental to their own practice.

H. Werner (1957) was among the first to introduce the concept of *psychological differentiation.* He theorized that human development followed a biological course from a global state to a state of differentiation, articulation and hierarchical integration. In other words, developmental changes in human growth are systematic and dependent upon earlier stages. In Werner's theory, the child's increase in foot size or arm length, for example, are quantitative changes and not particularly important developmental issues. To Werner, only qualitative changes, such as those associated with basic underlying biological structures, are truly developmental. He theorized that the human organism develops in predetermined steps and stages that are influenced more by internal structures than environmental experiences. From a global (undifferentiated) relationship between the individual and the environment, the system progressively develops biological structures that become independent (differentiated) in their function. As the human system processes further, it becomes more efficient at maximizing cooperation between the underlying subsystems. In this advanced stage of maturity the human system is able to differentiate external from internal stimuli, and process information derived from these sources appropriately.

Finally, these underlying biological systems mature and become independently capable of setting goals and rejecting distractions. In this regard, Werner's approach to developmental systems has been called orthogenetic—the theory that individuals in all cultures pass through a series of steps and stages. The orthogenetic approach to describing human development is also central to the work of Mahler (social adaptation), Sigmund Freud (psychosexual), and Jean Piaget and Erik Erikson (psychosocial). Building upon theories of psychological differentiation, professionals in various fields of education and psychology have pursued a set of ideas that have similar philosophical and theoretical foundations that they have termed cognitive styles.

Education is not an academic discipline in the traditional conceptualization of the word. In a more realistic sense, education borrows extensively from fields of study that are generally accepted as disciplines of scholarly activity. Those fields include anatomy, anthropology, biology, chemistry, psychology, sociology, and the humanities in general. To the benefit of the scientific community, and the general well-being of humankind, several disciplines have combined their scholarly work to produce advanced knowledge of an integrated nature. The field of neurobiology, for example, is providing descriptions of the brain and central nervous system to provide a basic understanding of how they function as the human organism processes information. A significant contribution to this endeavor is a book edited by Jeanne S. Chall and Allan F. Mirsky, *Education and the Brain,* published by the National Society for the Study of Education.

Earlier studies of the principles underlying how we process new information come primarily from the field of psychology. These early works, however, avoided discussions of brain function and other internal human systems other than to acknowledge that they had some role in the process. As scholars in anatomy, biology, chemistry, neurology, physiology, and psychology, just to name a few, started to interrelate in a scientific manner, a greater understanding of the total process of how we know started to emerge.

It is rather remarkable that Sigmund Freud in the late 1800s discovered the need for interdisciplinary approaches to an understanding of the inner workings of human knowledge acquisition. Freud embarked upon what he called a Project for a Scientific Psychology, in an attempt to describe what he considered an interrelated role of anatomical, physiological, and neural function of the brain in our conscious deliberations. The project was aimed at an understanding of the objective transmission of information by the human organism, which he thought would lead to a more comprehensive understanding of the subjective categories of psychopathology.

Freud hypothesized that the ego must require a physiological and psychical presence in the human organism. He surmised that the ego probably consisted of a cluster of neurons with ego characteristics that flowed through the central nervous system to the brain as a function of normal processing of information by the organism. If this neural system could be scientifically analyzed, Freud thought, an understanding of the physiology of the ego and its pathway to the brain in normal individuals would be useful in the treatment of ego dysfunction. He conceptualized the ego as an organism possessed of constant energy, integrated with neural functions, neuroses, and the physiology of the brain, thereby providing a basic structure for future psychoanalytic studies. The influence of Freud's studies toward an understanding of cognition and cognitive style is described by Cantor and Kihlstrom:

> The early cognitive style theorists were very much influenced by the ego psychology tradition in psychoanalytic thinking. Therefore, styles of perceiving and thinking were associated in their work with the regulating functions of the ego—hence the term *cognitive controls.* Cognitive styles like leveling-sharpening or impulsive-reflective thinking were assumed to serve critical functions in modulating the expression of motivational drives (defensive functions) and in providing for comfortable ways in which to find personal gratification (adaptive functions). On the one hand, characteristic styles of perceiving and thinking reflected characteristic ways of defending against overwhelming intrapsychic drives, as, for example, when the "leveler" engaged in repression. On the other hand, cognitive styles also demonstrated the more adaptive functions of the ego, as the individual worked (unconsciously) to adapt to reality demands from the social world (e.g., repression can also be a functional way of handling personal loss or injury). Cognitive styles reflected the ego's activity as the regulator of

motives and the mediator between the person and his or her environment. . . . Cognitive styles reflected the person's attempts to regulate and fulfill intrapsychic drives and interpersonal demands. (Cantor and Kihlstrom, 1987, 12-13)

Freud exhausted his knowledge of physiology prior to what he considered a unified and complete theory of neural function of the brain in human emotions. With the Project for a Scientific Psychology, in Freud's view, mired in theoretical frustration, he started to correspond with Wilhelm Fleiss—a colleague and highly respected physician. Freud sought help from Fleiss because he thought that his friend and colleague had a better understanding of physiology than he himself had. During a time when professionals were more guarded of their territory than today, Fleiss was less than enthusiastic about Freud's "project." He declined his colleague's request, declaring that he was too busy with his own projects and had too little interest in what he considered a waste of time for Freud.

A major part of Freud's confusion rested upon his not being able to solve the practical problems posed by the manner in which the brain—after receiving an impulse traveling through the central nervous system—could simultaneously be available to constantly occurring drives, like sex and hunger, on the same "track." How does the human neural system and the brain negotiate the diversion of impulses to the brain or prevent the damming-up of information to the brain from the outside world, and from itself? Freud's notes from 1895 point out his theoretical dilemma in the following manner:

From the very first, however, the principle of inertia is upset by another set of circumstances. As the internal complexity of the organism increases, the neurotic system receives stimuli from the somatic element itself—endogenous stimuli, which calls forth for discharge. These have their origin in the cells of the body and give rise to the major needs: hunger, respiration, and sexuality. The organism cannot withdraw itself from them as it does from external stimuli; it cannot employ their quantity (Q) for the purpose of flight from the stimuli. They only cease if certain definite conditions are realized in the external world. (Take, for example, the case of the need for nourishment.) To carry out an action (that will bring these conditions about)—an action which deserves to be called "specific"—requires an effort which is independent of endogenous quantities and is generally greater than they are, since the individual is placed under conditions which may be described as "the exigencies of life." The neuronic system is consequently obliged to abandon its original trend towards inertia (than is, towards a reduction of its level of tension to zero). It must learn to tolerate a store of quantity sufficient to meet the demands for specific action. In so far as it does so, however, the same trend will persist in the modified form of a tendency to keep the quantity down, at least, so far as possible and avoid any increase in it (that is, to keep its level of tension constant). All the performances of the neuronic system are to be comprised under the heading either of the primary function or of the secondary function imposed by the exigencies of life. (Freud, 1954, 357-358)

In the absence of assistance from other learned colleagues, Freud abandoned the project short of satisfactory completion, concluding that it had captured too much of his time. Currently, our understanding of the role of the central nervous system in how we process information come from studies in neurobiology. It is remarkable that Freud's basic concepts that were formulated in the late 1800's are the roots of neurobiological research in the field of brain function today. His basic thesis from the following notes from one of his papers in 1887 is strikingly similar to descriptions of information processing by the human organism found in college texts in the 1990s.

The essence of this new knowledge that the neuronic system consists of dystinct but similarly constructed neurons which only have contact with one another through an intervening foreign substance and which terminate on one another in the same manner as on a piece of foreign tissue; that certain lines of conduction are laid down on them, in so far as they receive excitations through a cell process (or dendrite) and discharge them through an axis cylinder (or axone); and furthermore, that they have numerous ramifications and diameters of various dimensions. . . . The structure of the neurone makes it possible that these resistances are in the contacts (between the neurones) which thus function as *barriers.* (Freud, 1954, 358)

What Freud termed "barriers" and "contact-barriers" in the late 1800s, was labeled "synapses" by Foster and Sherrington in 1897. The search for an understanding of how knowledge is acquired by individuals should begin with a discussion of the nature and function of the brain. The brain weighs approximately one pound at birth and will double in size within a 12 month period. By the time a child reaches the age of 17, the brain has increased an additional pound in weight. It is believed that this growth is nonlinear, in that, brain growth has periods of acceleration usually followed by plateaus of synthesizing what has been learned. What makes this theory troublesome for educators of young children is that scheduling of schooling can conflict with the accelerated periods of growth in the child's information processing mechanisms. For example, H. Epstein (1978) has reported that there are several critical periods of acceleration in brain growth, followed by plateau periods when the brain synthesizes previously acquired information—one being between the ages of four and six. During this period, the synapse (to be discussed later in this chapter), a critical connection for the passage of information, has just undergone an accelerated phase of development.

One problem that Epstein's work highlights is that following a period of accelerated development (ages 2 to 4), the child is being asked to perform school entry learning tasks, and negotiate separation from family for several hours a day, while encountering emotional changes associated with taking up daytime residence in a strange institution called school. All of this at a time when the brain is in a state of recovery from an accelerated period of growth. Theories of growth and plateau periods are not fully understood at this time, but from what we now know, the possible implications that it holds for children who are developing are worthy of serious consideration.

A lack of agreement in the field is not a prevalent condition, but what does prevail is a need for more knowledge and coordinated investigations in a variety of fields that provide information regarding the acquisition of knowledge.

Studies that focus on the function of the brain are now occurring in a variety of disciplines like neurology, neurobiology, anatomy, biochemistry, physiology, and cognitive science. In a scientific environment where new knowledge is being introduced frequently at the annual conferences of the aforementioned disciplines, there seems to be a relatively stable agreement among the various scientists that information processing starts with our sensory systems (seeing, hearing, touching, smelling), and reach our brain through the central nervous system. The structure of the brain is composed of *laminae* and rounded sheets called *nuclei,* both designed to manage billions of neurons (Figure 2.1).

Neurons are arranged in the human organism in a variety of complex patterns called *maps.* The interconnectedness of neurons and their patterns are not wired like a telephone system as some have theorized. It has also been popular to describe the CNS as analogous to the computer. The fact that information is transmitted through a network of complex patterns does have similarities to the telephone and computer, but beyond this point likenesses are merely metaphoric. Electronic instruments like the telephone and computer are capable of processing information that has been programmed for their input and output capacities. Information, however, is not the same as knowledge and wisdom which as of now exist as solely human qualities.

Fundamental differences also exist because the computer and telephone are hard-wired in that when these devices are in need of repair, for example, wiring can be traced in a point-to-point pattern. If it were possible to number the axon branches of each neuron and the associated dendritic extensions of a neuron(s) with which it communicates, this network would not be the same for any two individuals—not even monozygote twins. Maps in individual central nervous systems differ as well. Some have suggested that this imprecise network of the central nervous system is due to a "code" that the system employs to facilitate higher order thinking. It is higher order information processing and the role of the brain in this function that remains unresolved by neuroscientists, biologists, cognitive scientists, psychologists, and others who conduct research in related fields. It is, after all, the brain within the body of the researcher(s) that must enable itself to understand its own function. Basic aspects of brain function that have yet to be fully understood have to do with the precise action of brain structures in the interpretation of an experience.

G. M. Edelman (1978) has proposed that variations in neuronal networks and maps are Darwinian, in that brain development is under change from individual to individual and from one generation to another. From his theory of neuronal group selection it is implied that neuronal variations are influenced by population adaptation. Accordingly, each generation has gone through a system of selection in order for the most recent generation of brains to improve upon the nature of living in previous generations. Individuals, therefore, start life with a brain that contains structures that are genetically developed independent of sensory inputs from the environment.

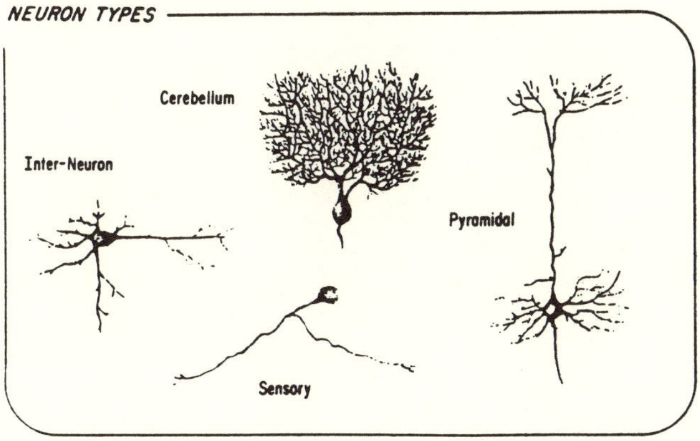

Figure 2.1 Various types of neurons located in the brain.

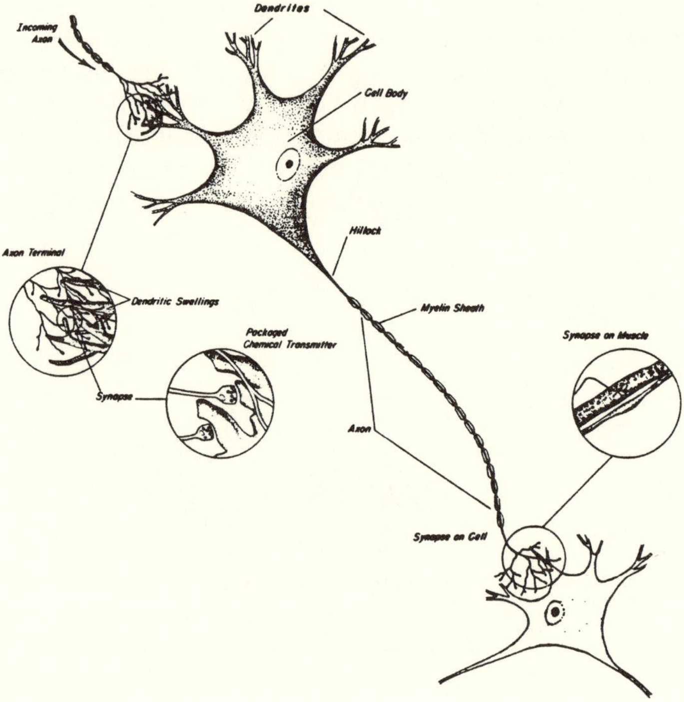

Figure 2.2. The neuron and its communication process(synapse), showing the axon and dendrite.

For some time now, theorists like N. Chomsky and L. S. Vygotsky have suggested that preexisting genetic structures provide for the early acquisition of such complex things as language. The environment, according to Edelman, "selects" capacities that were present in the organism from birth.

The nervous system of animals capable of carrying out complex sensorimotor acts can successfully adapt to complexes of information input that have never been encountered before in the history of an individual or its species. This premise is difficult to prove but is probably most defensible in man. Perhaps the most dramatic examples are the capabilities of some individuals to solve highly abstract problems in mathematics, to generate new symbol structures of the complexity of a symphony, or to analyze such unique structures in a surprisingly efficient fashion upon seeing them for the first time. (Edelman, 1978, 55)

The central nervous system is composed of the brain, and the billions of cells that are mostly located in the brain, and the spinal cord. Billions of cells also exist throughout the body in complex neural branches. These cells are neurons that exist along pathways, often in bundles, that help to comprise the central nervous system. The neuron is the central factor in the organism's capacity to transmit information. It is an elongated microscopic cell that transmits information to other cells. In its construction, it has extended parts at both ends of the cell body (Figure 2.1). On the receiving end it has branches called *dendrites,* and as information passes from the dendrites through the cell body and a protective myelin sheath, it exits out the other end through its axon branches, thus passing information to the adjoining neuron's dendrites (Figure 2.2). The dendrites from one neuron are separated by microscopic distances and do not actually touch the axons from other neurons. Rather, this transmission occurs over a small gap between the axon of one neuron and the dendrite of the other neuron. This point of transmission is an electrical and chemical process called a *synapse* (Figure 2.2). The frequent transmissions of information between particular neurons can establish a permanent relationship between them.

Anatomically some individuals have more dendrites and axons to talk across transmission lines thereby processing information of greater quantity and quality. It has been reported that interacting experiences can increase the information transmission potential of the synapse (Diamond, 1967).

The sensory organs are the brain's connection to the outside world. Things that we decide to attend to, and intrusions beyond our control, will enter our brain through our central nervous system. These sensory organs actually refuse entry to more sensations than they allow to enter the human information processing system. They are extremely sensitive receptors, each tuned to its own speciality; sight, sound, smell, and touch (Figure 2.3).

Short-term memory is actively recruiting the words and meanings that we frequently use. This can include vocabulary involved in daily/weekly experiences, common odors, basic arithmetic skills, and other tasks that are called for in recurring interactions in our environment.

Long-term memory stores information that forms our knowledge content that has been acquired from past experiences. It serves to guide our entire information processing system. Its structure is derived from our recognition that we have acquired the meaning of an experience prior to what is occurring in the immediate environment. This previous acquisition is, of the moment, providing the content and understanding for the new experiences. Long term memory grows with age because the more experiences we have, the larger the pool of events that are available to capture our attention (perception), and the more we store in our long-term memory. This type of memory starts at birth and continues to expand. A twenty-four-month-old child, for example, will store in long-term memory the meaning of large symbols that are displayed outside of fast food restaurants and request something from their menu while in a passing car. Even children several months old will attempt to put on their rainwear when they look out of their window and see the rain.

Motoric processing is a major part of our coded system that informs the organism that some performance is required. The information processing system determines the appropriate motoric response that could call forth writing a poem, riding a bicycle, ice skating, ballet, or playing basketball. Some theorists have identified motivation as a factor related to perception. They have suggested that personality and levels of interest, which involves motivation, can influence our selection of experiences in which to participate (Figure 2.4).

In the earlier discussion, regarding the development and growth of the brain in entry-age school children, it was mentioned from the work of Epstein that during one of the early periods (2-4 years), axon, dendrite, and myelin growth is accelerated forming millions of neural connections. Following this period (4-6 years), a great deal of the organism's energy is consumed in synthesizing already acquired growth and knowledge and is not completely available for consuming new information.

There are five basic elements involved in the acquisition of knowledge; perception, sensory organs, short term memory, long term memory, and motoric systems. These elements represent stages that are involved in the process of knowing, but they are not exclusively cast in a straight line, but rather in complex interactive configurations throughout the central nervous system. Perception is a function of how we decide to employ our attention. Sensory organs are primarily muscles in our eyes, ears, nose and on our skin surface. Short-term memory is often called working memory, and is used by the organism to hold a limited amount of information for a short time. Long-term memory stores a great deal of information that is retained and probably remains with us over our lifetime.

Perception is the entry point for the variety of experiences that we select to attend to and many that intrude. As we age there are fewer things to entrap our attention than during our younger years. One reason for this is the role of *novelty* in perception. As we age more experiences are commonplace. An infant usually finds most experiences worthy of attention, at least more so than six-year-olds. Even in infancy, though, once the luster of novelty has passed, some repetitive experiences capture only a passing glance. Investigators of infant attention behavior have found that a noise made by a ringing bell, for example, will result in the infant giving attention to the sound through eye and/or body movement. After repeated rings, the infant will start to ignore the sound.

The neurological basis for attention starts with a description of how brain structures maintain consciousness. The highest portions of the spinal cord (anterior) and the lowest section of the brain (brain stem) form the area that is generally referred to as the brain stem. Lower portions of the midbrain also share parts of the anatomical domain. It is believed that the maintenance of consciousness lies deep within the brain stem area in what is called the reticular formation. The reticular system contains millions of neurons that transmit impulses within itself and to other parts of the brain (Figure 2.3).

The reticular system is thought to maintain consciousness because it has a critical role in regulating and modifying all transmissions of impulses from the sensory receptors to the brain, as well as the brain's responses to impulses through muscles and glands. It is a system that operates as a screen between the brain and our communication to the outside world. Within the brain, there are many complex connections between the reticular formation and the cerebral cortex that have an interactive role in consciousness, thinking, and structuring responses to experiences. This raises a major point in Edelman's (1978) "selection" theory, in which he theorizes that as a part of our evolutionary development the brain contains preexisting cellular structures of its own for certain higher order thinking. In the absence of such preexisting structures, according to Edelman, the brain is less able to assure its own survival.

A practical understanding of this phenomenon is provided for the classroom teacher from the work of Elanore Gibson (1969). She has proposed a proactive role for perception and consciousness. She theorized that individuals explore their experiences for cues that aid them in making meaning of phenomena. The meaning that emerges from our variety of experiences enables us to determine what elements in our environment can afford us. "The affordables," according to Gibson, are sought out by our perception, and enable us to discover, for example, that shoes afford our feet protection from hard surfaces like the floor and pavement; a blanket affords us warmth, and language affords us a means of communicating our needs and desires to significant others.

Our exploring perception continually increases our knowledge of affordables and this process becomes more systematic with age. In a variety of ways, Gibson's ideas are compatible with Edelman's theory of preexisting cellular brain structures that in part lead to higher order thinking. The absence of such preexisting structures, according to Edelman, "puts the brain too much at the mercy of the outside world."

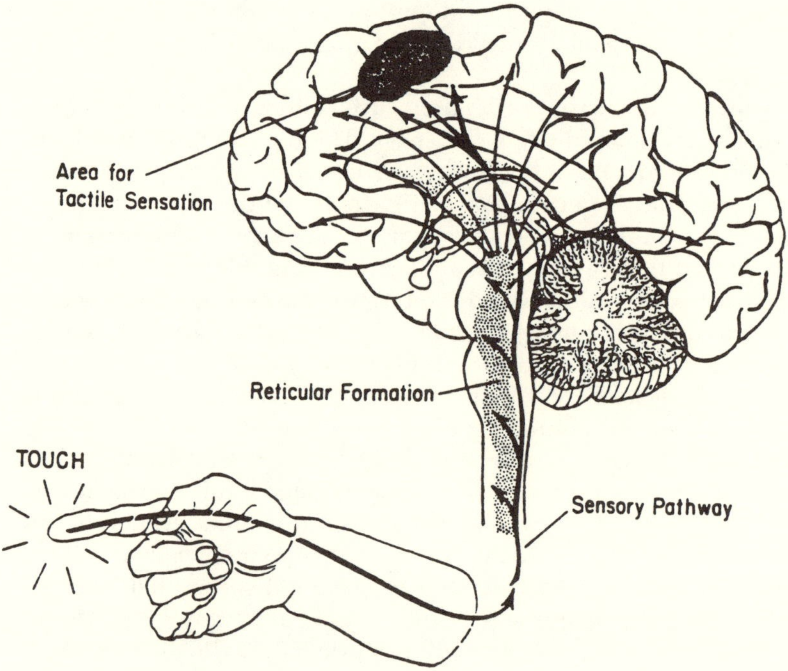

Figure 2.3. Sensory information from touch receptors (finger), is fed into the reticular formation that in turn activates the cortex. Touch information is transmitted by the thalmus (shaded portions), to the cortical area for tactile sensation.

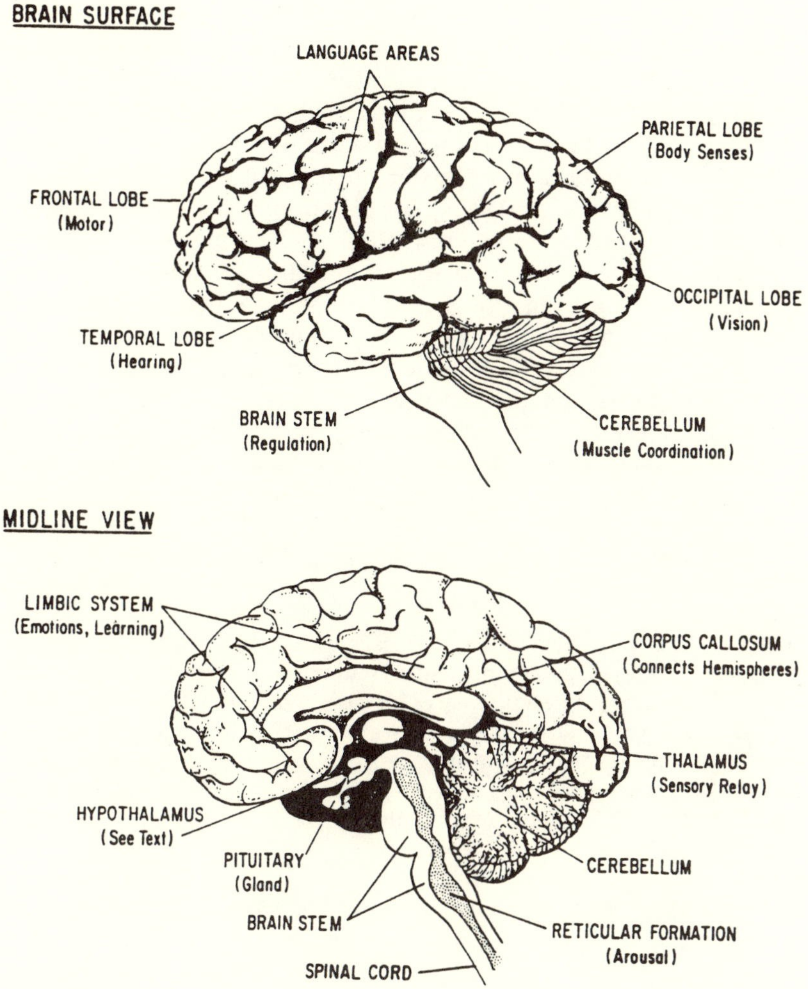

Figure 2.4. Top: The flow of sensory information to brain areas from receptors like the finger. Bottom: Some of the areas involved in motor response commands issued to muscles of the hand and finger.

As mentioned previously, some texts attempt to describe the brain with analogies associated with telephone or computer networks, and the graphic illustration in Figure 2.3 should not be construed as a support for such ideas. These comparisons break down very early in the discourse because science has yet to find hard-wired, point-to-point connections that are responsible for a particular neuro-transmission. For example, we now know that a touch on the nose and one on the bottom of one's foot would send an impulse through the same transmitting network, and register in different areas of the brain. A point to point tracking for each input is not possible because dendrites and axons are sent out in diverse patterns by the cell body (neuron), and even they are structured in divergent, overlapping patterns.

Interesting reports regarding gender differences in brain function and the importance of these patterns to cognitive style theory are emerging from the work of Bruce R. Dunn at the Laboratory for Advanced Studies in Neurocognition at the University of West Florida, along with Marlin L. Languis, Denise A. Dunn, and D. B. Andrews at the Brain/Behavior Laboratory at the Ohio State University. While female and male students performed a series of tasks associated with memory and recognition, their EEG (electrical brain activity) was recorded. From studies conducted on college students it was reported that:

> Topographic Brain Imaging (computer generated images of EEG activity across the cerebral cortex of the brain) coupled with discriminate analyses of the EEG data, showed clear gender differences in patterns of EEG activity for each of the acquisition tasks. Gender differences were also obtained with the recall data generated from the serial learning task which indicates that men recalled significantly more words than did women. The results were discussed in terms of possible differential strategy used by the sexes during the performance of the tasks. (1988, 1)

From studies that were initiated in the late 1960s, Marian Diamond, a researcher in the department of anatomy and physiology at the University of California-Berkeley, conducted a variety of studies on colonies of rats and reported that experience could expand human potentials by increasing axons and dendrites. Diamond structured three different residential colonies in which rats spent a period of time. One colony of twelve rats was maintained in a large "enriched" cage with a collection of twelve objects that were alternated with other objects on a daily basis. The enriched rats were also removed from the cage for thirty minutes a day for exercise in a larger area of open field mazes.

A second colony of rats was placed in a standard cage that was mid-sized and contained three rats. A third environment was labeled "impoverished" because a single rat was placed in a smaller cage and could not see or touch other rats. Compared to the standard colony, subjects in the enriched environment advanced in synaptic growth, and subjects in the impoverished environment lost synaptic fibers. The Diamond study (1967) reported that synaptic structure can be increased in number and size when the organism is exposed to interacting experiences.

Among the various approaches to the study of knowledge acquisition, new challenges are emerging that question the validity of the scientifically assumed role of long-term memory. As described previously, there has been considerable belief among scholars that human experiences led to the storage of information in long-term memory, and that stored information was available to individuals as they made meaning of new experiences. Researchers in cognitive science and fields related to psychology and social science have been reporting on Situated Cognition, which expands considerably a role for human perception and interpretation of experiences. The theory that the role of perception and the interpretation of a learning experience is more a creation of immediacy, rather than of long term stored information, is described by Clancey and Roschelle:

> Situated cognition claims that all processing behavior, including speech, problem solving, and physical skills, are generated on the spot, not by mechanical application of scripts or rules previously stored in the brain. . . . Knowledge is a capacity to behave adaptively within an environment; it cannot be reduced to representations of behavior or the environment. Representations are created by an *interaction* of neural and external processes in what we call perception. As the product of interactions with the environment (sensory, gestural, and interpersonal), representations cannot *correspond* to an external, objective reality. Representations are themselves interpreted interactively, in cycles of perceiving and acting—they are always outside the main loop; they are the *product* of interactions, not a fixed substrate from which behavior is generated. Cognition, like all human behavior, is *situated*. (1991, 1)

Situated learning, a related area of study, has also been of interest to researchers from the perspective of examples of informal childhood learning that were cited in the introduction to this book. From that perspective, examples of children having skills available to them during out-of-school experiences, that were not necessarily available to them to perform in-school assignments, were described. Studies of situational learning theories have examined the extent to which knowledge acquisition depends upon the context in which the knowledge is embedded (Lave, 1988; Greeno, Smith and Moore, 1992). For example, a study of women who performed well on tasks of calculating money-saving shopping skills in making food market purchases, reported that the same women were less successful in carry-over these skills to paper-and-pencil performance in classroom type math calculations (Carraher, Carraher, and Schlemann, 1995).

In related studies involving children, Lave reported that young street vendors in Brazil were able to make error-free money calculations in their curb-side transactions but were unable to solve math problems of equal difficulty in classroom settings (1988).

The role of experience as a factor in information processing is central to an understanding of cognition and cognitive style. There are various schools of thought that describe the complex nature of the role of perception and human behavior that emerges from experience.

Studies by psychologist Arthur Jensen (1966) have reported some capacities for learning might be available to children under certain designed conditions that might not be translated into abilities available to them to solve problems in the general environment of the classroom. To demonstrate this phenomenon, Jensen designed an experiment to show that some learning abilities are unrelated to IQ and/or skills tapped by achievement tests.

From various socioeconomic backgrounds, children were selected who were diagnosed as slow learners, average, and gifted. Children from each of the three groups were assigned the same tasks, which involved pushing a button in response to triangles, squares, and other geometric forms displayed on a screen. Children had to make problem-solving choices between twelve buttons and twelve different geometric forms. As expected, gifted children performed better than both groups, and the "average" children responded better than children in the slow learners as a group. However, one of the children with an IQ of 65—and below average in academic achievement—was among the fastest learners alongside a gifted pupil with an IQ of 145. Also, for the entire group, four children in the slow learner group scored above average for fast learning. Jensen differentiated the experience of learning from the content to be learned. The experience of learning, according to Jensen, involves the elements of learning abilities, learning to learn, learning sets, and labeling behavior. These abilities, though minimally related to IQ, can mean the difference between slow or fast processing of information. Jensen and others have suggested that labeling behavior is essential for learning because one must know how to refer to objects in their absence. Information processing abilities are also enhanced when individuals understand symbolic representations and abstract forms. A slow achieving individual can acquire these abilities through particularized teaching/learning experiences.

The school of thought termed Gestalt psychology invited educators to consider a human encounter as a unified whole that provides meaning for each individual segment of an experience. Gestalt psychologists believe that an experience is comprised of a pattern, or form. They suggest that the pattern or form provides meaning for each individual part. The often-heard statement that the "whole is more than the sum of its parts" has been used by some to describe Gestalt theory. P. E. Vernon (1972) has referred to cognitive styles as Dynamic

Gestalt.

Gestalt psychology was in part a response to prevailing psychological thought about the role of experience in thinking during the early 1900s. Behaviorists argued that experiences should be objectively controlled, observed, and measured. Structuralism, another school of psychological thought that was popular in Europe at about the same time, believed that a study of individual thought processes should be approached by studying the individual parts of the process.

Founded in the early 1900s by German psychologist Max Wertheimer (1880-1943), Gestalt psychology emerged as an important theoretical construct. In the language of his country, Gestalt meant form, pattern, or shape. Wertheimer is credited with originating the movement, however, it was Kurt Koffka (1886-1941) and Wolfgang Köhler (1887-1967), his classmates at the University of Berlin and close colleagues later in life, who made Gestalt psychology known to scholars around the world.

In the United States psychologists who were rejecting prevailing theories of behaviorism and structuralism, were experimenting with their own school of thought called *cognitivism.* Psychologists who were active in this domain were interested in studying the mental processes involved in problem solving through information processing, decision making, awareness, and perception. It was not long before psychologists who were pursuing these two areas of scholarly activity, cognitive psychologists, and Gestalt psychologists, recognized similarities in their interests.

It was problem solving and insight that brought Köhler to formulate concepts embodied in Gestalt psychology. These two concepts emerged from observations that Wolfgang Köhler made during his stay on an island off the coast of Africa. Köhler spent approximately forty-eight months on the island of Tenerife, which was inhabited by apes. In his book, *The Mentality of the Apes,* Köhler described the problem-solving behavior of apes who had been placed in cages. The apes had to use their "thinking skills" to retrieve food that was placed just beyond their reach outside the cages.

In one situation, a bunch of bananas was placed overhead beyond their reach. In another situation, the ape had to employ either one or two sticks to retrieve bananas that were beyond reach. To Köhler's surprise the apes did not use trial and error as might be expected, but they used insight. In this regard, they sought to understand the relationship between self and others, as well as between objects and events.

Their success came after the apes relaxed and contemplated the approach to solving their food retrieval problem. Even when it appeared that the hungry ape employed some trial and error strategy, in reality, each trial was preceded by a short period of thought from which some insight emerged.

Köhler concluded that apes and people utilize insight in problem-solving situations. He described Gestalt theory as the use of insight and the perception of relationships among elements in solving a problematic situation. The principles of insight and perception would be central themes in the theoretical work of Koffka, Köhler, and Wertheimer. Gestaltism theorizes the whole as being made up of parts, but the whole cannot be fully understood by merely examining its individual parts. In a classroom of thirty children, for example, the class as a group cannot be understood by analyzing each child individually, apart from the group. Because, when children come together as a group, the group becomes a social context that assumes a dynamic role of its own. When an adult called "teacher" is included, the group assumes a different dynamic identity.

In the initial stages of the Gestalt movement, Kurt Lewin (1890-1947) was an active participant along with Wertheimer, Koffka, and Köhler, in establishing principles of Gestalt Psychology. Lewin, however, was more concerned about motivation and social interaction than with perception and memory. Lewin's research interests turned more toward individual perceptions that tend to emerge in environmental contexts. He termed this line of interest field studies. Here, Lewin defined the field as ground, and the objects in the environment as figures. In field theory, individual perceptions alternate so that we either perceive figure or ground, but not both simultaneously. Lewin theorized that learning implanted traces in the memory of the organism. This learned information (memory) will format the perceived material in the best possible manner. Individuals, therefore, remember a better Gestalt than what was originally perceived. According to Lewin, the cognitive processes involved in newly organized memories have been described as leveling, sharpening, and normalizing—concepts that will be discussed later in Chapter 7, along with cognitive styles, that share the same labels.

The next steps in describing Lewin's theory starts with the philosophy of phenomenology, in that he introduced the term life space to describe the environment in which individual experiences are enacted. Life space, as defined by Lewin, is the environment as perceived by the individual, which is also a fundamental principal of phenomenology. Lewin's work is also central to the ideas embodied in various approaches to group therapy, theories of self-actualizing, and humanistic psychology. Occasionally, life space has been referred to as personal Gestalt.

In the early 1900s, Katherine C. Briggs became a keen observer of personality types through observations of human interactions and individual behavior related to experience and information processing.

At the same time, she devoted a great deal of time to reading biographies. With the emergence of the work of Carl Gustav Jung (1875-1961), she began to realize that his descriptions of *psychological types* were highly compatible with her own interests that included personality typologies. The Myers-Briggs work will be discussed in greater detail in Chapter 6.

Jung, a Swiss psychologist and psychiatrist, influenced many scholars in philosophy, anthropology, sociology, psychotherapy, and education. He developed the terms *introvert* to describe an individual personality type that is able to satisfy their own needs, and extrovert, one who needs the support of others for gratification. His psychoanalytic approach to clients was to enable them to balance these two at-variance dimensions within their own personality.

He was a contemporary of Freud, and became a strong supporter of the psychoanalytic movement utilizing Freud's psychoanalytic theories in his work. Jung believed that sexual drives were not as important in human development as Freud had theorized. Jung suggested to Freud that the personality of parents posed a more important pathway for the study of childhood development than did studies of early sexuality. This posed a serious dilemma for both theorists, particularly for Freud, because sexuality formed the foundation for his approach to work, and he was emphatic in his disagreement with Jung over this issue. Freud thought that infantile sexual fantasies emerged in the thoughts and dreams of adults and the behavior of patients he diagnosed as neurotic. Ultimately, differences in Freud's and Jung's views regarding sexual implications for child growth and development led to a serious break in their relationship.

Jung dedicated a great deal of his time to what he termed the collective unconscious. In this regard, he theorized that all humans have memories of early experiences embedded in their unconscious. These early memories, he suggested, also have thought patterns that have been passed down to each generation through their ancestors, and the collective nature of these memory patterns leads us to respond to experiences in a manner similar to our ancestors. According to Jung, individuals have different patterns of response to experiences—based upon their ancestral connections—and he calls these differences archetypes. Psychoanalysis, he theorized, could bring clients in touch with the wisdom of the centuries that is embedded in the collective unconscious. From a life-long interest in superstition and mythology, Jung came to the conclusion that religion had a critical role in human development because it enabled individuals to express an underlying need for this type of experience.

With a specific focus on learning experiences of children, Urie Bronfenbrenner's (1917-) ecological theory utilizes fundamental principles found in phenomenology, and in Lewin's theory of Life Space.

Bronfenbrenner's theory of child development examines the child's environment from the perspectives of a variety of social settings. In each setting—home, neighborhood, school, and so forth—the influences on the interacting child are not necessarily the objectively observed experiences, but the influences that emerge from the child's interpretations of encounters. These encounters that influence the child's development come from events, interpersonal relations, and various roles that are enacted by significant persons in the child's environment.

According to Bronfenbrenner, there are three Microsystems (home, school, and peer group), that host various childhood experiences. These Microsystems form a single Mesosystem which embodies childhood experiences beyond the first protective tier. Then, there are other components that influence the child's experiences from a more global Exosystem. This aspect of the child's social system includes, but is not limited to, school authorities who set policies that ultimately influence the child's school and community life; neighborhood adults and professionals who occasionally interact with adults in the child's family; and the parent's work place. In this system, the child's experiences are examined in light of the child's interpretation of influences and interactions in the various Microsystems (school, home, and peer group).

The variations on existentialism and phenomenology that were embedded in the theories of Lewin, Bronfenbrenner, cognitivism, and Gestalt psychology, created a worldwide scholarly environment within which humanistic psychology, and humanistic education, could emerge. Equally important to the popularity of humanistic approaches to individual and group experience was the political climate of the 1960s and 1970s.

Politically, the 1960s brought our attention to the importance of the self in human development, as opposed to the notion that government and institution should be the major forces in directing our lives. Here again, we encounter the value of the individual as central to the study of human experiences as proposed by existentialists and phenomenologists years earlier. The concept of self has received considerable attention in scholarly literature.

By the age of twelve, children are aware of a "self" that will endure over time regardless of changes in their stature or appearance. They are also capable of making distinctions between their subjective self (the kind of person I am) and their objective self (how I am perceived by others).

The construct known as self-esteem (used interchangeably in the literature with self-concept) has been the interest of educational professionals for some time. Harter (1982) suggested that during the middle years a child's self-concept becomes more complex. She identified four performance areas that contribute toward the learner's self-worth: (a) cognitive competence (performance of school work), (b) social competence (popularity and social skills), (c) physical competence (performance in sports/games), and (d) general self worth (sure/unsure of one's self in general). A child can feel competent in one or more areas or, unfortunately in some cases, none. Cognitive style theorists have investigated the relationship between certain cognitive preferences and individual perceptions of self.

> Persons with a more articulated or more global mode of cognitive functioning have also been found to differ in an important aspect of the self, namely, *sense of separate identity.* Persons with an articulated cognitive style give evidence of a developed sense of separate identity—that is to say, they have an awareness of needs, feelings and attributes which they recognize as their own and which they identify as distinct from those of others. Sense of separate identity implies experience of the self as segregated from nonself: it also implies experience of the self as structured. (Witkin, et al. 1971, 8)

Educators have focused on self-concept in learners as a means of enabling them to value their competence positively and, thereby, to maximize their classroom performance. It is often reported that Black children, because of high rates of poverty, single parent homes, and too few male role models, tend to demonstrate less positive self-valuing than do their White peers. The arguments continue along these lines to identify this phenomenon as a possible source for Black/White school achievement differences, when they occur. Recent studies have failed to confirm these widely accepted views. There are significant indications from self-reports to suggest that Black males in particular, and Black pupils in general, possess a greater positive valuing than did their White classmates. As pointed out earlier, these contradictory findings have been analyzed at various intervals; Adam (1978) presented the most compelling analysis.

Humanistic theorists also give serious consideration to the thoughts and feelings that individuals take to—and receive from—their experiences. It is their view that the actuality of an experience cannot be fully explained by an objective observer. The essence of an experience, according to humanistic theorists, should be interpreted only by the experiencer. Therefore, the experiencer must be given the opportunity to explore the meanings that they derive from their encounters. In the classroom, this means that the environment must be open and responsive to the needs and interests of learners, because the learner is in the most strategic position to determine their own needs.

Early humanistic classroom practices were often labeled the open classroom approach. Despite the fact that humanistic education is mentioned less in scholarly circles today, their theories are still recognized in classroom practice in such things as invented spelling, whole language, affective curriculum, the child-centered approach, and cooperative learning. In each of these approaches to understanding human development, curriculum design and teaching practices, the child's observations and interpretations are highly respected. Humanistic theorists believed that educators, and those who direct programs for children, should focus on the self and create a variety of experiences from which learners can acquire information. In this endeavor, many humanistic teachers discovered the philosophy of John Dewey who had espoused similar practices in the early 1900s.

As of now, humanistic education is seldom spoken of in current educational forums, but curriculum reforms that emerged from its 1960s and 1970s popularity have left us with an enriched collection of affective teaching and learning improvements.

Present-day educational programs and practices have also been enriched by the philosophical and theoretical variations that have been described in literature and made available to educational planners and practitioners. This literature has, among other things, informed educators that an understanding of the role of self and experience in human development is essential. It is within this context that cognitive style theory has emerged as an important development in professional approaches to classroom teaching and learning.

REFERENCES

Abeles, M., and Schilder, P. (1935). "Psychogenic Loss of Personal Identity." *Archives of Neurology and Psychiatry* 34, 587-604.

Adam, B. D. (1978). "Inferiorization and Self-Esteem." *Social Psychology* 41, 47-53.

Alpert-Gillis, L. J., and Connell, J. P. (1989). "Gender and Sex-Role Influences on Children's Self-Esteem." *Journal of Personality* 57, 97-114.

Anderson, J. R. (1983). *The Architecture of Cognition*. Cambridge. MA: Harvard University Press.

Anderson, J. R. (1990). *Cognitive Psychology and its Implications.* New York: W. H. Freeman.

Astington, J. W., Harris, P. L., and Olson, D. R. (1988). *Developing Theories of Mind.* New York: Cambridge University Press.

Bargar, R. R., and Hoover, R. L. (1984). "Psychological Type and the Matching of Cognitive Styles." *Theory Into Practice* 23 (1), 56-63.

Barker, R. G. (1978) *Habitats, Environments, and Human Behavior.* San Francisco, CA: Jossey-Bass.

Bateson, G. (1988). *Mind and Nature: A Necessary Unity.* New York: Bantam.

Bennett, E. L., Diamond, M. C., Krech, D., and Rosenzweig, M. R.

(1964). "Chemical and Anatomical Plasticity." *Science* 146, 610-619.

Bennett, E. L., Rosenzweig, M. R., Diamond, M. C., Morimoto, H., and Hebert, M. (1974). "Effects of Successive Environments on Brain Measures." *Physiology and Behavior* 12, 621-631.

Bickard, M. H., and Ritchie, D. M. (1983). *On the Nature of Representation: A Case Study of James Gibson's Theory of Perception.* New York: Praeger.

Bode, B. H. (1940). *How We Learn.* New York: D. C. Heath.

Brainerd, C. J. (1983). *Recent Advancement in Recent Cognitive Developmental Theory.* New York: Springer-Verlag.

Bronfenbrenner, U. (1979). *The Ecology of Human Development.* Cambridge, MA: Macmillan.

Broughton, J. (1978). "Development of Concepts of Self, Mind, Reality, and Knowledge." *New Directions for Child Development* 1, 75-100.

Buhler, C., and Allen, M. (1972). *Introduction to Humanistic Psychology.* Monterey, CA: Brooks/Cole.

Cantor, N., and Kihlstrom, J. F. (1987). *Personality and Social Intelligence.* Englewood Cliffs, NJ: Prentice Hall, Inc.

Carey, J. C., Fleming, S. D., and Roberts, D. Y. (1989). "The Myers-Briggs Type Indicator as a Measure of Aspects of Cognitive Style." *Measurement and Evaluation in Counseling and Development* 22, 94-99.

Carraher, T. N. Carraher, D. W., and Schilemann, D. D. (1985). Mathematics in the Streets and in the Schools." *British Journal of Developmental Psychology* 3, 21-29.

Combs, A. W., and Snygg, D. (1959). *Individual Behavior.* New York: Harper and Row.

Chall, J. S., and Mirsky, A. F. eds., (1978). *Education and the Brain.* Chicago, Ill: The University of Chicago Press.

Chomsky, N. (1957). *Syntactic Structures.* The Hague: Mouton.

Clancey, W. J., and Roschelle, J. eds., (1991). "Situated Cognition: How Representations are Created and Given Meaning." *Implications of Cognitive Theories of How the Nervous System Functions for Research and Practice in Education.* Symposium Conducted at the Annual meeting of the American Educational Research Association, Chicago, IL.

Crandall, R. (1973). "The Measurement of Self-Esteem and Related Concepts." In J. P. Robinson and P. R. Shaver, eds., *Measures of Social Psychological Attitudes.* Ann Arbor, MI: Institute for Social Research.

Damon, W. (1983). *Social and Personality Development: Infancy Through Adolescence.* New York: W. W. Norton.

Diamond, M. C. (1967). "Extensive Cortical Depth Measurements and Neuron Size Increases in the Cortex of Environmentally Enriched Rats." *Journal of Comparative Neurology* 3, 357-364.

Dunn, B. R., Languis, L. L., Dunn, D. A., and Andrews, D. B. (1988). "Gender Differences in EEG Patterns: Are They Indexes of Different Cognitive Styles?" Paper presented at the annual meeting of the American Educational Research Association, New Orleans, LA.

Edelman, G. M. (1978). "Group Selection and Phasic Reentrant Signaling: A Theory of Higher Brain Function." In G. M. Edelman and V. Mountcastle, eds., *The Mindful Brain.* Cambridge, MA: MIT Press.

Edelman, G. M. (1987). *Neural Darwinism: The Theory of Neuronal Group Selection.* New York: Basic Books.

Epstein, H. (1978). "Growth Spurts During Brain Development: Implications for Educational Policy and Practice." In J. Chall and Mirsky, eds., *Education and the Brain,* Chicago, IL: University of Chicago Press.

Franz, M. L., and Hilman, J. (1979). *Jung's Typology.* Dallas: Spring Pub-lications.

Freud, S. (1977). *The Origins of Psychoanalysis: Letters to Wilhelm Fliess, Drafts and Notes:* 1887-1902. Trans. by E. Moisbacher and J. Strachey. New York: Basic Books.

Gagne, R. M. (1962). The Acquisition of Knowledge. *Psychological Review* 69, 355-365.

Gibson, E. J. (1969). *Principles of Perceptual Learning and Development.* New York: Appleton.

Greeno, J. G., Smith, D. R., and Moore, G. L. (1992). "Transfer of Situated Learning." In D. Detterman and R. J. Sternberg, eds., *Transfer on Trial: Intelligence, Cognition, and Instruction.* Norwood: NJ: Ablex.

Hall, C., and Nordby, V. (1973). *A Primer of Jungian Psychology.* New York: New American Library.

Harter, S. (1982). "The Perceived Competence Scale for Children." *Child Development* 53 , 87-97.

Jensen, A. R. (1966). "Individual Differences in Concept Learning." In *Analyses of Concept Learning.* H. J. Klausmeier and C. W. Harris eds., New York: Academic Press.

Jung, C. G. (1923). *Psychological Types.* London: Rutledge and Kegan Paul.

Kagan, J. (1965). "Impulsive and Reflective Children: Significance of Conceptual Tempo." In J. D. Krumholtz ed., *Learning and the Eduational Process.* Chicago, IL: Rand McNally.

Klatsky, R. L. (1980). *Human Memory: Structures and Process.* San Francisco: W. H. Freeman.

Klausmeir, J., and Harris C. W. (1966). *Analyses of Concept Learning.* New York: Academic Press.

Koffka, K. (1922). "Perception: An Introduction to Gestalt Theory." *Psychological Bulletin* 19, 531-585.

Koffka, K. (1935). *Principles of Gestalt Psychology.* New York: Harcourt Brace & World.

Köhler, W. (1927). *The Mentality of Apes*. New York: Harcourt Brace & World.

Köhler, W., and Wertheimer, M. (1959). "Gestalt Psychology Today."*American Psychologist* 14, 727-734.

Lave, J. (1988). *Cognition in Practice.: Mind, Mathematics, and Culture in Everyday Life.* Cambridge, MA: Cambridge University Press.

Lave, J., and Wenger, E. (1991). *Situated Learning: Legitimate Peripheral Participation.* Cambridge, MA: Cambridge University Press.

Lewin, K. (1947). "Frontiers in Group Dynamics." *Human Relations* 1, 5-41.

Lewin, K. (1951). *Field Theory in Social Science.* New York: Harper & Row.

Macphail, E. M. (1982). *Brain and Intelligence in Vertebrates.* London: Clarendon Press.

Mazola, A. H. (1968). *Toward a Psychology of Being.* New York: Van Nostrand & Reinhold.

Marsh, H. W. and Shavelson, R. J. (1985). "Self-Concept: Its Multifacated, Hierarchical Structure." *Educational Psychologist* 20, 107-125.

Mayr, E. (1982). *The Growth of Biological Thought: Diversity, Evolution, and Inheritance.* Cambridge, MA: Harvard University Press.

McCaulley, M. H. (1981). "Jung's Theory of Psychological Types and the Myers-Briggs Type Indicator." In P. Reynolds, ed., *Advances in Personality Assessment.* (Vol. 5), 294-352. San Francisco: Jossey-Bass.

Myers, I. B. (1962). *Manual: The Myers-Briggs Type Indicator.* Palo Alto, CA: Consulting Psychologists Press.

Neisser, U (1976). *Cognition and Reality: Principles and Implications of Cognitive Psychology.* New York: W. H. Freeman.

Nickerson, R. S. (1965). "Short-Term Memory for Complex Meaningful Visual Configurations, a Demonstration of Capacity." *Canadian Journal of Psychology* 19, 155-150.

Norman, D. A. (1982). *Learning and Memory.* New York: W. H. Freeman.

Read, D. A., and Simon, S. B. (1975) *Humanistic Education Sourcebook.* Englewood Cliffs, NJ: Prentice-Hall.

Rosenfield, I. (1988). *The Invention of Memory: A New View of the Brain.* New York: Basic Books.

Schon, D. A. (1987). *Educating the Reflective Practitioner.* San Francisco: Jossey-Bass.

Sheerer, M. (1965). *Cognition: Theory, Research, Promise.* New York: Harper & Row.

Shepherd, G. M. (1983). *Neurobiology.* New York: Oxford University Press.

Sperry, R. W. (1969). "A Modified Concept of Consciousness." *Psychological Review,* 76, 532-536.

Sperry, R. W. (1970). "An Objective Approach to Subjective Experience." *Psychological Review* 77, 585-590.

Staddon, J. E. R. (1974). "Temporal Control, Attention and Memory." *Psychological Review* 81, 375-391.

Staddon, J. E. R. (1983). *Adaptive Behavior and Learning.* New York: Cambridge University Press.

Staddon, J. E. R. (1984). "Time and Memory." *Annals of the New York Academy of Sciences* 423, 322-324.

Tyler, S. (1978). *The Said and the Unsaid: Mind, Meaning, and Culture.* New York: Academic Press.

Vernon, P. E. (1972). "The Distinctiveness of Field Independence." *Journal of Personality* 40, 366-391.

Vygotsky, L. S. (1962). *Thought and Language.* Cambridge, MA: MIT Press.

Werner, H. (1937). "Process and Achievement." *Harvard Educational Review* 7, 353-368.

Werner, H. (1948). *Comparative Psychology of Mental Development.* Chicago: Follet.

Werner, H. (1957). "The Concept of Development From a Comparative and Organismic Point of View." In D. B. Harris, ed., *The Concept of Development: An Issue in the Study of Behavior.* Minneapolis: University of Minnesota Press.

Wertheimer, M. (1959). *Productive Thinking.* New York: Harper & Row.

Witkin, H. A., Dyk, R. B., Faterson, H. F., Goodenough, D. R., and Karp, S. A. (1974). *Psychological Differentiation.* Potomac, MD: Lawrence Erlbaum.

Witkin, H. A. , Oltman, P. K. , Raskin, E., and Karp, S. A. (1971). "Manual: Embedded Figures Test." Palo Alto, CA: *Consulting Psychologist Press.*

Worden, F. G., Swazey, J. P., and Adelman, G., eds. (1975). *Neuroscience: Paths of Discovery.* Cambridge, MA: MIT Press.

3

Field Independent and Field Dependent Cognitive Styles

> The most complex form of expression is called "style"—the particular individualized manner of execution that permeates any highly integrated volitional activity. Though most conspicuous and most celebrated in the fields of esthetic creation, style is also apparent in economic, domestic and social conduct—wherever, in fact, the fundamental traits of personality are operative. Though the roots of style are no doubt to be traced to native temperament, the interaction of mature traits with one another, and their confluent effect upon creative and adaptive acts, are the immediate sources of the stylistic idiom.
>
> —Gordon W. Allport

Field independent and field dependent cognitive styles have received more attention from scholars in education and psychology than any other cognitive styles. These two styles are frequently paired for discussion because they represent an individual information processing mode along a bipolar plane—at either end of a continuum. This does not mean that there are two distinctively different types of individuals—field independent and field dependent. A continuum in this context means that there are persons with variations of these traits at different points between the two extremes, on each side of a central point. From a psychological differentiation perspective, Witkin describes these two domains in the following manner:

> The person with a more field independent way of perceiving tends to experience his surroundings analytically, with objects experienced as discrete from their backgrounds. The person with a more field dependent way of perceiving tends to experience his surroundings in a relatively global fashion, passively conforming to the influence of the prevailing field or context. (Witkin, et al. 1974, 35)

Historically, the concept of psychological differentiation, first introduced by Werner in 1957, preceded the term cognitive style. Werner's theories were developmental in nature and have been referred to as orthogenetic. In this regard, the orthogenetic approach to conceptualizing human growth and development is central to the work of Freud (psychosexual), Piaget and Erikson (psychosocial), and Mahler (social adaptation).

Werner theorized that the biological course followed by the growth pattern of all humans followed a pathway from a global state to one of differentiation, articulation, and hierarchical integration. He stressed that, developmental changes in the human growth system advanced systematically taking advantage of earlier stages of growth. Werner was rather specific about how growth changes were defined. In his view, a child's change in height or weight represented only quantitative changes which were not particularly important to study. What was important to Werner's theory were systematic qualitative changes found in basic underlying biological structures. These internal structures, he theorized, emerged in predetermined stages with minimal influence from environmental experiences in the early stages of growth.

Internal structures, according to Werner, begin with an undifferentiated (global) relationship between the individual and the environment. As biological structures grow they become more independent (differentiated), and the human organism becomes more efficient at creating cooperative interactions between the underlying subsystems.

In maturity, the individual is capable of differentiating external from internal stimuli and processing them appropriately. Finally, individual underlying biological structures become independent and mature to the point of acquiring the capability to set goals and reject distractions.

At this point in structuring an understanding of the relationship between psychological differentiation—factors that are central to Lewin's life space, and constructs of self-concept— the work of Green on social structures, can bring together these concepts as they interface with field independent/field dependent theory.

Part of an ongoing project on the reciprocal effects of persons and social boundaries, examines effective reactions of relatively undifferentiated (field dependent) and relatively differentiated individuals following their participation in two social situations designed to differ primarily in group size. . . . Large groups, especially those that are relatively free, are perceived by the individual as boundless, amorphous, and. . . . Difficulties in establishing discrete rules, in preserving a comfortable interactive distance between self and others, in simply being heard and responded to can lead to complete withdrawal or fusion. In comparison, small groups, even those with minimal, explicit social structure, are considered much less threatening for the individual partly because they are said to afford greater opportunities for creating powerful, covert structures. (1979, 81)

By 1962 concepts associated with psychological differentiation were fully integrated into the work of psychologists who were exploring various aspects of field dependence and field independence (Witkin, Dyk, et al.).

In general, individuals who are more field independent are able to delineate objects or details that have surroundings that might obscure them from view. For example, field independent persons are more capable of identifying fruit on a vine or tree even though the colors might not be very different from the leaves and branches. This is also true for the understanding of issues that might be embedded in a Socratic argument. In other words, field independent persons are better able to detect objects in a manner that such objects are independent from other parts of the scene. On the other hand, field dependent learners are less likely to view things separate from the overall environment and would have greater difficulty viewing a single piece of fruit as standing apart from the tree or surrounding foliage. Therefore, field dependent learners might prefer that things remain within their field to enable them to better examine the meaning of their individual parts, while remaining embedded in their environment. In social settings, the field dependent-style person might process information more proficiently during group interaction, while the field independent-style person could prefer to interact with individuals or work alone.

An understanding of these bipolar cognitive styles can also be derived from instruments designed to measure these traits in individuals. Central to the fundamental concepts underlying the development of these instruments is that the downward pull of gravity gives us an internal sense of uprightness. Second, individuals have a visual awareness of direction from objects in their visual field of experience. When we put the visual awareness of the environment together with our internal gravitational sense of uprightness, this congruence provides a sense of orientation. What would happen if one were asked to determine the uprightness of an object in an environment where the visual field did not exist? One instrument, which is designed on this principle, asked subjects under test to determine their upright position in an environment where a sense of body status and visual cues were eliminated. The subject is placed in a completely darkened room where the visual component is a luminous frame that can be rotated left or right on a central axis. On the same axis is a luminous rod that can be pivoted in the same directions of choice. The frame and rod are all that the subject can see or manipulate in the completely darkened room. With the frame in a tilted position, the subject is asked to orient the rod to an upright position without moving the frame. Some subjects used the frame as a reference for uprightness and aligned it with the surrounding frame. For example, when the frame was tilted 30 degrees to the right, they tilted the rod 30 degrees to the right. This group was considered field dependent, in that they based their decision on the surrounding field. While others ignored the frame's tilt and placed the rod in a position closely resembling the uprightness of the outside world. This latter group was determined field independent based upon their perception of internal body orientation being influenced less by the frame of reference.

After many studies were conducted with the rod and frame device, over time a less complex table-top model was developed. Such instruments have been designed to accommodate individuals age three and older. The traditional instruments that required a dark room would be inappropriate for young children.

A second approach to field independent field dependent assessment uses the orientation of the body in space rather than a rod. The subject is placed in a chair that can be tilted mechanically within a small room which can also be tilted. The chair and the room are tilted to the same degree, and the examiner asks the subject to alter the orientation of the chair in a manner that feels upright (while the room remains in a tilt). Some subjects experience their own bodies as being upright when it is in common with the tilt of the room. These subjects are determined to be influenced profoundly by their surroundings. Then there are subjects at the other extreme who are not influenced by the tilted room; they orient their bodies similar to gravitational uprightness.

For both assessments, The rod and frame test and the body adjustment test, people score along a continuum between the two extremes, with most subjects being reported closer to the mean. All subjects however, achieve accurate scores when asked to orient their bodies upright, with their eyes closed. It is the intrusion or exclusion of the environment that tends to make a difference in individual body adjustment assessments. A portable rod and frame test was later developed that provided a less cumbersome instrument more suitable for administration in limited space and less intrusive when children are subjects under test.

A sense of uprightness examined by the two previous instruments was employed as an index to determine the extent to which a person might be field independent or field dependent. Other instruments have also used the senses as the foundation for assessing these cognitive styles. They have usually measured the extent to which an individual could discern a simple sound, design, or tactile element once it was removed from its more complex surroundings. One type of embedded-figures task requires the subject to feel out a simple figure of raised contours and establish its rightful position in a larger context of raised contours. Another embedded-figures test employs music by playing a simple tune for the subject and requesting that they place it in its proper place in the more complex melody from which it came. The embedded-figures task that has been more popular than the latter two asks the subject to place a small geometrically shaped figure in its proper place in a larger more complex figure from which it came. Each is concerned with the extent to which an individual is influenced by the surrounding field in situations.

After the basic constructs of cognitive style received a great deal of interest from the research community, the children's embedded-figures test was developed, and the portable rod and frame test provided a less intrusive means to test preschool children's cognitive styles. Developmentally, it would not be particularly useful to test children below school age. We now know from the work of Piaget and others that children are not only egocentric, but they also have an undeveloped sense of object permanence. For example, by the age of three, children are aware of a sense of self apart from others, as well as gender differences among significant others. It is not until they reach the age of five or six, however, that they are aware that these conditions are permanent. Here, socialization is a critical factor because of the influence that it imposes on perception and individual values. The growing child's experiences enhance their perceptions regarding gender typing. Their knowledge about gender emerges from their observations of what men and women do in relation to their own experiences, their observations of gender specific likes/dislikes (values), their perceptions of their own values and sexual preferences, patterns of friendship, and their own sense of self.

Socializing experiences of young children are still greatly influenced by gender role stereotyping. Despite the fact that professionals who work with young children are taught to focus upon the actual attributes that children bring to the school experience—rather than an adult imposed, preconceived characteristic—there still remains considerable stereotypical gender classification of some children. In this regard, some teachers expect that boys are more likely to say taboo words, be aggressive and tough, dominant, and ambitious. It is also true that girls are often expected to be more meek, submissive, gentle, and affectionate. Children get cues and signals from their experiences with adults; and when unexpected characteristics are exposed, as when a seven-year-old boy displays affectionate, gentle behavior, or a girl playmate is aggressive and dominant., adults will discourage these children from continuing along their selected pathways. Nonetheless, regardless of adult influence in either direction, socialization with its own idiosyncrasies is taking place.

Socialization, it is believed, also accounts for many variations in cognitive styles. The family, being our first social context, provides the environment for all early experiences. Many studies have reported that variations in these experiences such as strict discipline, strong demands for obedience, patriarchal authority—as opposed to encouragement of self-expression, unlimited wait-time for toilet training, and access to choices without gender stereotyping—will influence the emergence of different cognitive styles.

Child-rearing practices have been the subject of thousands of studies in psychology, sociology, anthropology, and education. Variations in these practices have been linked to the development of particular cognitive preferences in children. It was reported by Dyk and Witkin (1965) that when parents encourage their children to act independently, more often than not, the children will be field independent. They go on to suggest that when children are encouraged to conform to authority, they tend to acquire field dependent cognitive preferences.

It has been reported that children of Hispanic descent are generally raised in homes where conformity to authority within the family, among neighbors, and in the school is encouraged and expected. It has also been reported that children raised in orthodox Jewish homes have fewer experiences with their father as an authority figure than with their mother in this role. The influences that these variations in socialization have upon cognitive style suggest that children from both of these environments would be more field dependent than field independent. Once cognitive preferences are established by individuals, Spiro and Tirre (1980) report from their study, that even when the experiences of readers are the same, their comprehension remains associated with an idiosyncratic cognitive preference.

Here, for teachers who highly value comprehension as an essential factor in learning to read, consider it important that students are able to make inferences about the text that is not explicit, but embedded in an understanding of the experience, called cognitive structures. These cognitive structures are thought to be stored in memory as generalized concepts. For example, when children are reading about a class that took a trip to the circus with their teacher, they will infer from the nature of the event that there was probably a charge for admission and that parents probably paid, even when it is not mentioned in the text. These inferences, according to Spiro and Tirre, will vary in idiosyncratic lines according to the cognitive style of the learner.

Fehrenbach (1994) also studied the implications that cognitive style might have for classroom performance in reading. She reported significant differences in the effectiveness of various strategies utilized by field dependent/independent children. For this study, the divisions of field dependent/independent were further divided into gifted and average readers. For gifted readers there appeared to be no significant differences in the reading processing strategies utilized by those who were field dependent and those who were field independent. It was also reported from this study that among average readers, there were no significant differences between reading processing strategies when field dependents were compared to field independents.

When the ability levels were ignored, and all field dependents as a group were compared to field independents, there were significant differences between the groups in the types of reading processing strategies used. In this regard, field independents summarized accurately, reread the text, analyzed the structure and/or the content of the story more often. On the other hand, field dependents more often summarized inaccurately and stated failure to understand the story.

Mansoor Niaz (1989) studied proportional reasoning competence among science majors at the Universidad de Oriente (Venezuela) to investigate differences in performance between field independent and field dependent students. From a group of over three hundred university students Niaz reported that during certain experiments field dependent students demonstrated less proportional reasoning skill than their field independent counterparts. Similar studies have been conducted in the United States at various grade levels (Wollman and Lawson, 1978; Nummedal and Collea, 1981).

Niaz recommended that science teachers should use a variety of techniques to accommodate the field dependent learner's proportional reasoning deficit. For example, information that depends upon perceptual field factors should not constitute the major emphasis in instruction, "correct" responses should not be completely embedded in field factors, and classroom activities should include teaching students how to translate sentences into algebraic equations.

Manuel Ramirez et al. (1974) were among the first scholars to investigate cognitive styles among American children of Spanish descent. Their work has reported consistently that learners from these families tend to be field dependent rather than field independent. Further, in Ramirez's more recent work he has preferred the term "field sensitive" in describing their preferred cognitive style (1982). The term field sensitive represents more than a mere semantic change; it represents, among other strategies, a shift away from the traditional assessment instruments like the embedded-figures tests and the rod and frame test. Ramirez has argued that for minority children, and possibly other children as well, observations of children's performance in the classroom setting provides more valid and reliable information about knowledge acquisition styles employed by minority children. Ramirez and others have developed programs that are infused with teacher and administrator multicultural awareness. This awareness has emerged from observational studies which in turn serves as a backdrop to educational planning for minority children in several areas of the United States including Southern California and Texas.

The goals and selected multicultural values identified by Ramirez, in working with learners of Spanish descent, are reminiscent of ideas regarding Black youth in higher education, expressed by Alain Locke, African American philosopher and professor at Howard University in the 1920s. Ramirez discussed these goals as he described a program designed to recognize the cognitive styles of minority children in the schools where such programs have been implemented.

> In these programs, the cognitive styles framework has been used to develop administrator, teacher, and staff self awareness as well as to work toward the goals specified for children. The cultural backgrounds of the children were respected and used through other strategies as well, including multiethnic social studies curriculum and use of Spanish and English for instruction. . . . Data from evaluations of this program show that by the end of third grade, math scores of children who participated were six months ahead of those children of comparable backgrounds in a school without the program. Furthermore, on standardized tests of academic achievement, the participating children performed as well, and in some cases better than, children in non-participating classes who were from homes of higher SES and more fluent English speaking backgrounds. Children participating in the program have shown annual improvement in self esteem and respect for cultural diversity, while teachers and staff implementing the program have shown increasing sensitivity and awareness of individual differences among children. (Ramirez, 1982, 8-9)

As multicultural variations occur in program implementation, there are two cautionary elements of concern. One suggests that care should be taken not to over interpret learner differences so that the identification of multicultural differences become stereotypes. In this regard, *differences* might be interpreted as *deficits* and harm the very students for whom multicultural programs are designed to help. The second concern is with curriculum content. In the absence of careful planning, programs designed for culturally different children might be lacking in the content that all children need to become competent learners.

Saracho (1991) investigated cognitive styles among Mexican American children from the perspectives of social competence, social role taking, social problem-solving, social play, and other socially oriented variables. She reported that Mexican American children were not overly field dependent as reported by earlier studies. She used a variety of instruments like the articulation of body concept, the Goodenough-Harris drawing test, the children's embedded-figures test, the preschool social behavior scale, a researcher developed picture sociometric test, and a role-taking, problem-solving instrument called perspective taking. From an assessment of various findings, Saracho suggested that it is premature, and often erroneous, to attribute field-dependency to Mexican Americans because variables like the quantity and quality of integrated Anglo experiences attribute to a normal distribution between field independent/dependent cognitive styles. It is worth noting however, that the instruments employed by Saracho were primarily socially oriented assessments—precisely the domain of field-dependence dominance. It is the interpretation of the results from socially oriented measures that led Saracho to conclude a significant distribution for Mexican American children among the domains of field independent/dependent cognitive preferences.

Cognitive style characteristics and how they influence the performance of African American and Hispanic children have been the subject of many studies. These investigations appear at a time when educators are attempting to identify what might satisfy the needs of a multicultural curriculum. Various approaches have emerged on this theme.

Anthropologist John Ogbu reminds us that any approach to developing academic multiculturalism must start with an awareness of how various immigrant groups came to the United States. He cites African Americans as one of several groups who did not come to the United States by choice. Many racial minorities were imported for the purpose of providing free labor, not as citizens with rights of participation in such things as commerce and politics. From the perspectives of community-based research, Ogbu discusses the relationships between school expectations, values, and interpretations of experiences, and those things that are imparted to children by minority family members and their communities.

> Taken together, multicultural education fosters pride in minority cultures, helps minority students develop new insights into their culture, reduces prejudice and stereotyping, and promotes intercultural understandings. But the critical question is to what extent will multicultural education improve the academic performance of those minorities who have not traditionally done well in school? Rarely do multicultural education models address this question explicitly. . . . Multicultural education may indeed improve school learning for some minority children, however, for several reasons it is not an adequate strategy to enhance the academic performance of those minorities who have traditionally not done well in school. . . . Multicultural education generally emphasizes changing teacher attitudes and practices. . . . School success depends not only on what schools and teachers do but also on what students do. . . . What is also instructive is that there are minority groups whose language expressions, mathematical and number systems, and overt cultural behaviors might be different from those of White Americans to be considered barriers to learning math and science but whose

members, nevertheless, learn more or less successfully. . . . To understand what it is about minority groups, their culture and languages that makes cross cultural boundaries and school learning difficult for some but not for others, we must recognize that there are different types of minority groups or minority status. . . . Castelike or involuntary minorities are people who were originally brought into the United States or in any other society against their will. For example, through slavery, conquest, colonization or forced labor. Thereafter, these minorities were often relegated to menial positions and denied true assimilation into the mainstream society. American Indians, Black Americans, Early Mexican Americans in the Southwest, and native Hawaiians are U.S. examples. (1992, 6)

Within this context, it is important to discuss perceptual preferences that surface in the classroom when the backgrounds of learners have been influenced by environments that are at variance with experiences that are common to most children. It is also important to study the unique learning qualities of children with whom newly educated teachers have had no experience and have read little or nothing about. Children who reside in the impoverished areas of our major cities and the children of migrant workers are among the most likely to become field dependent.

In regards to the children of inner-city and poor families, Jonathan Kozol has spent a great deal of time promoting their interests and bringing our attention to racial isolation and debilitating circumstances under which they attend school. From observations during visits to schools between 1988 and 1990, Kozol recorded the following:

Oyler Elementary School, unlike so many of the schools I have seen in poor black neighborhoods, is not so much intense and crowded, as it is depleted, bleak and bare. The eyes of the children, many of whom have white-blond hair and almost all of whom seem rather pale and gaunt, appear depleted too. During several hours in the school I rarely saw a child with a good big smile. Bleakness was the order of the day in fifth grade science.The children were studying plant biology when I came in, but not with lab equipment. There was none. There was a single sink that may have worked but was not being used, a couple of test tubes were locked up in a cupboard, and a skeleton was also behind glass windows. The nearly total blankness of the walls was interrupted only by a fire safety poster. The window shades were badly torn. . . . "The Elements" on the wall behind the teacher listed no elements discovered in the past four decades. (1991, 230-231)

For children in some immigrant and migrant-worker families, their life experiences are not unlike those of children described by Kozol. Their frequent change in school environments due to seasonal opportunities for family work, and variations in work sites, place them at risk in a subsistence income family with uncertain and impermanent living conditions, with too few opportunities for sustained socialization in peer environments. It is likely that the child's modest schooling experiences in the agriculturally migrant way of life, along with observation and conversations with family members, will induce referents that are field dependent.

When the entire migrant family is focused on one primary goal (getting in the crop), with each person expected to fulfill an essential role that contributes to group success, individualization is obscured. Rather than a detailed analysis of events around them, field dependent individuals are more likely to be social and group oriented. Field dependence is compatible with the nomadic, agricultural context within which migrant children make meaning from their experiences.

Luis Rodriguez, a political activist involved in educational and community issues, has described the existential nature of his own childhood.

> I came from Mexico when I was two years old, and I spoke perfect Spanish when I entered the Los Angeles schools. I had a command of a language. I had a sense of who I was. My first day of school was the beginning of the downfall. The first thing they did was take my language away. People find this hard to believe. It wasn't just people not teaching you the value of your language. The language was literally beaten out of you. I use to think this doesn't happen any more, but I have been in schools where this continues. The problem is, they also don't teach us English very well. I began to realize what was happening, that they were taking away a power that people have. Because if you don't have language, you don't have power. It wasn't just a small number of us who had our Spanish taken away and told we were nothing. It was a whole generation of children. When I was 11, there was a gang that came into school with chains and bats and zip guns and they terrorized the whole school. Teachers were scared and students were scared, but I wasn't scared. I was intrigued. I wanted that power. Soon after that, I got into my own little gang, although it was more like a club. It wasn't about fighting as much as it was about ourselves and who we were. It was about a respect we couldn't get anywhere else. It was about love. . . . And it was about belonging somewhere. (1996, 3)

James Banks, who was among the first to promote the need for multiculturalism in the classroom, has argued for educators to study the fundamental nature of values attached to knowledge. He has described variations in multicultural discourse that lead to the manner in which issues of diversity are integrated into school programs and classroom activities. Banks does not believe that theoretical frameworks for multicultural education have been made clear to teachers, because groups involved have staked out philosophical positions with differing points of view that usually remain misunderstood or unshared with other groups. He also believes that, despite variations in multicultural curriculum, it is the role of the classroom teacher to become knowledgeable enough to understand that information reflects values of what is considered important by the intellectual world.

Teachers should help students to understand all types of knowledge. Students should be involved in the debates about knowledge construction and conflicting interpretations, such as the extent to which Egypt and Phoenicia influenced Greek civilization. Students should also be taught how to create their own interpretations of the past and present, as well as how to identify their own positions, interests, ideologies and assumptions. . . . Multicultural education is an education for functioning effectively in a pluralistic democratic society. (Banks, 1993, 5)

In addition to Banks identifying teacher interactions with individual students as being central to the interpretation of what constitutes valued knowledge, he suggests that experience and the interpretation of that experience is fundamental to what is considered worth knowing. And ultimately, students make their own meaning. Banks describes this concept in the traditions of existentialism and phenomenology.

My conceptualization of knowledge is broad and is used the way in which it is usually used in the sociology of knowledge literature to include ideas, values, and interpretations. As postmodern theorists have pointed out, knowledge is socially constructed and reflects human interests, values, and actions. Although many complex factors influence the knowledge that is created by an individual or group, including the actuality of what occurred, the knowledge that people create is heavily influenced by their interpretation of their experiences and their positions within particular social, economic, and political systems and structures of society. (Banks, 1993, 5)

Studies and theories that focus on African Americans as a minority group often report similar findings after examining other minority groups. This pattern would bear out that Ogbu's theory which related to the different ways in which certain minority groups were brought to the United States can have significant implications for the below-average school performance of their children. In this regard, he cited early Mexican Americans in the Southeast, American Indians and native Hawaiians, as being members of castelike societies in the United States.

Educators and other professionals have also been the topic of various cognitive style studies. In this regard, the field dependent/independent construct has been found to be useful as a career choice indicator. Studies have reported that field independent college and university students tend to select areas of study associated with the sciences and field dependent students are more likely to choose fields of human service like teaching and social work. It has also been reported that when field dependent persons choose a college major in the sciences, and their field independent peers in a likewise crossover select a major in the humanities, each group of individuals is more likely than not to change over to opposite majors prior to the completion of their college careers. In other words, when they make the "unexpected" choices, these decisions are corrected prior to graduation.

In the 1980s personality type and occupational choice were linked in studies of cognitive style, perception, and decision-making style (York and Tinsley, 1986; Holland, 1985; Osipow, 1983). In their work that established a correlation between cognitive style and personality type, York and Tinsley reported that:

> Research has indicated that field independent persons tend to show interests in careers requiring competence in articulation or in analysis and structuring (e. g. mathematics, science, health professions, and art). In contrast, field dependent persons tend to favor careers requiring interpersonal relations with people (e. g., helping, humanitarian, persuasive, and administrative activities). (1986, 535)

Macnab (1991) and his associates have pointed out that field dependent/independent cognitive preferences should be an important area of interest for classroom teachers of science, because "In many areas of biology and the other sciences, it is necessary to abstract information, to reorganize it, and then to use it in a different situation." The Macnab team established an elaborate set of tests, some that were similar to The Matching Familiar Figures Test, and other sets including variations of geometric designs in which 82 single shapes were hidden, to be disembedded and recognized by the subjects. The test was designed to measure information retrieving abilities (not biological content), that are thought to be essential for success in processing information related to understanding the biological sciences.

The subjects were grade school children, graduate students, post graduates, and college teachers. The post-secondary groups contained science and nonscience majors. It was concluded that, "There are few areas in a biology syllabus that do not demand some level of competence in analysis. This should be systematically taught and not left to chance."

In most classroom activities, students are frequently presented with problem-solving activities. Occasionally the student will have all of the material at hand. There are also times when the situation calls for the student to manipulate materials to solve a math problem, for example. There are other times when students must use such things as globes, charts, maps, and numerical tables in problem-solving. At the same time, directions must be read and interpreted as a part of the problem at hand. The problem can be perceived as a single complex challenge, or in Gestalt terms, can be divided into its parts with each part analyzed in turn, and later returned to its whole for an interpretation of the answer.

The student might decide to write down the steps taken for the step-by-step examination, or commit each small part to memory. The styles that are employed in problem-solving are often influenced by a particular way of thinking that is necessary for resolution in a reasonable period of time. The type of problem that requires the student to take an element (or think about it in his manner), out of its whole context to be used and/or understood in a restructured form will be more difficult for the field dependent learner than the field independent learner.

This is also true when an object or idea is removed from its usual context. The field independent learner, being more analytically prone, would enjoy the challenge; the field dependent learner, on the other hand, would experience greater difficulty with the types of problems that separate an element from its common field.

Perceptual differences (the manner in which the problem is perceived), between field dependent and field independent persons that have been documented from the rod and frame tests, embedded-figures tests, and others, suggest that differences in problem-solving are directly related to measurable differences in perception.

There are valuable lessons for the classroom teacher who is willing to recognize and plan for such differences. For example, by now teachers are aware of the teaching approach called cooperative learning. Cooperative learning requires that the teacher assign a small group of students to a learning task. There are various models of this approach to classroom teaching and management.

In most models of cooperative learning, the teacher designates group membership and assigns the members of that group a learning task. The task(s) is presented to the group by a designated student leader/participant who initiates a discussion on how the assignment can be completed. Either by choice or volunteering, individuals and the group share in the completion of the task. In this particular arrangement, both field dependent and field independent students would have the opportunity to volunteer for the task that they are better able to satisfy, given their way of perceiving and solving a problem. An awareness of the variations employed by students in their approach to classroom assignments would also enable a teacher to orient assignments toward the problem-solving strengths of particular students.

Studies that have reported more field dependent learners among Black and Hispanic students have also pinpointed the desire for more social interaction in their learning environment. In addition to group learning situations like cooperative learning, there are indications that the teacher's role as social participant in the classroom fosters a greater interest in classroom activities for minority children. Interest toward classroom learning also appears heightened for minority children when the content is social or has a social context. In social studies where the subject under study involves human interaction and consequences closely related to that subject, minority children also show greater interest. Given this awareness, the skillful teacher could expand this approach across the curriculum. Math concepts, for example, could be presented as word problems within a social context where people are interacting or problem-solving. Interest could be enriched if names of local people and famous ones were infused into the printed descriptions or substituted for the book's standard script. Variations on this approach could involve children in small group projects, where their interactions promoted peer learning in a socially interactive atmosphere. Teacher participation would expand student interest and at the same time provide an unobtrusive diagnostic opportunity for the teacher.

It is also believed that field dependent learners are dominated perceptually by the surrounding field of an object or in a social setting with others. It has also been shown that when the field is not firmly organized, as in Rorschach's aperception inkblots, the field dependent person is more likely to interpret the material as it is, and their field independent peers will more than likely impose a structure.

In the therapeutic setting, differences have been reported concerning the professional's approach to work. Here, therapists who are field independent tend to use treatment modalities that are directive with established lines of separation from the client. Field dependent therapists, on the other hand, select more non-directive therapies that call for more interaction with clients who are also granted more opportunities to talk.

The concept of *self* as discussed in Chapter 2 is important to consider here. The roles enacted by teachers and professionals in other helping professions are modified to a degree in relation to the extent the professional is field dependent or independent along that bipolar plane. The human service provider (teacher, nurse, social worker, therapist), who is more field dependent has a global sense of self with a tendency to blur the distinction between the objective self and the subjective self. Field independent professionals have a greater tendency to identify objective self (the outer self, what others see) as a separate entity from the self they presume to be (inner self). This differentiated sense of self enables the field independent professional to create a distinct separation between the role of therapist/teacher and client/student.

The preschool setting has also been an area of interest to investigators of cognitive style theory. Studies have been conducted to determine the relationship between field dependent/independent style and intellectual performance in preschool classrooms. Coates (1975) conducted a study involving 169 children with the average age of four and one-half. Using selected subtests from the Wechsler intelligence scale for children (WISC), and the preschool embedded-figures test, she reported a significant relationship between the children's intellectual functioning in the analytical domain on the WISC and their field independent status in the cognitive style domain.

Since these investigations have been reported, the WISC has undergone several revisions. The new version, The Wechsler intelligence scale for children revised (WISC-R), is among the most commonly used tests to measure individual functioning in young children. It is designed for subjects ages six to sixteen, and consists of twelve subtests (two are optional). Half the items are verbal, and half nonverbal, and it is administered individually. In the 1990s the state of the art in measuring intelligence among school children for various purposes, like screening for candidates to be placed in classrooms for the gifted, has led to the selection of the Wechsler intelligence scale for children-III (WISC-III), as well as the Wechsler preschool and primary scale of intelligence-revised (WPPSI-R).

These instruments are designed primarily to be administered individually, and several studies have investigated the test-taking environment. It has been reported that field dependent/independent early childhood subjects are responsive to various cues that can emerge from the examiner effect. When the examiner provided facial cues, field independent subjects performed less adequately in the testing environment than their field dependent peers. Field dependent children were more attentive to the examiner's facial expressions during questioning. This supports the view that field dependent learners are more sensitive to social interactions than their counterparts. When the testing situation called for a demonstration of problem-solving tasks by the examiner, Ruble and Nakamura (1972) reported that field dependent children rated lower.

There are also significant gender differences in cognitive style acquisition related to maturational stability. Maturational stability of cognitive preference seems to appear in preschool girls eighteen months ahead of preschool boys. The data are so compelling in the direction of females that reports of male dominance in this area are rare.

Prior to the revision of the WISC-lll and the WPPSI-R, both designed to measure intellectual functioning in children, several studies identified areas of compatibility between these tests and instruments designed to measure cognitive style. Coates and Bromberg (1973) reported significant correlations between intellectual abilities of four to six year old children, as measured by the WPPSI, and field independent indicators for the same subjects' cognitive style index.

Using the children's embedded-figures test, Goodenough and Karp

(1961) found that for nine- to twelve-year-old children, their scores on the analytical sub-test of the WISC correlated significantly with field independent scores for the same subjects.

For the classroom teacher there are some important lessons in these reports. One, when children appear not to perform well in solving math problems of an analytic nature, or appear not to understand material of a social studies nature when an analysis of a set of circumstances or events are required, it does not mean that they are less intelligent than their classroom peers.

Indications should guide the teacher to expand the number of ways in which the material can be presented. When the content is embedded in a larger context from which ideas, solutions, and descriptions must be extracted, field dependent children are likely to perform less well than their field independent age mates. Disembedding issues, ideas, or answers requiring quantification from its "field" (surroundings) might be a welcome challenge for field independent children; on the other hand, it can be a difficult and complex experience for the field dependent learner.

Finally, the bipolar construct known as field dependent/field independent cognitive styles should not be viewed as negative/positive poles along a continuum, but rather, different dimensions of cognitive preferences with linear inclinations around a single mean, both employing important characteristics.

In general, preferences for field dependent modes of information processing will likely be persons who are socially sensitive, preferring group environments, for example. This does not mean that persons with field independent cognitive preferences are not socially sensitive, but that their cognitive preferences are more commonly found to be more analytical with preferences toward acting alone or with fewer people.

The intensity of these information processing, problem-solving, and personality variables can be characterized in terms of their distance from the aggregate mean, established by characteristics derived from both groups.

An interesting perspective from which to analyze field independent/dependent cognitive preference has emerged from scholars who study imagery. These approaches have their roots in the work of Kant, Husserl, Sartre, and others who blended existentialism and phenomenology. The work of Fleming and Hutton (1983) advanced the study of imagery as it relates to cognitive style theory. From the edited publication, Mental Imagery and Learning, imagery is divided into two perceptual categories. Type I imagery is related to phenomenology, in that, it is defined as individual reconstruction of the perception of a previous experience. Type II imagery is that which is generated by individuals at the time of an experience (reading a novel, observing a play, and so forth).

Imagery is important for cognitive preferences related to field-independent/dependent perceptions because it suggests that field independent individuals are adept at reorganizing information for higher meaning when such analyses are called for. When individual performance in a particular problem-solving situation is called for, imagery is essential because one must use what is at hand (present experience), together with images that are reconstructed from previous experiences, to achieve an intelligent resolution. Studies suggest that field dependent individuals primarily employ Type II imagery; therefore, when problem-solving calls for the reconstruction of previous experiences, they perform less well than their field independent counterparts.

Studies related to verbal information processing have been of interest to those who have studied hemispheric functions of the brain. It has been suggested that within the complex cooperative relationship between the cortical hemispheres, encoding and memory are processed differently. Encoding is the facility to convert the "code," inherent in information being presented, to knowledge that the individual can process and understand. It also implies that one can convert information from one system (the teaching methods that children experience the first time they encounter classroom activities) to another system (the manner in which family members communicate with each other).

Approximately 60 percent of right-handed persons and most all left-hand individuals show preferences for left cortical hemisphere learning which emphasizes imagery and remembering verbal information. For these same individuals, the right cortical hemisphere often assumes a Gestalt approach to information processing, in that they demonstrate capabilities to examine the parts of an experience and analyze their meaning from the perspective of the relationships among and between the parts. Perceiving and interpreting a design, drawing, or other visuals are examples. In this regard, we now know that phenomenologists would accept the individual's perceptual interpretation as being valid, and reject an "expert" objective interpretation as having any greater authenticity than the experiencer's version.

For the classroom teacher, the left cortical hemispheric information processing preferred by some learners has implications for the teaching of reading. Reading is a left to right visual activity that requires the learner to process words placed sequentially on a printed page. These individuals also possess a right cortical hemispheric facility for grasping meaning from words and phrases because of their preferences for verbal imagery (their Gestalt, in this case) processing. This group also demonstrates capability in analytical, sequential, and serational organization.

The relationship between field independent/dependent cognitive styles, loneliness, and coping strategies was studied by Woodward and Kalyan-Masih (1990) as it pertains to gifted rural adolescents. This study utilized the group embedded-figures test and a loneliness inventory scale designed by the researchers. Important implications for teachers and counselors of adolescents in rural environments were pointed out. It was suggested, for example, that being gifted does not prevent adolescents from experiencing feelings of rejection, isolation, and alienation.

Reports of groups (field independent/dependent) were compatible with earlier studies by others—about adolescents who were not labeled gifted—but indicated that field dependent rural gifted adolescents were less lonely when in a group. Also, field independent adolescents, from the same setting, were not relieved of loneliness when in a group.

Woodward and Kalyan-Masih also reported that field independent adolescents in a rural environment sought individual pursuits, showed more autonomy and self-reliance. On the other hand, field dependent adolescents relied more on external sources and were more likely to seek professional help to cope with loneliness and to pursue physical and religious activities.

The preschool embedded-figures test (PEFT), designed to measure field independence/dependence in young children, was employed by Allen, Watson and Howard (1993) in a study to examine problem-solving strategies that might be unique to the cognitive styles of minority children. The children under study were enrolled in an academic enrichment-type program where teachers used "High Scope" in their approach to work. This particular academic model is designed to plan for learner exploration and discovery that can be found in the theoretical work of Jean Piaget.

In such programs children are encouraged to explore their environment and resolve critical issues on their own with classroom adults at hand to respond to their queries. Adults are discouraged from rendering praise that might resemble "behavior modification," but rather, they encourage learners to value the intrinsic qualities in their work from their own perspective.

The prekindergarten program under study enrolled four-year-old children, ten boys and six girls. The results from the PEFT yielded nine field independent and seven field dependent subjects. One unique aspect of this study was employment of a computer program—Logo—that was designed for the purpose of problem-solving in educational settings. Logo was developed in the 1960s by artificial intelligence theorists to facilitate the learning of mathematical concepts by children. It was viewed by many as a positive alternative to the drill and rote memorization methods of teaching mathematics that were common in classrooms of that period. There were others in those early days of computer literacy who were fearful of "teaching machines" replacing the human element in teaching and learning, and looked upon Logo as a step in that direction. Unknown to these critics was the role that Logo was designed to enact in encouraging problem-solving, creativity, and exploration, among young learners. In this regard, its purpose was highly compatible with the High Scope classroom involved in the Allen, Watson, and Howard study.

The study investigated the extent to which minority preschool children could develop Logo computer skills, how these skills compared with demonstrated competence of their counterparts in other environments, and to what extent these children might employ cognitive styles thought to be common among minority children. From their results, the researchers reported:

> It was hypothesized that children would perform significantly better on the problems that were suited to their preferred cognitive style. It was also hypothesized that after being trained in specific problem-solving strategies the children would perform significantly better on tasks oriented toward their opposing cognitive styles. Results showed that when concepts of programming and command were presented at developmentally appropriate levels, this sample population performed as well as any other preschool aged sample in a Logo paradigm. (Allen, et al., 1993, 203)

Other studies have reported that in some settings where computer literacy is a variable, it does make a difference in the rate and quality of computer learning when the teaching approaches take into account the learner's cognitive style (Hoffman and Waters, 1982; Stevens, 1983). Studies on the relationship between cognitive preferences and success in computer science courses for college-level learners have suggested that field independent students be given specific assignments early in their course work and should be encouraged to progress at their own pace, while field dependent learners should have their course work structured in formal teaching segments.

Finally, psychological differentiations as defined as constructs of field-dependent/independent cognitive preferences, seem to be a complex interaction between social competences, problem-solving issues embedded in teaching and learning, and abilities associated with restructuring. Field independent individuals by nature of their ability to perceive issues and events and to invoke their problem-solving skills with specificity without the intrusion of the "field" (related factors that compete for individual attention), are more successful in teaching/learning environments that are traditionally structured. The traditional classroom structure rewards analytical thinkers who are capable of working independently on tasks. Students who spend more time on classroom tasks as autonomous thinkers are positively valued and encouraged.

Individuals who are independent of "field" influences, which could be social interactions and process related, or a specific academic assignment and more often content related, can demonstrate essential skills in cognitive restructuring. An analysis of the task at hand and the approach toward problem-solving often require restructuring at various levels of perception and response. Cognitive restructuring places the task at hand into a workable context for resolution.

Individuals who demonstrate field dependent cognitive preferences possess interpersonal competences that tend to extract the high cost of being captured by the "field" of perception. This field could be composed of an informal social gathering or a classroom.

When the classroom teacher invests the time and inclination toward establishing a classroom environment that rewards cooperative interpersonal approaches to school work, field dependent students who are less analytical, autonomous, and independent, are less likely to suffer because of these differences. There is an important discussion of psychological issues related to individual autonomy, cognitive restructuring skills, and interpersonal competences by Witkin and Goodenough in *Cognitive Styles: Essence and Origins* (1981). Their discovery of the linkages between psychological differentiation and field independent/field dependent cognitive styles occurred after extensive investigations of individual responses to the rod and frame test, the body adjustment test, the embedded-figures test and similar instruments. While this work was in progress Witkin and Goodenough reported the following:

> Subsequent research linked the individual differences described so far to differences in a still wider array of areas, including, in particular, areas ordinarily subsumed under personality, such as controls and defenses, body concept and the self. When it became clear that these areas could not be accommodated within the articulated-global construct, another theoretical step had to be taken. "Differentiation" recommended itself, on several grounds, as a useful construct for conceptualizing the enlarged picture of self-consistency that had now emerged. First, each of the constituents of the cluster of characteristics found to be associated with one another showed a definite ordering during ontogenetic development. Second, the characteristics that had been implicated were clearly formal rather than content properties of the psychological system—that is, typical ways of functioning based on given structural arrangements. Third, as may be expected of characteristics of a formal nature, they were stable over time. Fourth, common to many of the characteristics was degree of specialization and function; others reflected degree of separateness of the self from the selves of others. All the features listed are in fact distinguishing properties of a relatively more differentiated psychological system, suggesting that the concept of differentiation was a useful one for characterizing commonality among the linked areas of psychological functioning and their common fate

during development. Field dependence-independence was accordingly now placed in the broader framework of differentiation. (1981, 18-19)

Finally, from time to time researchers have investigated the relationship between problem-solving success and feelings about self (Bloom and Broder, 1951; Coor and Somerfield, 1975). In general, studies report that pupils who are successful at problem-solving tasks make positive comments about themselves. On the other hand, pupils who find problem solving tasks troublesome make negative comments about themselves. Indications are that self-rejecting attitudes can produce negative consequences for learning; while self-supporting attitudes can ensure positive consequences. Classroom demands for problem-solving call for thoughtful preparation and presentation of content by teachers together with the utilization of a variety of media and teaching styles, supported by well-balanced testing procedures that enable field dependent and field independent pupils to demonstrate through their performance that learning has occurred.

REFERENCES

Allen, J., Watson, J. A., and Howard, J. R. (1993). "The Impact of Cognitive Styles on the Problem-Solving Strategies Used by Pre-school Minority Children in Logo Microworlds." *Journal of Computing in Childhood Education* 4 (3), 203-217.

Allen, M. J., and Cholet, M. E. (1978). "Strength of Association Between Sex and Field Dependence." *Perceptual and Motor Skills* 47, 419-421.

Allport, Gordon. (1937). *Personality: A Psychological Interpretation.* New York: Henry Holt and Company.

Bandura, A. (1986). *Social Foundations of Thought and Action.* Englewood Cliffs, NJ: Prentice-Hall.

Banks, J. (1993). "The Canon Debate, Knowledge Construction, and Multicultural Education." *Educational Researcher* 22 (5) 4-14.

Bennett, N., and Deforges, C. (1988). "Matching Classroom Tasks to Student Attainments." *Elementary School Journal* 88 (3), 221-234.

Berger, E., and Goldberger, L. (1979). "Field Dependence and Short-Term Memory." *Perceptual and Motor Skills* 49, 87-96.

Berry, J. W. (1981). *Comparative Studies of Cognitive Styles: Implications for the Education of Immigrant Students.* Paper presented at the Conference on Ethnic Minority Immigrants. (Dec.) Miami, FL.

Bertini, M., Pizzamiglo, L., and Wapner, S. (1986). *Field Dependence in Psychological Theory, Research, and Application.* Hillside, NJ: Erlbaum.

Bigelow, G. S. (1971). "Field Dependence-Field Independence in 5- to 10-Year-Old-Children." *Journal of Educational Research* 9, 397-400.

Bloom, B. S., and Broder, L., (1950). *Problem-Solving Process of College Students.* Chicago: University of Chicago Press.

Brumby, M. (1982). "Consistent Differences in Cognitive Styles Shown for Qualitative Biology Problem-Solving." *British Journal of Educational Psychology* 52 (2), 244-257.

Cairns, E. D., Malone, S., Johnston, J., and Cammock, T. (1985). "Sex Differences in Children's Group Embedded Figures Group Performance." *Personality and Individual Differences* 66, 653-654.

Castenada, A., Ramirez, M., Cortez, C. F., and Barrea, M. (1974). *Mexican American and Educational Change.* New York: Arno Press.

Coates, S., (1972). *The Preschool Embedded Figures Test.* Palo Alto, CA: Consulting Psychologist Press.

Coates, S. (1975). "Field Independence and Intellectual Functioning in Preschool Children." *Perceptual and Motor Skills* 41, 251-245.

Coates, S. and Bromberg, P. M. (1973). "Factorial Structure of the WPPSI Between the Ages of 4 and 6 1/2." *The Journal of Consulting Clinical Psychology* 40, 365-370.

Coates, S., Lord, M., and Jakabovics, E. (1975). "Field Independence-Dependence, Social-Nonsocial Play, and Sex Differences in Preschool Children." *Perceptual and Motor Skills* 40, 195-202.

Cohen, J. (1959). "The Factorial of the WISC at Age 7-6, 10-6 and 6." *Journal of Consulting Psychology* 23, 285-299.

Cooperman, R. W. (1980). "Field Differentiation and Intelligence." *Journal of Psychology* 23, 295-299.

Couch, R. A., and Moore, D. M. (1992). "The Effects of Imagery Rehearsal Strategy and Cognitive Style on the Learning of Different Levels of Instructional Objectives." *Journal of Instructional Media* 19 (1), 53-63.

Davey, B., and Menke, D. (1989). "The Importance of Cognitive Style in Children's Acquisition of Reading Skill." *Early Child Development and Care* 51, 49-64.

Davis, J. K., and Cochran, K. F. (1989). "An Information Processing View of Field Dependence-Independence." *Early Child Development and Care* 51, 31-47.

Davis, J. K., and Frank, B. M. (1979). "Learning and Memory of Field Independent Individuals." *Journal of Research in Personality* 17, 89-96.

Dewey, J. (1956). *The Child and the Curriculum.* Chicago: University of Chicago Press.

Doyle, W. (1983). "Academic Work." *Review of Educational Research* 53, 159-199.

Doyle, W., and Carter, K. (1984). "Academic Tasks in Classroom." *Curriculum Inquiry* 14, 129-149.

Dubois, T. E., and Cohen, W. (1970). "Relationship Between Measures of Psychological Differentiation and Intellectual Ability." *Percep-*

tual and Motor Skills 31, 411-416.

Dyk, R. B., and Witkin, H. A. (1965). "Family Experiences Related to the Development of Differentiation in Children." *Child Development* 30, 21-55.

Fehrenbach, C. R. (1994). "Cognitive Style of Gifted and Average Readers." *Roeper Review* 16 (4), 290-292.

Fehrenbach, C. R. (1991). "Gifted and Average Readers. Do They Use the Same Reading Strategies?" *Gifted Child Quarterly* 35 (3), 125-127.

Finke, R. A. (1980). "Levels of Equivalence in Imagery and Perception." *Psychology Review* 87 (2), 113-132.

Fiske, S., and Taylor, S. (1984). *Social Cognition.* Reading, MA: Addison-Wesley.

Fleming, M. L., and Hutton, D. W. (1987). *"Mental Imagery and Learning."* Englewood Cliffs, NJ: Educational Technology Publications.

Goodenough, D. R., Gandini, E., Olkin, I., Pizzamiglio, L., Thayer, D., and Witkin, H. A. (1977). "A Study of X-Chromosome Linkage with Field Dependence and Spatial-Visualization." *Behavior Genetics* 7, 373-387.

Goodenough, D. R., and Karp, S. A. (1961). "Field Dependence and Intellectual Functioning." *Journal of Abnormal and Social Psychology* 63, 243-246.

Goor, A., and Sommerfield, R. (1975). "A Comparison of Problem-Solving Process of Creative Students and Noncreative Students." *Journal of Educational Psychology* 67, 495-505.

Gough, H. G., and Olton, R. M. (1972). "Field Independence as Related to Nonverbal Measures of Perceptual Performance and Cognitive Ability." *Journal of Consulting and Clinical Psychology* 38, 338-342.

Greene, L. R. (1979). "Psychological Differentiation and Social Structure." *The Journal of Social Psychology* 109, 79-85.

Harren, V. A. (1979). "A Model of Career Decision Making for College Students." *Journal of Vocational Behavior* 14, 119-133.

Hess, R. D., and Shipman, V. C. (1965) "Early Experiences and the Socialization of Children." *Child Development* 36, 869-886.

Hoffman, P. A. (1978). "Field Independence and Intelligence: Their Relation to Leadership and Self-Concept in Sixth-Grade Boys." *Journal of Educational Psychology* 70, 827-832.

Hoffman, J. L. and Waters, K. (1982). "Some Effects of Student Personality on Success With Computer-Assisted Instruction." *Educational Technology* (March).

Holland, J. L. (1985). *Making Vocational Choices: A Theory of Vocational Personalities and Work Environments.* Englewood Cliffs, NJ: Prentice-Hall.

Holland, J. L., and Gottfriedson, G. D. (1975). "Predictive Value and

Psychological Meaning of Vocational Aspirations." *Journal of Vocational Behavior* 6, 349-363.

Holtzman, W., Diaz-Guerrero, R., and Swartz, J. D. (1975). *Personality Development in Two Cultures: A Cross-Cultural Longitudinal Study of School Children in Mexico and the United States.* Austin, Texas: University of Texas Press.

Jolly, P., and Strawitz, B. M. (1984). "Teacher Student Cognitive Style and Achievement in Biology." *Science Education* 68 (4), 485-490.

Kirchner, T. (1988). "Sex Differences Among Children on the Embedded Figures Test." *Perceptual and Motor Skills* 678, 972-974.

League, B. J., and Jackson, D. N. (1961). Activity and Passivity as Correlates of Field-Independence. *Perceptual Motor Skills* 12, 291-298.

Locke, E. A., and Latham, G. P. (1990). *A Theory of Goal Setting and Task Performance.* Englewwood Cliffs, NJ: Prentice-Hall.

Macnab, W., Hansell, M. H., and Johnstone, A. H. (1991). "Cognitive Style and Analytical Ability and Their Relationship to Competence in the Biological Sciences." *Journal of Biological Education* 25 (2), 135-139.

Mahler, M., Pine, F., and Bergman, A. (1975). *The Psychological Birth of the Human Infant.* New York: Basic Books.

Marlowe, D. (1958). "Some Psychological Correlates of Field Independence." *Journal of Consulting Psychology* 22, 334.

Marx, R. W., and Walsh, J. (1988). "Learning from Academic Tasks." *Elementary School Journal* 88 (3), 207-219.

Meyer, C., and Sallee, T. (1983). *Make it Simpler: A Practical Guide to Problem Solving in Mathematics.* Menlo Park, CA: Addison Wesley.

Niaz, M. (1989). "The Role of Cognitive Style and its Influence on Proportional Reasoning." *Journal of Research in Science Teaching* 26 (3), 221-235.

Nummedal, S. G., and Collea, F. P. (1981). "Field Independence, Task Ambiguity, and Performance on a Proportional Reasoning Task." *Journal of Research in Science Teaching* 18 (3), 255-260.

Ogbu, J. (1992). "Understanding Cultural Diversity and Learning." *Educational Researcher* 21 (8), 5-14.

Oltman, P. K., Ehrlichman, H., and Cox, P. W. (1977). "Field Independence and Laterality in the Perception of Faces." *Perceptual and Motor Skills* 45, 255-260.

Osipow, S. H. (1983). *Theories of Career Development.* Englewood Cliffs, NJ: Prentice-Hall.

Polya, G. (1973). *How To Solve It.* Princeton, NJ: Princeton University Press.

Provost, G. L. (1981). "Teaching Strategies, Modes of Evaluation, and Field-Independence Factor." *Perceptual and Motor Skills* 52, 163-

173.

Ramirez, M. III, (1982). "Cognitive Styles and Diversity." Paper presented at the annual meeting of the American Educational Research Association. (March) New York: NY.

Ramirez, M., and Castaneda, A. (1974). *Cultural Democracy, Bicognitive Development and Education.* New York, NY: Academic Press.

Ramirez, M., Costaneda, A., and Herold, L. P. (1974). "The Relationship of Acculturation to Cognitive Style Among Mexican Americans." *Journal of Cross-cultural Psychology* 5, 424-431.

Resnick, L. (1987). *Education and Learning to Think.* Washington, DC: National Academy Press.

Richardson, J. T. (1980). *Mental Imagery and Human Learning.* New York: St. Martins Press.

Ritchley, P. A., and La Shier, W. S. (1981). "The Relationship Between Cognitive Style, Intelligence and Instructional Mode to Achievement of College Science Students." *Journal of Research in Science Teaching* 18 (1), 41-45.

Rivas, M. (1984). "Cognitive Styles of Mexican-American and Anglo American Five, Eight, and Ten Year Old Boys and Girls." *Texas Tech Journal of Education* 2 (1), 67-76.

Roberge, J. J., and Flexer, B. K. (1984). "Cognitive Style, Operativity and Reading Achievement." *American Educational Research Journal* 21, 227-236.

Rodriguez, L. (1996). "How Society Helps Some Kids Succeed and Others Fail: Our Kids Are Being Set Up." *Rethinking Schools* 10 (4), 1996.

Roeper, A (1982). "How the Gifted Cope with Their Emotions." *Roeper Review* 51 (3), 21-24.

Ruble, D. N. and Nakamura C. Y. (1972). "Task Orientation Versus Social Orientation in Young Children and Their Attention to Relevant Social Cues." *Child Development* 43, 471-480.

Rudin, S. A., and Stagner, R. (1958). "Figure Ground Phenomena in the Perception of Physical and Social Phenomena." Journal of Psychology 45, 213-225.

Saracho, O. N. (1991). "Cognitive Style and Social Behavior in Young Mexican American Children." *International Journal of Early Childhood* 2 (23), 21-38.

Shulman, J. P. (1987). "Knowledge and Teaching: Foundations of the New Reform." *Harvard Educational Review* 57, 1-22.

Silver, E. A. (1985). *Teaching and Learning Mathematical Problem Solving: Multiple Research Perspectives.* Hillsdale, NJ: Erlbaum.

Spiro, R. J., and Tirre, W. C. (1980). "Individual Differences in Schema Utilization During Discourse Processing." *Journal of Educational Psychology* 72, 204-208.

Steele, C. (1989). "Cognitive Style and the Gifted Young Child." *Early Child Development and Care* 51, 157-174.

Stevens, D. J., (1983). Cognitive Processes and Success of Students in Instructional Computer Courses. *AEDS Journal* (Summer), 228-233.

Thurstone, L. L. (1944). *A Factoral Study of Perception.* Chicago: University of Chicago Press.

Tichener, E. B. (1908). *Feeling and Attention.* New York: Macmillan.

Vaidya, S., and Chansky, N. (1980). "Cognitive Development and Cognitive Style as Factors in Mathematics Achievement." *Journal of Educational Psychology* 72, 326-330.

Wallach, M. A., and Kogan, N. (1965). *Modes of Thinking in Young Children.* New York: Holt, Rinehart and Winston.

Wenckstern, S., Weizman, F., and Leenaars, A. A. (1984). "Temperment and Tempo of Play in Eight-Month-Old Infants." *Child Development* 55, 1195-1199.

Werner, H. (1948). *Comparative Psychology of Mental Development.* New York: Science Editions.

Werner, H. (1957). "The Concept of Development From a Comparative and Organism Point of View." In D. B. Harris, ed., *The Concept of Development: An Issue in the Study of Human Behavior.* Minneapolis: University of Minnesota Press.

Witkin, H. A. (1950). "Personality Differences in Ease of Perception of Embedded Figures." *Journal of Personality* 19, 1-15.

Witkin, H. A., and Berry, J. W. (1975). "Psychological Differentiation in Cross-Cultural Perspective." *Journal of Cross-Cultural Psychology* 6, 4-87.

Witkin, H. A., Dyk, R. B., Faterson, H. F., Goodenough, D. R., and Karp, S. A. (1962). *Psychological Differentiation.* New York: Wiley.

Witkin, H. A., and Goodenough, D. R. (1981). *Cognitive Styles: Essence and Origins.* New York: International Universities Press.

Witkin, H. A., Moore, C. A., Oltman, P. K., Goodenough, D. R., Friedman, F., Owen, D. R., and Raskin, E. (1977). "Role of the Field-Dependent and Field-Independent Cognitive Styles in Academic Evolution: A Longitudinal Study." *Journal of Educational Psychology* 69 (3), 197-211.

Witkin, H. A., and Oltman, P. K. (1967). "Cognitive Style." *International Journal of Neurology* 6, 119-137.

Witkin, H. A., Oltman, P. K., Raskin, E., and Karp, S. A. (1971). *A Manual For The Embedded Figures Test.* Palo Alto, CA: Consulting Psychologist Press.

Witkin, H. A., Price-Williams, D., Bertini, M., Christiansen, B., Oltman, P. D., Ramirez, M. and Meel, J. V. (1974). "Social Conformity and Psychological Differentiation." *International Journal of Psychology* 9, 11-29.

Wollman, W. (1983). "Determining the Sources of Error in a Translation From Sentence to Equation." *Journal for Research in Mathematics Education* 14 (3),169-181.

Wollman, W., and Lawson, A. E. (1978). "The Influence of Instruction on Proportional Reasoning in Seventh Graders." *Journal of Research in Science Teaching* 15 (3), 227-232.

Woodward, J. C., and Kalyan-Masih, V. (1990). "Loneliness, Coping Strategies and Cognitive Styles of the Gifted Rural Adolescent." *Adolescence* 25 (100), 977-987.

Wright, J. C., and Kagan, J. (1963). *Basic Cognitive Processing in Children.* Chicago: University of Chicago Press.

York, D. C., and Tinsley, H. E. A. (1986). "The Relationship Between Cognitive Styles and Holland's Personality Types." *Journal of College Student Personnel* (Nov.), 535-541.

Young, H. H. (1959). A Test of Witkin's Field-Dependence Hypothesis. *Journal of Abnormal Social Psychology* 59, 188-192.

4

The Cognitive Style Context of Reflectivity and Impulsivity

> If you bind or prune an organism so it can move only in limited ways, it will move rather excessively in that way. If you lace a man into a straight jacket so he can only wiggle his toes, he will wiggle them *hard*. Since in school children are necessarily constrained to limited human expression, under the direction of the teacher, they will have a natural tendency to do with exaggerated enthusiasm what they are permitted to do. They are like the man in the straight jacket. In class children are usually not permitted to talk much, to walk around much, to put their arms around each other during lessons, to whistle or sing. But they are permitted to raise their hands and go to the pencil sharpener almost at will.
>
> —Jules Henry

As an important topic in scholarly works, cognitive styles have attracted greater interest from psychologists and educators than researchers and practitioners in other fields. Personality traits of cognitive preferences that employ reflection or its counterpart, impulsiveness, have been studied in psychiatry, psychology, education and their allied fields for some time. Early writings about these two characteristics often implied that the term analytical was practically the same as reflectivity, and nonanalytical implied the same meaning as impulsivity.

Historically, persons who demonstrated patience in a time-consuming approach to problem-solving tasks were considered analytical. Their counterparts who were observed to approach tasks with accelerated fervor, and reached conclusions early in their problem-solving process, were often labeled nonanalytical. In assessing analytical and nonanalytical cognitive preferences as personality traits, tempo and time-on-task were viewed as principal variables.

In schooling, analytical characteristics were preferred personality traits for pupils because nonanalytical approaches often yield greater activeness and a higher error rate on the part of the student.

The primary concern of scholars who were involved in examining the cognitive style dimension of reflectivity/impulsivity rested in the information processing stages of human cognition, as opposed to the initial stage of perception that seemed to guide studies of other cognitive styles.

As described in the chapter on theoretical perspectives, cognitive-style theory is interrelated with theories of knowledge acquisition. Knowledge acquisition involves several basic elements: perception, sensory organs, short-term memory, long-term memory, and motoric systems (Chapter 2). Various studies of cognitive styles approach the examination of this inter-relationship from educational and/or psychological perspectives.

Studies of reflective/impulsivity employ a psychological perspective with an emphasis on personality development. Studies of other cognitive styles like field dependent/independent, for example, focus primarily upon perception, which is the initial phase of knowledge acquisition. Studies concerned with reflective/impulsivity, however, go beyond the initial phase of the acquisition of knowledge. Unlike field independent and field dependent constructs where the emphasis is on styles of perception and interpretation, reflectivity/impulsivity is concerned with information processing further along in the problem-solving chain. In other words, reflectivity and impulsivity embody the manner in which individuals think about a problem, how they explore alternatives, and the tempo of their problem-solving style. Tempo also becomes central to the design and implementation of assessment procedures. Measurement procedures that are commonly used direct subjects to match a correct pattern with its counterpart which is displayed among multiple alternatives. Calculations are then made of the subject's speed and accuracy. It is assumed that impulsive children will take less time with the task at hand and respond quickly, resulting in a greater likelihood of error. On the other hand, their counterparts will spend more time reflecting on alternative solutions, and for that reason, experience fewer errors.

Children who were labeled nonanalytical (those observed to display unusually short periods of time on task) were occasionally labeled "overactive," "aggressive," "hyperactive," "impulsive," and/or "distractible." This process of labeling attracted the attention of counselors and therapists through referrals from classroom teachers and school authorities.

As early as 1929, Harthshorne, May, and Miller discussed impulsivity as a problem of self-control, while others labeled it "inhibition," "anxiety," and/or "motor-diliberation." In 1938, H. A. Murray in his book *Explorations in Personality,* identified this characteristic as "impulsive deliberation." By 1959, using observed behavior as primary criteria, Sutton-Smith and Rosenberg had developed a scale to identify impulsiveness as a childhood dysfunction. This scale employed a single-step procedure that identified, within a specified group, only those who could be labeled impulsive, and it was then assumed that the remaining children in that group were reflective.

In the early 1950s psychologists, social workers, classroom teachers, and practitioners in associated fields of human service were viewing impulsivity as a behavior disorder. In other words, what we refer to in current literature as impulsivity, was historically referenced in pathological contexts. Early in the 1900s childhood behavior problems were viewed as one aspect of family dysfunction. From the influence of Sigmund Freud and his daughter Anna Freud, psychoanalysts in the United States sought understandings of child development primarily from their adult client's descriptions of their own childhood.

It was common practice to approach the treatment of mental disorders among children through "play therapy" and similar psychoanalytical sessions involving the child and a clinical psychologist or psychiatrist. During the same time period at a different site, a counselor or social worker would conduct individual therapy sessions with the child's parents (usually the mother). By the mid-1960s, this therapeutic approach started to include family therapy as the modality of choice for troubled children. What family therapists most have in common they also share with a number of behavioral scientists in the world today:

> There is an increasing awareness that psychiatric problems are social problems which involve the total ecological system. There is concern with, and an attempt to change, what happens with the family and also the interlocking systems of the family and the social institutions in which the family is embedded. The fragmentation of the individual into parts, is being abandoned, and there is growing consensus that a new ecological framework defines problems in new ways and calls for new ways in therapy. (Haley, 270)

These treatment modalities continued over such extended periods of time that it was not unusual for families to be in therapy long after they were no longer in contact with the social worker or teacher who referred them in the first place. Teachers and school authorities were growing impatient with this psychosocial model that relied upon "talk therapy" and were poised for less time-consuming methods to deal with troublesome pupils.

During the 1940s, mental institutions for adults were also being criticized from within the professions by advocacy groups and from the general public because of the use of restraining devices and isolation cells to maintain seriously disruptive mental patients. By the 1950s remarkable results were emerging from the use of drugs that dramatically reduced the acting-out behavior of adult psychotic patients. The success of antipsychotic drugs for the treatment of adult mental disorders were accompanied by studies investigating how these treatments effected the brain and central nervous system. Investigations along these lines were enhanced through the use of the electroencephalogram (EEG) to study institutionalized youth and adults. This activity attracted the attention of psychologists and social workers who worked with troubled families and youth around problems in school. Gradually, talk therapy as a treatment for the problems of troubled youth would be partially abandoned in favor of drug treatment that had proved successful with troublesome institutionalized patients. For institutionalized adults, the new drug treatment was a part of a larger program to release them into their community with appropriate medication. It is the view of many social agencies that in the 1980s this policy led to the increase in homelessness.

These trends created a professional climate that gradually employed the medical model in the treatment of child development problems and a gradual reduction in the use of the Freudian "dysfunctional family" approach, which previously required extensive social work and psychoanalysis.

Along with the aforementioned developments, and throughout the 1960s, greater interest grew in the relationship between brain function and abnormal behavior in children. EEG data were used to develop profiles of "brain damaged" children from examinations of those who had been institutionalized for various reasons. From these investigations, and as early as 1955, Ounsted described epileptic children in the same clinical contexts with children who demonstrated "pervasive short attention span," "aggressive outbursts," and children who were labeled "distractible."

Following the great success that institutions were having with the use of tranquilizing drugs to calm patients who previously had to be isolated or physically restrained, the medical community, universities, governmental health agencies, and drug companies sponsored workshops, institutes and conferences aimed at expanding the application of psychoactive behavior-altering drugs. Members of the medical community usually associated with child development, like psychiatrists and pediatricians, gradually introduced the term "minimal brain dysfunction" to bring into their sphere the diagnosis and treatment of the school's most chronic "behavior problems" as neurological and not psychosocial.

Throughout the 1960s psychiatric literature identifying "minimal brain dysfunction" as a neuropsychological problem listed various behaviors as common symptoms for which educators and practitioners should be on the alert. S. D. Clements not only authored a health service bulletin for the U.S. Department of Health Education and Welfare titled "Minimal Brain Dysfunction" in children (MBD), but authored and co-authored many scientific reports on the subject. Among the common characteristics of MBD that were cited in Clement's work included "impulsivity," "hyperactivity," "short attention span," and "distractibility."

These developments had been aided in 1966 by the creation of a task force by the National Institute of Neurological Diseases and Blindness to develop a diagnostic term for children who demonstrated impulsive, overactive behavior that was generally troublesome for parents and teachers. The task force created the term "minimal brain dysfunction." The word minimal was important here because, at that time, no hard neurological evidence was found to substantiate such a distinction. Previous terms like "neurological disorder," "hyperactivity," and "brain damage" were now included under minimal brain dysfunction diagnoses.

The practice of employing pathological labels to officially group childhood impulsivity among other behaviors diagnosed as "hyperkinetic," or "hyperactive," created an enormous market for the sale of drugs purported to control undesirable acting-out behavior of children. The American Psychiatric Association had by now created "hyperkinetic syndrome of childhood" as the official descriptor for research, diagnosis, and treatment of these "disorders" in children.

Throughout the 1970s, this "official" label was conveniently available to teachers and other school personnel who were exasperated with children whose classroom demeanor was active and generally annoying. Parents, some of whom had only a general understanding of the subject from popular media, made frequent requests of physicians to prescribe Ritalin for their children so that "they will get better grades in school."

By 1980 it was estimated that over one million school children, mostly boys, were regularly prescribed drugs to modify their "hyperkinetic" behavior in school. The scientific community discovered that the body's normal flow of dopamine to the frontal lobe of the brain served to regulate impulsivity and attention. Without any direct evidence that children demonstrating impulsive behavior had an organic problem related to frontal lobe dysfunction, the modified behavior induced by various drugs that increased the flow of dopamine to the brain was sufficient justification for their use. The most popularly prescribed drugs were Dexedrine (dextroamphetamine), Ritalin (methylphenidate), and Cylert (permoline).

Companies that profited from the sale of these drugs mailed an avalanche of literature to physicians, sponsored research projects, professional seminars, workshops, and sent professionals to address parent-teacher meetings to promote the use of their products.

There was a persistent lack of clinical evidence that could confirm a hard link between specific central nervous system dysfunction and the listed behaviors that were attached to the hyperkinetic syndrome, under which tremendous amounts of psychoactive drugs were being dispensed to children. Annually, the number of children between the ages of five and seventeen who were diagnosed as hyperkinetic and/or hyperactive began to experience a rapid growth after 1970. A relatively small number of pediatricians, psychologists, psychiatrists, parents, and educators were becoming alarmed at the high rate of school children that were being given behavior controlling medication, and they started to question the practice of labeling impulsive behavior as a brain disorder.

In 1975 Peter Schrag and Diane Divoky published an important book, *The Myth of the Hyperactive Child: and Other Means of Child Control,* that captured the attention of professionals and the informed public. The timing of their publication witnessed troubling increases in medical diagnoses of hyperactivity and minimal brain dysfunction.

> In less than a decade, the ailment spread from virtual obscurity to something well beyond epidemic proportions. It has no single name, no universally accepted symptoms, and no discernible anatomical or biochemical characteristics which can be diagnosed in a clinic or laboratory, yet it is said to affect as many as 40 percent of all American children, to reflect an organic or chemical dysfunction of the brain or the nervous system and to be the cause of most, if not all, pediatric problems in learning and behavior. Its most common name . . . is "learning disabilities" (LD) . . . sometimes synonymous with "minimal brain dysfunction" (MBD), "hyperkineses," "impulse disorder" and a substantial number of other conditions and "syndromes." (1975, 30)

The Schrag and Divoky publication created a great deal of interest among the general public, especially among parents with school age children. As is often the case, concerns of the general public can stir interest in the professional community and stimulate research activity where little or none previously existed.

In this regard, some of the more interesting research literature appeared after the work of Schrag and Divoky. Among those studies that questioned the practice of utilizing broad and inclusive childhood behaviors as descriptions for highly active children, Schachar, Rutter and Smith pointed out that :

> The very existence of "hyperactivity" as a behavior which is independent of the observer value system has been called into question. It has been argued that the diagnosis is no more than an artificially created "medical" label applied to

children whose behavior is annoying to adults because it does not comply with the demands of the home or school environment. This definition of the "hyperkinetic syndrome" has also been challenged empirically. Studies have failed to demonstrate the interrelatedness of the behaviors usually attributed to the syndrome. . . . The concept of the syndrome has also been challenged on clinical grounds. . . . In Great Britain and Europe, clinicians have tended to reserve the diagnosis of "hyperkinetic syndrome" for the very few children who show severe overactivity and inattentiveness in nearly all situations. (1981, 376)

Among the most troublesome behaviors that tended to unnerve parents and teachers was the child's lack of attention to assigned tasks. It was only a matter of time before the professional community would recognize this and eventually incorporate it among its already litany of "symptoms." The earlier descriptions for hyperactivity as a brain disorder had employed the term "distractibility," and like impulsivity, it also implied a lack of sustained attention.

By 1980 Minimal Brain Dysfunction (MBD) was expanded to Attention Deficit Disorder (ADD), marking a point when the therapeutic community expanded the pool of children well beyond the earlier American Psychiatric Association's diagnostic label of the Hyperkinetic Childhood Syndrome. The inability or refusal by a pupil to sustain attention with specificity was thought to be a neurological deficit. Sustained attention, for many educators, psychiatrists, and psychologists, gradually became the center piece of hyperactive behavior in children. In the 1990s the research community focused considerably on issues related to attention deficit disorders.

A sustained attention deficit is thought by many to be the cardinal component of hyperactivity. On tests of vigilance, lasting anything from 5 to 30 min., hyperactive children tend to have poorer concentration and so make many more mistakes in absolute terms than control children. However, poor performance on vigilance tasks does not necessarily imply a sustained attention deficit. The greater number of errors made by hyperactive children may be due to a whole host of unrelated motivational and cognitive variables. In order to isolate such a deficit one must show that hyperactive children's attention decays more quickly over time than that of non hyperactive controls. (Sonuga-Barke and Taylor, 1992 1091)

For various complex reasons, from the early 1950s, impulsivity and hyperactivity were consistently mentioned in various ways in clinical descriptions. In 1996 children who had been previously labeled MBH and ADH were being diagnosed as having an attention deficit disorder with hyperactivity (ADDH). Characteristics for ADDH were remarkably similar to those from MBD and ADD: including, "inattentiveness," "failure to complete tasks," "unable (or unwilling) to concentrate," "impulsiveness," and "frequent shifting of interests and attention."

By the 1990s ADDH settled into professional and public literature as attention deficit hyperactive disorder (ADHD) and the published symptoms remained the same. There seemed to be concerted efforts by school authorities, frustrated parents, drug companies, and physicians, to match diagnosis and treatment to accommodate troubling childhood behaviors as identified by teachers and parents. The list of these "behaviors" tend to grow annually.

As late as 1994 scholars were still engaged in trying to disentangle the impulsivity and reflectivity paradigm from the general discussion of active versus passive children in learning environments in a dysfunctional context. That year, an important study was published that asked a significant question in its title, *When Is "Impulsiveness" Not Impulsive? The Case of Hyperactive Children's Cognitive Style*. In introducing this study, Sonuga-Barke, Houlberg, and Hall informed us that:

> Philosophers of science have become increasingly aware of the way in which normative assumptions embodied in scientific terminology influence research strategy. This is particularly clear in the human sciences where terms are often borrowed from everyday speech. For instance, the term impulsive, when understood as a symptom of childhood psychopathology, has both a descriptive and an explanatory significance. It couples a description of a response in favour of immediacy and certain assumptions about both the dysfunctional character and the constitutional origins of that response. In short, the assumption is that children "don't wait not because they don't want to wait but because they can't wait." In this way, hyperactive children's apparently maladaptive and unconditional preference for response or reward immediacy, has been assumed by psychopathologists to reflect a deficit in regulative functioning or inhibitory processes thought by many to lie at the heart of their problem. (1994, 1247-1248)

By 1996, amid a serious debate among professionals regarding over-diagnoses, more than three million children in the United States, mostly boys, had been diagnosed as having ADHD. Over 60 per cent of children diagnosed as ADHD are prescribed drugs (primarily Ritalin), and the remainder are treated through behavior modification and family therapy. Several studies have reported that hyperactivity in young children often disappears with adolescent maturation. It has also been suggested that academic and emotional problems can persist and these children remain on medication for reasons more related to impulsivity than hyperactivity (Laufer, 1962; Menkes, Rowe and Menkes 1967; Cohen, Weiss, and Minde, 1972).

Since the 1950s impulsivity has been entangled with labels attributed to undesirable behaviors like, "distractibility," "hyperkinetic," "attention deficit" and "hyperactive." This chapter describes the etiology of the trends that created a dysfunction context for impulsivity, the use of brain altering drugs like Ritalin to sequester active children, and current research on this paradigm.

It still remains difficult to view impulsivity as a desirable trait by educators because of the assumed high error rate among impulsive individuals. There are new studies, however, that attempt to separate learners who approach their school work with intensity and sincerity of early resolution, and those who lack the control to perform in any other way.

It is also likely, if given the choice, teachers would prefer students who are reflective, thoughtful, and patient. Such characteristics seem to embody all that is good about scholarship in particular and academia in general. Because this is probably true, several studies have focused upon modifying the information processing of impulsively oriented individuals to a more reflective cognitive style.

IMPULSIVITY AND REFLECTIVITY AS COGNITIVE STYLES

In an atmosphere where impulsive behavior was being viewed in a pejorative context, scholars in education and psychology were maintaining a steady flow of cognitive style literature that defined a normative status for reflectivity and impulsivity as a cognitive preference construct. Previously, they had been identified as analytical and nonanalytical cognitive preferences.

Early in the 1960s, and primarily through the work of Jerome Kagan at Harvard University, reflectivity and impulsivity as cognitive preferences displayed by individuals in problem-solving experiences emerged as cognitive style constructs within the range of "normal" behaviors.

In general, studies that have continued to investigate reflective and impulsive behaviors have been concerned with the tempo employed by individuals in teaching/learning experiences. The impulsive modalities have been identified as a person's inclination—when presented with a hypothesis of uncertainty—to respond hurriedly in reaching a solution in a problem-solving situation. In critical thinking situations, impulsive style individuals usually consider fewer alternatives and gather information less systematically than reflective style individuals.

Reflective individuals employ modalities that tend to invest the time, inclination and/or ability to reflect on hypotheses, and respond more thoughtfully than their impulsive counterparts. Jerome Kagan defined this cognitive style as:

> The dramatic differences in problem-solving among children of the same age or among children of different ages have been attributed to two categories of constructs—motivational variables and/or adequacy of conceptual skills. In

effect differences in quality of cognitive products have been explained by assuming either that one child cared more about his performance, or that one child had more knowledge relevant to the task. However, other cognitive processes are an intimate part of problem-solving activity. One of these processes concerns the degree to which the child reflects over the adequacy of a solution hypothesis.

Some children—and adults—select and report solution hypotheses quickly with minimal consideration for their probable accuracy. Other children, of equal intelligence, take more time to decide about the validity of solutions. The former group has been called impulsive, the latter reflective. (1966, 17)

In the 1960s Kagan and others developed the matching familiar figures test (MFFT) for preschool children, older children, and adults, to identify individual cognitive styles within the reflectivity and impulsivity paradigm.

The test format presents a set of familiar figures that are common to every day life, along with four, six, or eight similar objects to which they must be matched. Objects to be matched on each of the test's twelve items has an exact facsimile in its matching group. The accuracy of the subject's choices and the time that it takes for choices to be made are calculated. Children who score above the median in accuracy, and below the median in errors are designated reflective. Those who score below the median on response time and above the median on errors are called impulsive.

Instruments that are designed to measure intellectual functioning in young children rely heavily upon the "correct" solution, therefore, impulsive responses by subjects will presumably yield a higher error rate than reflective responses. Such instruments, even in the 1990s, were designed to give extra credit for speed while maintaining a penalty for errors. For the small group of fast accurate individuals, their impulsive responses can be beneficial. In this regard, current intelligence tests are undergoing frequent modification and sometimes speed is designed into the scoring. For example, the Wechsler preschool and primary scale of intelligence-revised (WIPPSI-R), includes 40 percent new items in the 1990s version, and bonus points are granted for fast-accurate performance to com-pensate for certain inequities in the instrument. In a review of WIPPSI-R by A. S. Kaufman it was suggested that:

Giving bonus points for speed to preschool children seems silly from a developmental and common-sense perspective. Sure, brighter children will tend to solve problems more quickly then less intelligent children, and that relationship will hold even at the preschool level. But young children sometimes respond slowly for a variety of reasons that have more to do with maturation and personality. For example, a young child might respond deliberately because of immaturity of experience in test taking, underdeveloped motor coordination, insecurity, or a reflective cognitive style. (1992, 158)

Thomas J. Banta, who has written extensively on existentialism and psychotherapy, approached the measuring of cognitive behavior in young children from the perspective of "the ways in which a child solves a problem, not just his ability to perform a task correctly." The work of Banta is cited here because, like Kagan, he studied individual "self regulating behaviors that facilitate effective problem-solving," in young children including impulsivity and reflectivity. Banta called these behaviors "autonomy" (1970).

Banta designed the Cincinnati autonomy test battery (CATB), to tap into abilities that children often utilize in their daily activities like play, as they encounter and solve problems. In addition to reflectivity, impulsivity, and field independence, the CATB variables included curiosity (the child's tendency to explore and investigate novel stimuli); Innovation (the tendency to discover alternative solutions); intentional cognition (the tendency to acquire the intended information); incidental cognition (the tendency to acquire information that was not necessarily intended); persistence (the tendency to pursue the specified cognitive goal); resistance to distraction (the tendency to pursue the cognitive goal despite competing distractions); task competence (cognitive competence to solve problems having different characteristics); social competence (the tendency not to be intimidated in the presence of adults); kindergarten prognosis (ability to work confidently in traditional kindergarten settings); curiosity verbalization (the tendency to discuss novel aspects of the test objects or the testing situation); fantasy-related verbalization (while engaging in curiosity verbalization, the tendency to introduce fantasy into the conversation).

> Ideas which have aided development of the CATB are found in diverse literature from the areas of personality, cognition and perception. There is a significant trend in each of these areas toward interest in aspects of what I call autonomous functioning, aspects especially concerning the style with which persons approach problems. The common element in these various perspectives can be stated briefly as interest in respect to which human functioning is not completely determined by internal impulses or conflicts (e.g., by compulsions, hostility, sex drive, guilt) or by external restraint (e.g., persuasion, punishment, oppression, deprivation). . . . There are numerous facets of functioning . . . enabling man not only to adapt to the average demands of living, but also to innovate—to find alternative ways of behaving and thinking. (Banta, 1970, 426-427)

There are various instruments that have been developed with the measurement of impulsive and reflective cognitive preferences as their goal. Among the most popular is the matching familiar figures test (MFFT). The MFFT is used to examine children's perceptual behavior. This instrument examines the ways in which children approach problem-solving tasks along a continuum between extremes of quick impulsive responses, and a more thoughtful reflective response. Impulsive children appear willing to sacrifice accuracy for speed, while reflective children are unwilling to make this sacrifice.

Banta's CABT modified some of the items in the MFFT to accommodate a younger group of subjects. To distinguish it from the MFFT, which was designed for older school children, Banta developed the early childhood matching familiar figures test (EC-MFFT). The EC-MFFT was intended for children from low-income families ages three to four.

Half of the test items were intended to be "social" in that it required the subject to match the drawing of a face to its likeness that is arranged among a group of faces. The other half, called "nonsocial" are matching common shapes and patterns like cars or airplanes.

Because preschool children have seldom acquired the etiquette of the testing environment, their responses are often random, playful and unreliable. For these reasons, instruments designed to measure variabilities among very young children need careful scaling and an experienced examiner to administer them. Tests that give credit for speed, for example, could be measuring cognitive style characteristics that the instrument does not purport to measure.

When the MFFT has been used to determine the extent to which a preschool child was reflective or impulsive, mixed results were reported. It has been reported that when the MFFT was presented to children under the age of six, the subjects were often too playful, carrying on unrelated discussions with the examiner and giving random responses for reasons other than those related to what the item intended to measure. For the MFFT to be effective, the subject must have some concept of error, and an awareness of the implications of providing a wrong response.

This level of understanding of the meaning of social consequences related to errors comes with maturation and an awareness of the relationship between school work and the learner. Reports about preschool children from impoverished families indicate that they seem to enjoy the attention that they are receiving from the examiner and will frequently make random selections based upon the proximity of test objects. While other subjects from similar families are intimidated by the strange examiner who is inviting them to add to their failure to do well in school. Others have reported that an experienced examiner and a proper setting can overcome these aforementioned problems with most preschool subjects.

A different measure, the Kansas reflection impulsivity scale for preschoolers (KRISP), presents the subject with ten items consisting of drawings that must be matched with four choices. A score is derived for time spent in making choices (latency) and for errors. Results tend to report that reflective individuals are also field independent with above-average IQ scores.

In his approach to the study of impulsivity/reflectivity in language and speech competence among white children, Schwebel (1966) questioned nine- to twelve- year-olds in middle- and lower-class neighborhoods. After careful distinctions were made between two different neighborhoods, the researcher entered the neighborhoods in search of children in the specific age group. After offering them fifty cents to participate, the subjects were asked to answer several questions and sort objects.

Schwebel reported that middle-class children "described more ideas and events, used longer and better developed sentences, gave more accurate and complete accounts and grouped objects more effectively" than their lower-class counterparts. In contrast, lower-class children were reported to be more anxious to get started and responded impulsively to instructions. Their haste precluded from their attention salient information that would have assisted in the accuracy of their responses.

Middle-class children in the study were patient and reflected on tasks and questions posed by the examiner. The study reported that this reflective style found among middle-class children contributed significantly toward their greater accuracy and better phrased responses.

In school activities that require problem-solving skills, it has been reported that impulsive children are less likely than their reflective peers to use effective strategies. Occasionally, during problem-solving experiences when impulsive children just happen to discover effective strategies, they seldom employ such strategies consistently. It has also been reported that impulsive children process perceptual information in a global manner, and their reflective counterparts are more analytical in this process. In other areas of classroom learning, like reading for example, children who were thought to be both impulsive and field dependent demonstrated difficulties in reading comprehension.

The reflective/impulsive dimensions, compared to the field dependent/independent dimensions, have received considerable attention from scholars with interests in early childhood and preschool development. It has also been demonstrated that aspects of personality development are revealed in the measures of reflectivity/impulsivity in preschool children. For example, researchers have reported that children who were taught by reflective teachers acquired social traits that were more reflective in nature.

In post secondary student groups it has been reported that impulsivity has been associated with characteristics of authoritarianism and reflectivity with intellectual and liberal dispositions. It is rather common in traditional classrooms to find that impulsive style children do not perform as well as reflective ones. Several studies, however, have reported that the performance of impulsive style children can be modified through the use of problem-solving strategies that enable them to become more reflective.

In their study, *The Effects of Teacher Tempo on the Child,* Yondo and Kagan reported that the modifying of impulsivity of young children can be achieved in a relatively short period of time by experienced teachers: "First grade children placed with experienced reflective teachers became more reflective than those placed with impulsive teachers (1968, 33)." They also reported from the same study that boys who spent a year with experienced reflective teachers showed greater gains toward reflectivity than those in classes of inexperienced impulsive teachers.

Kagan, Rosman, et al. have provided compelling reasons for classroom teachers to seriously consider encouraging students prone to impulsivity to modify their behavior toward a more reflective mode. The consequences that they cite support their point of view.

> The child who does not reflect upon the differential validity of several solution possibilities is apt to implement mentally the first idea that occurs to him. This strategy is more likely to end up in failure than one that is characterized by reflection. For the impulsive child who reaches a *cul-de-sac* in a problem-solving sequence, and recognizes that he has not solved the problem is likely to become more anxious than he was initially. As a result of the increased anxiety his selection and evaluation of a second solution path is apt to be impaired, and the probability of success attenuated. This maladaptive cycle may become entrenched with time and after 5 years of experiencing the sequence; problem>>> impulsive selection of invalid solution sequence>>> failure>>> anxiety>>> selection of second sequence>>> failure . . . etc., the child may gradually withdraw involvement from problem situations and become apathetic or hostile toward intellectual situations. (1964, 35)

In the 1960s another interesting perspective on the study of reflectivity and impulsivity in childhood education was added to the various ways in which these personality attributes were investigated. Scholars began to turn their attention to the child's delay of gratification (Jones, 1966; Michel and Ebbesen, 1970; Michel, 1974; Rapport, et al. 1986; Sonuga-Barle, et al. 1992, 1996). Fundamental to this approach was a measure of the child's tendency to prefer an immediate reward following an assigned task, rather than wait for a reward of greater value sometime after the completion of the task. Here, the concept of impulsiveness was extended to include frustration, choice, and self-control. It is assumed that the longer children are able to postpone the reward (gratification), the greater their level of self-control. In this regard, Rapport (1986) and his colleagues paired several related variables in a study involving thirty two males between the ages of six and eight, to examine the consequences and reported:

> The primary purpose of the present investigation was to determine whether hyperactive and normal children differ in their ability to delay gratification and hence tolerate frustration. In this regard it was predicted that, when faced with a free choice conflict situation involving smaller-immediate and larger-delayed rewards, hyperactive children would choose the former. The second purpose ... was to assess whether having some control over the imposed delay period influences a child's ability or willingness to delay gratification. (1986, 193)

As expected, Rapport and his colleagues found that hyperactive children choose smaller immediate rewards and preferred not to complete all of the assigned tasks. This style, they suggested, compromised the teaching learning environment. It was also their view, from this experience, that variations in teaching approaches could be designed to encourage children to be more reflective in problem-solving situations. Teaching practices that employ programmed workbooks, classroom assignments divided into smaller units, and computer assisted instruction, were recommended by Rapport and his colleagues (1986).

Educators should also resist the tendency to place children at the extremes of impulsive or reflective, but rather, conceptualize these dimensions along a continuum with a central tendency factor. In other words, teachers should avoid classifying children either/or reflective/impulsive because there are individual characteristics that vary along a continuum, as well as perceptual choices that enable some children to be selective as problem-solving situations change.

REFERENCES

Ault, R. L., Crawford, D. E., and Jeffrey, W. E. (1972). "Visual Scanning Strategies of Reflective, Impulsive, Fast-Accurate, and Slow- Inaccurate Children in the Matching Familiar Figures Test." *Child Development* 43, 1412-1417.

Banta, T. J. (1966). "Educating Children for Adulthood." *Young Children* 21, 272-280.

Banta, T. J. (1967). "Existentialism, Morality, and Psychotherapy." *The Humanist* 27, 44-48.

Banta, T. J. (1970). "Tests for the Evaluation of Early Childhood Education: Cincinnati Autonomy Test Battery." In J. Hellmuth, ed., *Cognitive Studies.* New York: Brunner/Mazel.

Barkley, R. A. (1981). *Hyperactive Children: A Handbook for Diagnosis and Treatment.* New York: Guildford.

Barkley, R. (1990). *Attention Deficit Disorder: A Handbook for Diagnosis and Treatment*. New York: Guilford.

Barratt, E. E. (1959). "Anxiety and Impulsiveness Related to Psych-Motor Efficiency."*Perceptual and Motor Skills* 9, 191-198.

Becker, L., Bender, N. and Morrison, G. (1970). "Measuring Impulsive-Reflection: A Critical Review." *Journal of Learning Disabilities* 10, 24-30.

Block, J. and Petersen, P. (1955). "Some Personality Correlates of Confidence, and Speed in Decision Situation." *Journal of Abnormal and Social Psychology* 51, 34-41.

Brodzinsky, D. M. (1975). "The Role of Conceptual Tempo and Stimulus Characteristics in Children's Humor Development." *Developmental Psychology* 11, 843-850.

Burks, H. F. (1960). "The Hyperkinetic Child." *Exceptional Children* 27, 18-26.

Burnham, W. H. (1908). "Attention and Interest." *American Journal of Psychology* 19, 14-18.

Campbell, S. B. (1973). "Cognitive Styles in Reflective, Impulsive, and Hyperactive Boys and Their Mothers." *Perceptual and Motor Skills* 36, 747-752.

Campbell, S. B., and Douglas, V. I. (1972). "Cognitive Styles and Response to the Threat of Frustration." *Canadian Journal of Behavioral Science* 4, 30-42.

Cohen, S., and Przybycien, C. A. (1974). "Some Effects of Sociometrically Selected Peer Models on the Cognitive Styles of Impulsive Children." *Journal of Genetic Psychology* 124, 213-220.

Cohen, N. J., Weiss, G., and Minde, K. (1972). "Cognitive Styles in Adolescents Previously Diagnosed as Hyperactive." *Journal of Child Psychology and Psychiatry* 13, 203-209.

Debus, R. L. (1970). "Effects of Brief Observation of Model Behavior on Perceptual Tempo of Impulsive Children." *Developmental Psychology* 2, 22-32.

Denney, D. R. (1971). "The Assessment of Differences in Conceptual Style." *Child Study Journal* 1, 142-155.

Denney, D. R. (1974). "The Relationship of Three Cognitive Style Dimensions to Elementary Reading Abilities." *Journal of Educational Psychology* 66, 702-709.

Denney, D. R. (1972). "Modeling Effects Upon Conceptual Style and Cognitive Tempo." *Child Development* 43, 105-119.

Douglas, V. I. (1965). "Children's Response to Frustration: A Developmental Study." *Canadian Journal of Psychology 19*, 160-171.

Drake, D. M. (1970). "Perceptual Correlates of Impulsive and Reflective Behavior." *Developmental Psychology* 2, 202-214.

Egeland, B. (1974). "Training Impulsive Children in the Use of More Efficient Scanning Techniques." *Child Development* 45, 165-171.

Eska, B., and Black, K. N. (1971). "Conceptual Tempo in Young Grade School Children."*Child Development* 42, 505-516.

Finch, A. J., Jr., Nelson, W. M. lll, Montgomery, L. E., and Stein, A. B. (1974). "Reflection-Impulsivity and Locus of Control in Emotionally Disturbed Children." *Journal of Genetic Psychology* 125, 273-275.

Finch, A. J., Jr., and Montgomery, L. E. (1973). Reflection-Impulsivity and Information Seeking in Emotionally Disturbed Children." *Journal of Abnormal Child Psychology* 1, 358-362.

Freibergs, V., and Douglas, V. I. (1969). "Concept Learning in Hyperactive and Normal Children." *Journal of Abnormal Psychology* 75, 388-395.

Fuhrman, M. J., and Kendall, P. C. (1986). "Cognitive Tempo and Behavioral Adjustment in Children."*Cognitive Therapy and Research 10*, 45-50.

Gozali, J. (1969). "Impulsive-Reflectivity as Problem-Solving Styles Among Educable Mentally Retarded Children." *American Journal of Mental Deficiency* 73, 854-867.

Grimes, J., and Allinsmith, W. (1961). "Compulsivity, Anxiety, and School Achievement."*Merrill-Palmer Quarterly of Behavior and Development* 1 (4), 247-271.

Haley, J. (1972). "Family Therapy." In, C. J. Sager and H. S. Kaplan eds., *Progress in Group and Family Therapy.* New York: Brunner/ Mazel.

Harrison, A., and Nadelman, L. (1972). "Concept Tempo and Inhibibitions of Movement in Black Preschool Children." *Child Development* 43, 657-668.

Harthshorne, H., May, M. A., and Miller, J. B. (1929). *Studies in Service and Self-Control.* New York, NY: MacMillan.

Heider, E. R. (1971). " Information Processing and the Modification of an Impulsive Conceptual Tempo."*Child Development* 42, 1276-1281.

Henry, F. (1973). "Effect of Reinforcement Conditions on a Discrimination Learning Task for Impulsive Versus Reflective Children." *Child Development* 44, 657-660.

Henry, J. (1965). *Culture Against Man.* New York: Vintage Books.

Hilgard, E. R. (1962). "Impulsive Versus Realistic Thinking: An Examination of the Distinction Between Primary and Secondary Process." *Psychological Bulletin* 59, 477-488.

Jones, R. L. (1966). "The Hyperkenitic Child: Some Consensually Validated Behavioral Correlates." *Exceptional Children* 32, 635-637.

Kagan, J. (1965). "Reflection-Impulsivity and Reading Ability in Primary Grade Children."*Child Development* 36, 609-628.

Kagan, J. (1966). "Reflection-Impulsivity: The Generality and Dynamics of Conceptual Tempo." *Journal of Abnormal Psychology* 71 (1), 17-24.

Kagan, J. (1984). *The Nature of the Child.* New York: Basic Books.

Kagan, J. (1989). "Temperamental Contributions to Social Behavior." *American Psychologist* 44, 674-688.

Kagan, J., Rosman, B., Day, D., Albert, J., and Phillips, W. (1964). "Information Processing in the Child: Significance of Analytic and Reflective Attitudes." *Psychological Monographs* 78, 1-37.

Katz, J. M. (1971). "Reflection-Impulsivity and Color-Form Sorting. *Child Development* 42, 745-754.

Kaufman, A. S. (1992). "Evaluation of the Icicle and WIPPSI-R for Gifted Children."*Roeper Review* (March). 156-160.

Kendall, P. C., and Finch, A. J. (1978). "A Cognitive Behavioral Treatment for Impulsivity: A Group Comparison Study." *Journal of Consulting and Clinical Psychology* 46, 110-118.

Knobel, M. (1962). "Psychopharmacology for the Hyperkinetic Child." *Archives of General Psychiatry* 6, 198-202.

Knobloch, H. and Pasamanick, B. (1959). "Syndrome of Minimal Cerebral Damage in Infancy." *Journal of The American Medical Association 170,* 1384-1387.

Laufer, N. W. (1962). "Cerebral Dysfunction and Behavior Disorders in Adolescents." *American Journal of Orthopschiatry* 32, 501-506.

Lewis, M., Rausch, M., Goldberg, S., and Dodd, C. (1968). "Error Response Time and IQ: Sex Differences in Cognitive Style of Preschool Children." *Perceptual and Motor Skills* 26, 563-5498.

Maccoby, E. E., Dowley, E. M., Hagen, J. W., and Dagerman, R. (1965). "Activity Level and Intellectual Functioning in Normal Preschool Children." *Journal of Genetic Psychology Child and Development* 36, 761-770.

Mann, L. (1973). "Differences Between Reflective and Impulsive Children in Tempo and Quality of Decision Making." *Child Development* 44, 274-279.

McKinney, J. D. (1973). "Problem Solving Strategies in Impulsive and Reflective Second Graders." *Developmental Psychology* 8, 145.

Meichenbaum, D. H., and Goodman, J. (1969). "Reflection-Impulsivity and Verbal Control of Motor Behavior."*Child Development* 40, 785-797.

Meichenbaum, D. H., and Goodman, J. (1971). "Training Impulsive Children to Talk to Themselves: A Means of Developing Self-Control." *Journal of Abnormal Psychology* 77, 115-126.

Menkes, M. M., Rowe, J. S., and Menkes, J. H. (1967). "A Twenty-Five Year Follow-Up Study on the Hyperkinetic Child with Minimal Brain Dysfunction." *Pediatrics* 39, 393-399.

Meredith, R. A. (1978). "Improved Oral Test Scores Through Delayed Response." *Modern Language Journal* 62, 321-327.

Messer, S. (1970). "The Effects of Anxiety Over Intellectual Performance in Reflection-Impulsivity in Children."*Child Development* 41, 723-735.

Messer, S. (1976). "Reflection-Impulsivity: A Review."*Psychological Bulletin* 86, 1026-1052.

Michel, W. (1974). "Process in Delay of Gratification." In L. Berkowitz ed., *Advances in Experimental Social Psychology,* Vol. 7, 249-292. New York: Academic Press.

Michel, W., and Ebbesen, E. (1970). "Attention in Delay of Gratification." *Journal of Personality and Social Psychology* 21, 204-218.

Minde, K., and Lewin, D., Weiss, G., Lavigeuer, V., and Sykes, E. (1971). "The Hyperactive Child in Elementary School: A 5 Year Controlled Follow-up." *Exceptional Children* 38, 215-221.

Montgomery, K. C. (1951). "Spontaneous Attention as a Function of TimeBetween Trials and Amount of Work." *Journal of Experimental Psychology* 42, 82-93.

Murray, H. A. (1938). *Explorations in Personality.* New York: Oxford University Press.

Ounsted, C. (1955). "Hyperkinetic Syndrome in Epileptic Children." *Lancet* 2, 303.

Parry, P. A., and Douglas, V. I. (1983). "Effects of Reinforcement on Concept Identification in Hyperactive Children." *Journal of Abnormal Psychology* 11, 327-340.

Rapport, M. D., Tucker, S. B., Dupaul, G. J., Merlo, M., and Stoner, G. (1986). "Hyperactivity and Frustration: The Influence of Control Over the Size of Rewards in Delaying Gratification." *Journal of Abnormal Child Psychology 14* (2), 191-204.

Reali, N., and Hall, V. (1970). "Effect of Success and Failure on the Reflective and Impulsive Child." *Developmental Psychology* 3, 394-402.

Ridberg, E. H., Parke, R. D., and Hetherington, E. M. (1971). "Modification of Impulsive and Reflective Cognitive Styles Through Observation of Film-Mediated Models."*Developmental Psychology* 5, 369-377.

Safer, D. J. (1971). "Drugs for Problem School Children." *Journal of School Health 41,* 491-495.

Salkind, N., and Wright, J. (1977). "The Development of Reflection-Impulsivity and Cognitive Efficiency." *Human Development* 20, 377-387.

Schachar, R., and Logan, G. D. (1990). "Impulsivity and Inhibitory Control in Normal Development and Child Psychopathology." *Developmental Psychology* (26) 5, 710-720.

Schachar, R., Rutter, M., and Smith, A. (1981). "The Characteristics of Situationally and Pervasively Hyperactive Children: Implications for Syndrome Definition." *Journal of Child Psychology and Psychiatry* 22 (4), 375-392.

Shacter, H. S. (1933). "A Method for Measuring the Sustained Attention of Preschool Children." *Journal of Genetic Psychology* 42, 339-

369.

Schwebel, A. I. (1966). "Effects of Impulsivity on Performance on Verbal Tasks on Middle-and Lower-Class Children." *American Journal of Orthopsychiatry* 36, 13-21.

Schrag, P., and Divoky, D. (1975). *The Myth of the Hyperactive Child: And Other Means of Child Control.* New York: Pantheon Books.

Siegelman, E. (1969). "Reflective and Impulsive Observing Behavior." *Child Development* 40, 1213-1222.

Sonuga-Barke, E. J. S., Houlberg, K., and Hall, M. (1994). "When is 'Impulsiveness' Not Impulsive? The Case of Hyperactive Children's Cognitive Style." *The Journal of Child Psychology and Psychiatry* 35 (7), 1247-1253.

Sonuga-Barke, E. J. S., and Taylor, E. (1992). "The Effect of Delay on Hyperactive and Non-Hyperactive Children's Response Times: A Research Note." *The Journal of Child Psychology and Psychiatry* 33 (6), 1091-1096.

Sonuga-Barke, E. J. S., Williams, E., Hall, M., and Saxton, T. (1996). "Hyperactivity and Delay of Aversion III: The Effects of Cognitive Style on Imposing Delay After Errors." *The Journal of Child Psyhology and Psychiatry* 37 (2), 189-194.

Sutton-Smith, B., and Rosenberg, B. G. (1959). "A Scale to Identify Impulsive Behavior in Children." *Journal of Genetic Psychology* 95, 211-216.

Ward, W. C. (1968). "Reflection-Impulsivity in Kindergarten Children."*Child Development* 39, 867-874.

Weiss, G., and Hechtman, L. (1979). " The Hyperactive Child Syndrome."*Science* 205, 1348-1353.

Yates, B. T., and Mischel, W. (1979). "Young Children's Preferred Attention Strategies for Delaying Gratification." *Journal of Personality and Social Psychology* 37, 286-300.

Yondo, R., and Kagan, J. (1968). "The Effects of Teacher Tempo on the Child." *Child Development* 39, 27-34.

Yondo, R., and Kagan, J. (1970). "The Effects of Task Complexity on Reflection-Impulsivity."*Cognitive Psychology* 1, 192-200.

Zeinker, T., Jeffrey T., Ault, R. and Parsons, J. (1972). "Analysis and Modification of Search Strategies of Impulsive and Reflective Children on the Matching Familiar Figures Test." *Child Development* 43, 321-335.

Zelniker, T., and Jeffrey, W. E. (1976). "Reflective and Impulsive Children: Strategies for Information Processing Underlying Differences in Problem-Solving." *Monographs of the Society for Research in Child Development* 41 (5), (Serial No. 168).

5

Cognitive Styles of Conceptualization

> The amplitude of our cultural heritage exceeds ten thousand times the carrying capacity of any human brain, and hence we must have ten thousand specialists to transmit it. To do away with the specialization of knowledge would be to produce a race of quiz winners and destroy our culture in favor of a universal dilettantism.
>
> —Michael Polanyi

Conceptualization is central to cognitive style theory in that one of the fundamental tenets of cognitive style is the consistent differences in the ways that individuals perceive and conceptualize their environment. Theories of perception, therefore, are important to an understanding of conceptualization as a cognitive style. How individuals interpret an experience will influence how future experiences will be perceived and evaluated. Over time, experiences influence individual perceptions of life's events and eventually serve as an index against which individuals make meaning of the world. Experiences not only provide opportunities for individuals to make meaning of the world, but in the process, experiences of the past provide knowledge for reflection.

Personality and self-concept are also linked to perception. In making sense of the world through how it is perceived, individuals are also evaluating *their* place within it. Experiences that undergird this perceptual process are essential to the emergence of individual self-concept formation. As individuals anticipate the future from past experiences, perceptions can undergo change and alter their values and self-concepts.

How individuals perceive events and issues is screened through human receptors that serve as entry points for information to our central nervous system. This is the brain's connection to the outside world. According to some theorists, they doubt that the brain would limit its own survival to these primary sensory elements. Nevertheless, it is believed that human perception serves as a filter for what the brain is asked to process, and this filtering system is further subject to how we conceptualize information to be processed.

Without a direct application of theories associated with perception and conceptualization, classroom teachers frequently interlace their teaching with these concepts. For example, early childhood teachers of reading, social studies, and mathematics have all used classroom activities designed to expand the number of ways in which children can organize materials and ideas. The teacher might introduce a container of objects like assorted buttons and ask the children to take a handful and place them in groups.

Some children might organize groups of buttons based upon color, the number of holes, size, whether they are smooth or embossed, or whether they are metal and not plastic. In most classrooms, at least one pupil will conceptualize a unique category that surprises everyone. The extent to which individuals can expand on such variations imply styles of conceptualization. Here, the intent is to encourage children to be thoughtful in the use of themes, categories, similarities, and representations. Following such an activity, pupils are then asked to discuss the reasons for their various choices and the actions that led to their formulated groupings.

During classroom discussions that follow such activities, teachers are sensitive to individual pupil contributions to the discussion. This process creates an environment that conveys to children that their ideas are important to the learning process and discovering what is important to be known. Children bring out-of-school experiences to such discussions and when their ideas are invited, the message is clear that their personal perceptions are of value. These in-school experiences are essential for the development of positive self-concept among pupils.

Conceptualization has been studied in a variety of ways. This variety emerged primarily for understanding and clarity as different scholars and researchers examined selected dimensions of this construct. Investigators have identified and attempted to measure conceptualization styles within the context of the following designations:

Breadth of categorization: studies the extent to which observers of events or participants in an experience will view these phenomena within a narrow or shallow specified range or category, or broad inclusive range with depth. Individuals inclined toward broad categorization will tolerate, and occasionally prefer, errors resulting from inclusion. On the other hand, individuals with tendencies toward narrow categorizations will tolerate, and also prefer, errors of exclusion.

Conceptual integration: studies individual information processing in categorizing and intellectually structuring issues and events through making comparisons, perceptualizing interrelationships, creating combinant variations and hierarchical perspectives.

Conceptual differentiation: examines the extent to which various sorting arrangements by individuals can yield larger numbers of differences and similarities among grouped objects or events. Creativity is often measured in a similar manner by observing and recording an individual's conceptual differentiation resulting from assigned tasks of sorting, classification, and/or reclassification.

Conceptual articulation: studies individual perceptual variations within a selected range of assessment, where distinctions to be made can be fine or course. It is concerned with the quality and quantity of dimensions employed by individuals in assessing events or issues within a single category.

Compartmentalization: studies individual perceptual limitations in the creation of ideas, and the tendency to reduce experiences into narrow particularized interpretations, rigid categories, and discrete compartments.

Complexity-Simplicity: is concerned with individual assessment of social experiences as influenced by one's world view. Individuals with tendencies toward cognitive complexity are thought to be more confident in diverse and interpersonal experiences that often require interrelated interpretations and responses. Such individuals also welcome social interactions that call for conflict resolution and values clarification. Individuals with tendencies toward simplicity prefer to avoid social contexts that require complex differentiations and layered multidimensional interactions that often require simultaneous interpretations. They are also more confident in intrapersonal experiences involving small group or individual encounters where social issues are clearly articulated and unidimensional. Studies of Multiple Intelligence have borrowed from the research in this domain and in the process cognitive complexity-simplicity was renamed "interpersonal" and "intrapersonal" intelligence (Morgan, 1996).

In their cognitive style study, Sigel, Jarman, and Hanesian (1967) studied styles of categorization among preschool and kindergarten children. They examined the extent to which this age group displayed such styles and whether or not a significant relationship existed between their styles of categorization and intellectual functioning. Their work discussed these issues from the perspective of personality theories derived from ideas first expressed by Allport (1937).

Three styles of categorization were selected for which subjects would be measured. These categories were defined in terms of behaviors expressed by subjects during sorting and matching tasks. One was described as descriptive and subdivided into two subgroups; one group being descriptive part-whole (similar to field independent and analytical), and the other descriptive global (where concern is with the total object much like field dependent). A second area of attention was defined as relational-contexual. Here the categorizing style utilizes inferences of functionality and theme. The third category included those items that were sorted according to "inferred characteristics of the stimuli."

The categorizing tasks were structured in various ways to the extent that the examiner assumed one approach to be more appropriate than another. In one setting the subjects were asked to choose two of the most similar objects from among three different ones. Another example offered a group of objects from which subjects made selections. Both procedures could be scored in a similar manner. This study reported significant gender differences within the descriptive, part-whole category, in that girls responded in a manner that varied from inattention to impulsive. Boys, on the other hand, were relaxed and emotionally under control.

Keeping in mind that this study was conducted in the 1960s, sometime prior to a general discourse concerning gender equity, the possibility of examiner bias could be a factor. This study, however, was well designed and the results were conservatively expressed so that one would not discern any obvious female bias.

For descriptive-global children, the study reported that girls were relaxed and inattentive, while boys displayed independence and tended to retain material. An interesting reversal was reported for the relational-contexual individuals. In this group the boys tended toward impulsivity, dependency, and inattentiveness, whereas the girls were more independent and attentive. These differences, though reported, were not deemed significant.

It is also interesting to note, that unlike other studies with very young children, these investigators reported a refreshing level of maturity among these four-and five-year-old subjects. They achieved a full understanding of what was being asked of them and provided a generous supply of responses. From the aspect of the Sigel, Jarman and Hanesian study concerned with intellectual functioning, it was reported that:

> The role of IQ in style for children is still an open question. Equivocal results have been found for children and for adults, particularly with relationships between descriptive part-whole responses and relational-contexual. . . .The significance of these findings rests in the support given to the proposition that styles of categorization may be integral to particular personality complexes, which are already beginning to be established at the kindergarten level. . . . For older children and adults it has been found earlier that styles of categorization relate to intelligence and to various personality variables. . . . The congruence

between these results and those found for older subjects suggests that styles of categorization may be relatively well established in the personality matrix at an early age. (1967, 13)

In addition to reporting on queries related to IQ and cognitive style, this particular quotation from the study by Sigel, et al also raise questions concerning developmental issues inherent in conceptualization. For professionals concerned with the acquisition of knowledge in early childhood, the circumstances under which teaching and learning is optimized are important to identify.

For example, we now know that infants as young as 8 weeks are capable of conceptualizing sensory experiences. The work of Piaget from which a great deal of early childhood theory is built, suggests that children are not aware of the permanent existence of objects until they are approximately 12 months of age. In general, prior to this age they will not search for a previously observed object that has been hidden from their view. As they approach 18 months of age, they will begin to search in the vicinity where it was last observed.

Finally, after 18 months infants will search for displaced objects that they observe being placed under a pillow, for example. Other scholars have raised questions about Piaget's conclusion that the child's active search for an object removed from view provides an indication of object permanence. Investigations along these lines are discussed in greater detail in Chapter 7.

After the acquisition of object permanence, infants advance to stages of perception where interests can be asserted. Piaget has theorized this next stage as the preoperational period. Symbolic functions are central to this phase in the child's development. Here, children are mentally able to allow an object in their presence to stand for something not within their purview. Such mental activity can be abstract as when a child is being read a story about a school, playground, and shopping center. Here, words on a page must satisfy the visual representation occurring in the child's thoughts. Symbolic references can also be more concrete as when young children imitate adult behavior in their play with dolls, toy trucks, and toy tools.

It is important to note here that children must reach the stage of symbolic functioning and achieve an appropriate vocabulary for conceptualization to be properly assessed. Language is essential for children to learn how things are ordered in their environment, and share that knowledge with others as a means of testing what they know and obtaining additional information. Children learn from experience how persons around them classify objects as well as things that symbolize other things.

During a variety of experiences, under myriad circumstances, children develop concepts of classes (plants, furniture, people, animals, etc.). They also learn that things can be further identified beyond class—flower, chair, adults, and dogs or cats, for example. Prior to classification and sorting tasks commonly administered to measure conceptualization, the chronological stages of development where symbolic representation is acquired must obviously be reached.

Among the various interrelationships between and among cognitive styles, there appears to be an important interaction between certain elements of scanning and reflective/impulsivity. It has been reported from several studies that the error rate of children who approach problem solving with impulsivity can be significantly reduced if they are taught scanning procedures. In the process, such individuals are able to increase response time (be more reflective) and reduce the rate of error (Drake, 1970; Siegelman, 1969; Egeland, 1974).

REFERENCES

Allport, Gordon. (1937). *Personality: A Psychological Interpretation.* New York: Henry Holt and Company.

Aschkenasy, J. R. and Odom, R. D. (1982). "Classification and Perceptual Development: Exploring Issues About Integrality and Different Sensitivity." *Journal of Experimental Child Psychology* 34, 435-448.

Asher, S. R., and Gorman, J. M. (1981). *The Development of Children's Friendships.* London: Cambridge University Press.

Bandura, A. L. (1977). *Social Learning Theory.* Englewood Cliffs, NJ: Prentice-Hall.

Banks, W. C. (1976). "White Preference in Blacks: A Paradigm in Search of a Phenomenon." *Psychological Bulletin* 83, 1179-1186.

Barrera, M. E., and Maurer, D. (1981). "Recognition of Mother's Photographed Face by the Three-Month-Old." *Child Development* 52, 714-716.

Benson, J. B., and Uzgiris, J. C. (1985). "Effect of Self-Initiated Locomotion on Infant Search Activity." *Developmental Psychology* 21, 923-931.

Bieri, J., Atkins, A. L., Briar, J. S., Leaman, R.L., Miller, H., and Tripodi, T. (1966). *Clinical and Social Judgment: The Discrimination of Behavioral Information.* New York: Wiley.

Bruner, J. S., Goodnow, J. J., and Austin, G. A. (1956). *A Study of Thinking.* New York: Wiley.

Bruner, J. S., and Tajfel, H. (1961). "Cognitive Risk and Environmental Change." *Journal of Abnormal Social Psychology* 62, 231-241.

Clayton, M. G., and Jackson, D. N. (1961). "Equivalence Range, Acquiescence, and Over Generalization." *Educational and Psychological Measurement* 21, 371-382.

Drake, D. M. (1970). "Perceptual Correlates of Impulsive and Reflective Behavior." *Developmental Psychology* 2, 202-214.

Egeland, B. (1974). "Training Impulsive Children in the Use of More Efficient Scanning Techniques."*Child Development* 45, 165-171.

Fillenbaum, S. (1959). "Some Stylistic Aspects of Categorizing Behavior." *Journal of Personality* 27, 187-195.

Gardner, R. W. (1953). "Cognitive Styles in Categorizing Behavior." *Journal of Personality* 22, 214-233.

Gelman, S. A., Collman, P., and Maccoby, E. E. (1986). "Inferring Properties From Categories vs Inferring Categories From Properties: The Case of Gender." *Child Development* 57, 396-404.

Haith, M. H., Bergman, T., and Moore, M. J. (1977). "Eye Contact and Face Scanning in Early Infancy." *Science* 198, 853-855.

Harvey, O. J., Hunt, D. E., and Shroder, H. M. (1961). *Conceptual Systems and Personality Organization.* New York: Wiley.

Hunt, J. McV. (1961). *Intelligence and Experience.* New York: Ronald.

Izard, C. E. (1960). "Personality Similarity and Friendship." *Journal of Abnormal Social Psychology* 61, 47-51.

Kagan, J., Moss, A., and Sigel, I. E. (1960). "Conceptual Style and the Use of Affect Labels." *Merrill-Palmer Quarterly* 6 (3), 261-278.

Kagan, J., Moss, A., and Sigel, I. E. (1963). "Psychological Significance of Styles of Conceptualization." *Monographs of the Society for Research in Child Development* 28(2, Serial No. 86), 73-112.

Kelly, G. A. (1955). *The Psychology of Personal Constructs.* New York: Norton.

Langley, C. W. (1971). "Differentiation and Integration of Systems of Personal Constructs." *Journal of Personality* 39, 10-25.

Messick, S. and Fritzky, C. F. (1963). "Dimensions of Analytic Attitude in Cognition and Personality." *Journal of Personality* 31, 313-318.

McGeoch, J. A. (1942). *The Psychology of Human Learning.* New York: Longmans.

Messick, S., and Kogan, N. (1963). "Differentiation and Compartmentalization on Object-Sorting Measures of Categorizing Style." *Perceptual and Motor Skills* 16, 47-61.

Messick, S., and Ross, J. (1962). *Measurement in Personality and Cognition.* New York: Wiley.

Morgan, H. (1996). "An Analysis of Gardner's Theory of Multiple Intelligence." *Roeper Review* 18 (4). 263-269.

Mos, L., Wardell, D., and Royce, J. R. (1974). A Factor Analysis of Some Measures of Cognitive Style." *Multivariate Behavioral Research* 9, 47-57.

Murphy, G. (1958). *Human Potentialities.* New York: Basic Books.

Pettigrew, T. F. (1958). "The Measurement and Correlates of Category Width as a Cognitive Variable." *Journal of Personality* 26, 532-544.

Piaget, J. (1936). *The Origins of Intelligence in Children.* New York: International Universities Press.

Piaget, J. (1937). *The Construction of Reality in the Child.* New York:

Basic Books.

Rosch, E., and Lloyd, B. B. *Cognition and Categorization.* Hillside, NJ: Lawrence Erlbaum.

Schroder, H. M., Driver, M. J., and Streufert, S. (1967). *Human Information Processing.* New York: Holt, Rinehart and Winston.

Scott, W. A. (1962). "Cognitive Complexity and Cognitive Flexibility." *Sociometry* 25, 405-414.

Signell, K. A. (1966). "Cognitive Complexity in Person Perception and Nation Perception: A Developmental Approach." *Journal of Personality* 34, 517-537.

Siegelman, E. (1969). Reflective and Impulsive Observing Behavior. *Child Development* 40, 1213-1222.

Sigel, J. I., Jarman, P. D., and Hanesian, H. (1967). "Styles of Categorization and Their Intellectual and Personality Correlates in Young Children."*Human Development* 10, 1-17.

Silver, A. A. (1978). Scanning, Diagnosis, and Intervention in the Prevention of Reading Disabilities. *Journal of Learning Disabilities* 11(7), 439-445.

Thompkins, S. S. (1962). *Affect Imagery Consciousness.* New York: Springer.

Tripodi, T., and Bieri, J. (1966). "Cognitive Complexity, Perceived Conflict, and Certainty." *Journal of Personality* 34, 144-153.

Vannoy, J. S. (1965). "Generality of Cognitive Complexity-Simplicity as a Personal Construct." *Journal of Personality and Social Psychology* 2, 385-396.

Wachtel, P. L (1968). Style and Capacity in Analytic Functioning."*Journal of Personality* 36, 202-212.

Wallach, M. A., and Kogan, N. (1966). *Modes of Thinking in Young Children.* New York: Holt Rinehart & Winston.

Witkin, H. A., Lewis, H. G., Hertzman, M., Machover., Meissner, P. B., and Wapner, S. (1954). *Personality Through Perception.* New York: Harper & Row.

Wyer, R. S. (1964). "Assessment and Correlates of Cognitive Differentiation and Integration." *Journal of Personality* 32, 394-409.

Ziller, R. C. (1973). *The Social Self.* New York, NY: Pergamon Press.

Zimiring, F. M. (1971). "Cognitive Simplicity-Complexity: Evidence for Discrete Processes." *Journal of Personality* 39, 1-9.

6

The Myers-Briggs Type Indicator

> All my life I had been looking for something, and everywhere I turned someone tried to tell me what it was. I accepted their answers too, though they were often in contradiction and even self-contridictory. I was naive, I was looking for myself and asking everyone except myself questions which I, and only I, could answer. It took me a long time and much boomeranging of my expectations to achieve a realization everyone else appears to have been born with: That I am nobody but myself.
>
> —Ralph Ellison

Theories of personality types that were developed by C. G. Jung, and described in Chapter 2 on theoretical influences of cognitive styles have direct implications for the development of The Myers-Briggs Type Indicator (MBTI), an instrument that is often used to assess personality and cognitive preferences. The MBTI is designed to identify individual cognitive preferences through the use of a self-report test for grades nine through college level and for adults.

> The MBTI is primarily concerned with the valuable differences in people that result from where they like to focus their attention, the way they like to take in information, the way they like to decide, and the kind of lifestyle they adopt. (Myers and Myers, 1980, 2)

In the early 1900s, Katherine C. Briggs started a systematic study of personality types in human interactions. Her focus was individual behavior related to experience and information processing. At the same time she spent a great deal of time reading biographies.

With her discovery of the work of Jung, she began to realize that his descriptions of psychological types were compatible with her interests in personality development. After a prolonged study of Jung's personality theory, Briggs and her daughter, Isabel Briggs Myers, during formal and informal encounters, began observations of personality types and cognitive styles.

In the early 1940s, Briggs and Myers started developing self-report questions that would lead to assessments of individual personality types. By 1975 the MBTI had gone through a series of field tests and modifications and was in widespread use by professionals in a variety of human service fields.

By now, even the general public is aware of the extraversion and introversion construct because over the years it has become the most widely discussed aspect of Jung's theory of personality types. Despite the popularity of the above constructs, the inventory does not end there. In a more complex manner, the MBTI includes other interacting domains, all derived from Carl Gustav Jung's theory of personality types.

In the MBTI, extraversion (E) and introversion (I) are conceptualized as cognitive preferences with extraversion at one end of the scale demonstrating outer-world preferences and introversion at the other end demonstrating inner-world preferences (Figure 6.1).

These two cognitive preferences are followed by two perceptual preferences for individual information acquisition. These perceptual types are defined within the context of how information is acquired. Sensing types (S) prefer the employment of their senses (visual, olfactory, etc.) in the processing of information. From a phenomenological perspective, the sensing individuals particularize experiences from their perception of "reality." Through the utilization of sensual preferences, such individuals are capable of considering vast amounts of information derived from immediately occurring events. At the other end of this bipolar scale, intuition types (N) prefer global perspectives and employ creative assessments in various ways of learning from an experience. They are more concerned with interactions and relationships than pinpointing specificities.

Following the acquisition of information through one or more of the aforementioned preferences (E, I, S, N), individuals usually act upon new knowledge in a way that changes their behavior. The next scale, thinking (T) and feeling (F), is designed to measure the ways in which individuals express their new knowledge. Thinking types use their new knowledge by objectively interpreting experiences from a cause and effect perspective. Whereas feeling types interpret their experiences more from an affective perspective. Impressions that take into account values and personal views of experiences are more important to F types than logical interpretations of experiences (Figure 6.1).

Finally, judgment types (J), and perception types (P) are posited on a scale that describes cognitive variations in how individuals interact with their environment.

E Extraversion People who prefer Extraversion tend to focus on the outer world of people and things.	**I Introversion** People who prefer Introversion tend to focus on the inner world of ideas and impressions.
S Sensing People who prefer Sensing tend to focus on the present and on concrete information gained from their senses.	**N iNtuition** People who prefer Intuition tend to focus on the future, with a view toward patterns and possibilities.
T Thinking People who prefer Thinking tend to base their decisions on logic and on objective analysis of cause and effect.	**F Feeling** People who prefer Feeling tend to base their decisions primarily on values and on subjective evaluation of person-centered concerns.
J Judging People who prefer Judging tend to like a planned and organized approach to life and prefer to have things settled.	**P Perceiving** People who prefer Perceiving tend to like a flexible and spontaneous approach to life and prefer to keep their options open.

Figure 6.1 Characteristics frequently associated with MBTI types.

Sensing Types

Introverts	**ISTJ** Serious, quiet, earn success by concentration and thoroughness. Practical, orderly, matter-of-fact, logical, realistic, and dependable. See to it that everything is well organized. Take responsibility. Make up their own minds as to what should be accomplished and work toward it steadily, regardless of protests or distractions.	**ISFJ** Quiet, friendly, responsible, and conscientious. Work devotedly to meet their obligations. Lend stability to any project or group. Thorough and painstaking, accurate. Their interests are usually not technical. Can be patient with necessary details. Loyal, considerate, perceptive, concerned with how other people feel.
	ISTP Cool onlookers—quiet, reserved, observing and analyzing life with detached curiosity and unexpected flashes of original humor. Usually interested in cause and effect, how and why mechanical things work, and in organizing facts using logical principles.	**ISFP** Retiring, quietly friendly, sensitive, kind, modest about their abilities. Shun disagreements, do not force their opinions or values on others. Usually do not care to lead but are often loyal followers. Often relaxed about getting things done because they enjoy the present moment and do not want to spoil it by undue haste or exertion.
Extraverts	**ESTP** Good at on-the-spot problem solving. Do not worry, enjoy whatever comes along. Tend to like mechanical things and sports, with friends on the side. Adaptable, tolerant, generally conservative in values. Dislike long explanations. Are best with real things that can be worked, handled, taken apart, or put together.	**ESFP** Outgoing, easygoing, accepting, friendly, enjoy everything and make things more fun for others by their enjoyment. Like sports and making things happen. Know what's going on and join in eagerly. Find remembering facts easier than mastering theories. Are best in situations that need sound common sense and practical ability with people as well as with things.
	ESTJ Practical, realistic, matter-of-fact, with a natural head for business or mechanics. Not interested in subjects they see no use for, but can apply themselves when necessary. Like to organize and run activities. May make good administrators, especially if they remember to consider others' feelings and points of view.	**ESFJ** Warm-hearted, talkative, popular, conscientious, born cooperators, active committee members. Need harmony and may be good at creating it. Always doing something nice for someone. Work best with encouragement and praise. Main interest is in things that directly and visibly affect people's lives.

Figure 6.2 MBTI categories frequently associated with sensing types.

Intuitive Types

Introverts	**INFJ** Succeed by perseverance, originality, and desire to do whatever is needed or wanted. Put their best efforts into their work. Quietly forceful, conscientious, concerned for others. Respected for their firm principles. Likely to be honored and followed for their clear convictions as to how best to serve the common good.	**INTJ** Usually have original minds and great drive for their own ideas and purposes. In fields that appeal to them, they have a fine power to organize a job and carry it through with or without help. Skeptical, critical, independent, determined, sometimes stubborn. Must learn to yield less important points to win the most important.
	INFP Full of enthusiasms and loyalties, but seldom talk of these until they know you well. Care about learning, ideas, language, and independent projects of their own. Tend to undertake too much, then somehow get it done. Friendly, but often too absorbed in what they are doing to be sociable. Little concerned with possessions or physical surroundings.	**INTP** Quiet and reserved. Especially enjoy theoretical or scientific pursuits. Like solving problems with logic and analysis. Usually interested mainly in ideas, with little liking for parties or small talk. Tend to have sharply defined interests. Need careers where some strong interest can be used and be useful.
Extraverts	**ENFP** Warmly enthusiastic, high-spirited, ingenious, imaginative. Able to do almost anything that interests them. Quick with a solution for any difficulty and ready to help anyone with a problem. Often rely on their ability to improvise instead of preparing in advance. Can usually find compelling reasons for whatever they want.	**ENTP** Quick, ingenious, good at many things. Stimulating company, alert and outspoken. May argue for fun on either side of a question. Resourceful in solving new and challenging problems, but may neglect routine assignments. Apt to turn to one new interest after another. Skillful in finding logical reasons for what they want.
	ENFJ Responsive and responsible. Generally feel real concern for what others think or want, and try to handle things with due regard for the other person's feelings. Can present a proposal or lead a group discussion with ease and tact. Sociable, popular, sympathetic. Responsive to praise and criticism.	**ENTJ** Frank, decisive, leaders in activities. Usually good in anything that requires reasoning and intelligent talk, such as public speaking. Are usually well-informed and enjoy adding to their fund of knowledge. May sometimes appear more positive and confident than their experience in an area warrants.

Figure 6.3 MBTI categories frequently associated with intuitive types.

These cognitive processes are described as "lifestyles" with specific references as to how one utilizes judgment, vis-á-vis thinking or feeling, and perception vis-á-vis sensing or intuition. Perception is how one becomes aware of meanings that emerge from experiences. Judgment encompasses the evaluation of experiences and the contemplation for responses (Figure 6.1). These four pairs (E/I, S/N, T/F, J/P) are each structured along a bi-polar plane appearing at various points along continuums that have true zero points. The individual's score will yield a cognitive preference that will appear at selected points between extreme dimensions (extraversion-introversion, for example).

These personality attitudes and functions can lead to the formation of 16 cells of cognitive styles (Figures 6.2 and 6.3). For example, if an individual is measured by the Myers-Briggs indicator to be an introvert, sensing, thinking, perceptual type (ISTP), this reports a cognitive style of a quiet, detached, curious, mechanically oriented individual who has a strong interest in cause and effect.

For all instruments that are designed to measure variables in human development, the basic requirement for construct validity prevails. Construct validity is the extent to which an assessment measures a nonempirical theory or trait(s). One of several methods employed to test for construct validity is to administer the test in question to groups of subjects who differ in respect to the variables being measured, to determine if the test scores of subjects differ in the direction of the hypothesis.

As discussed in Chapters 1 and 2, professional practice evolves from particular theories and philosophies in order for individuals in the profession to ensure consistent and common understandings throughout their scholarly field. Likewise, assessment instruments have theoretical structures to ensure that the practice (developing a test to be scored and interpreted, for example) is congruent with its stated philosophy and/or theory. The MBTI has been highly regarded and utilized frequently because it meets the most stringent demands of construct validity. The various forms of the MBTI are true to the personality theory of C. G. Jung, therefore, scholars and practitioners can have confidence in the belief that the MBTI measures what it purports to measure.

Several studies have reported a relationship between selected subcategories on the MBTI and traditional measures of cognitive styles. In this regard, a study by Carey, Fleming, and Roberts reported:

> The J-P (Judging-Perceptual) and S-N (Sensing-Intuition) scales both proved to be significantly related to the GEFT (Group Embedded Figures Test), Perceptual and Intuitive types tend to be more field independent than the judging and Sensing types. . . . The field dependent-independent trait seems to be related to, but not identical to, MBTI measured traits. (1989, 97)

Similar findings have been reported by Carlson, 1985; Stricker and Ross, 1963; and Holsworth, 1985. The MBTI represents an important area of cognitive styles because of its potential usefulness for classroom teachers, career counselors, educators of the gifted, and therapists in the public domain. For example, Carland and Carland reported from their study of 92 (54 males, 38 females) college level students enrolled in a computer information program, designed for business majors, that:

> SP students have special problems. SP students in higher education tend to have the lowest correlation between academic ability and grade point averages of all types. . . . They are underachievers. SP students need physical involvement in learning, hands-on experience, activity and competition, and to entertain and be entertained. . . . Such students can be a source of frustration for the instructor. SP students tend to be fraternal and egalitarian, to rebel against close supervision, and view instructions as things to outwit. Because the SP student needs a constant change of pace, attempting to hold him or her to a routine can result in absenteeism or disruptive behavior in the classroom. . . . Assigning homework to an SP is frequently futile, resulting only in conflict between student and instructor. (1990, 123-124)

The Carland study also reported significant gender differences as to type. From the MBTI scale, the composite score for males in the study indicated an ISFP cognitive style, but for women, the composite score indicated an ESFP cognitive style. Studies have also reported a higher than average drop-out rate among SP types, especially among women.

Using the MBTI indicators, a study at the Naval Technical Training Center reported that sensing types completed computer related tasks at a faster rate than intuitive types. They also reported that people with personality types who are concerned with details and can maintain interest in singular issues in memory and performance tend to do well in computer courses (Hoffman and Waters, 1982).

Barger and Hoover (1984) have explored the implications that the mismatch of cognitive style and psychological type between teacher and learner might have for child learning. They have suggested that the greatest difficulty between teacher and learner can surface when one is a dominant thinking type and the other is a dominant feeling type. They also suggest that It is equally difficult for intuitive/feeling learners to be successful when teachers approach their work from unrelenting sensing/thinking typologies. Whatever differences might prevail, conflicts between unrealistic teacher expectations and pupil performance, that are influenced by cognitive style differences, can have serious effects upon the learner. Barger and Hoover suggest that "damaging effects" can result from teacher assumptions in such situations that there is a lack of learner motivation or ability. In the interpersonal domain, regarding conflicts between teacher and pupil, the authors suggest that:

> Persons strongly opposite in type can react negatively to each other. . . . A typical example in the classroom is the dominantly feeling student who has difficulty with analytical reasoning (thinking function) and who not only prefers to avoid it, but may discredit its value. Dominant thinking types, often awkward in human relationships, may try to avoid such relationships or will try to conduct their human affairs on a strictly logical basis. Analogous examples could be cited for sensing and intuitive types. (1984, 60)

From the perspectives of Jung's philosophy and the theoretical structures of MBTI, Mamchur (1981) devised an instrument to determine selected cognitive styles through systematic observations. The instrument was labeled "action oriented, reflection oriented" (AORO). The development of the instrument assumes an interrelated relationship between personality traits, cognitive style, and classroom performance. Further, it places learners into two categories—those who are active (extravert) and those who are not. Inactive learners are assumed to be the reflective (introvert) ones.

Specifically, Action Oriented (extraverts) pupils act first then think. Observers look for characteristic pupil preferences for learning by doing, by interacting, by talking, and by concluding that the product or activity has practical applications. Reflection oriented (introvert) pupils are expected to think, then act. Their characteristics include preferences to work alone, learning independently with preferences for non-oral tasks, and self-motivation.

In devising the AORO, Mamshur used classroom teachers as observers and recorders, thus deriving an accompanying benefit of sensitizing teachers to accept pupil differences. Several recommendations for classroom organization and curriculum implementation emerged from the study. For action oriented learners, it was suggested that they be arranged in discussion groups that encourage oral interaction around serious topics. Opportunities for working on group projects and freedom to move about the classroom and explore practical applications for their work should also be provided. It was also suggested that the teacher should provide oral encouragement, orally evaluate their work, and give patient, but specific guidelines in an environment that allows them to study each other's work.

For reflection oriented students, emphasis should be placed on written assignments where the teacher also writes questions for display in the classroom prior to questioning them about their work. These students should have access to private space in the classroom where they can perform written tasks in isolation, if by choice. They might occasionally wish to work in pairs or small groups and these opportunities should be available. The teacher should also be willing to wait for an extended period of time between pupil assignments and pupil performance, with less emphasis upon oral presentations from these pupils.

MBTI as a cognitive style paradigm is in keeping with studies of personality, individuality, and social environments. George A. Kelly (1963) was among the first scholars to bring our attention to cognitive activity that constructs personal assessments of events and individuals, and ideas about self. He suggested that individuals, in various ways, are "naive scientists" who establish expectations from experiences that are then present in what we take to future experiences. In other words, individuals do not merely place information derived from experiences into long-term memory in an amorphous state, but rather, we utilize content from previous experiences to formulate an anticipation of future experiences. This anticipatory activity, according to Kelly, is similar to hypothesis setting found in scientific studies. Individual hypothesis setting derived from various experiences will lead to a personalized repertoire.

For example, there are numerous variations that exist in individual perceptions of beauty. There are individuals who are so deeply affected after learning about her work, consider Mother Theresa a "beautiful" person because of her altruistic spirit. Then there are others who would seek "beauty" solely from the pages of fashion magazines. Kelly suggests that we bring these "personal constructs" to our experiences. Individuals with the aforementioned contrasting views of "beauty" are likely to respond differently to an experience where the conceptualization of beauty is a serious variable. Over time, each individual has developed personalized constructs that dictate their reactions to issues and events.

With these examples describing one interpretation of personal constructs, George Kelly has given additional perspectives.

> A construct is a way in which some things are construed as being alike and yet different from others. . . . For example, suppose a person construes in terms of a *black vs. white construct.* His field comprises a number of things. Some of them, such as his shirt, his shoes, his house, the paper on which he writes, the skin of his neighbor, and so on, are amenable to the black vs. white construct. The construct may be misapplied; he may call his shirt white when his wife *sees* it as black. It may be inappropriate; merely to construe his neighbor's skin as black may not be a very enlightened way to look at his neighbor. But, all in all, the construct is applicable to those things which for him can be either black or white. Yet there are other things in the person's life. There is the time of day, his affection for his children, the distance to his office, and so on, for which the *black vs. white* construct is patently irrelevant. . . . Now conventional logic would say that black and white should be treated as separate concepts. Moreover, it would say that the opposite of *black* can only be stated as *not black,* and the opposite of *white* can only be stated as *not white.* Thus the person whose field we mentioned would have shoes which would be just as much *not white* as the time of day, and he would write on paper which would be just as *not black* as the distance to his office. (1963, 105-106)

The MBTI is designed to indirectly provide educators and psychologists insight into an individual's "personal construct" and its underlying meanings. According to Kelly, these individual variations significantly influence our social interactions as well as our view of self. He has referred to this overall pattern of individual differentiation as "Fundamental Postulate," a label which imposes a sense of invariant permanence. MBTI provides opportunities for psychologists, counselors, and teachers to measure the extent to which Kelly's personal construct theory, which focuses on individual difference in interpreting experiences, contribute to establishing personality types with consistent ways of viewing the self in society. It is important to know whether certain personality attributes are malleable through self-awareness, whether they change with maturation, or are generally permanent over the course of one's life.

After studying the philosophy and theory of Jung, Katherine C. Briggs and Isabel Briggs Myers placed themselves in social situations to observe and catalog various personality traits along the lines of Jung's work. From this empirical activity, Briggs and Myers designed instruments to measure personality types that were highly compatible with the philosophy and theory of George Kelly. Their work has provided insight into some of the complex intersections between cognitive style, personality, and classroom learning for psychologists, counselors, and educators.

REFERENCES

Bargar, R. B. and Hoover, R. L. (1984). "Psychological Type and the Matching of Cognitive Styles." *Theory Into Practice* 23 (1), 56-63.

Brody, L. R. (1985). "Gender Differences in Emotional Development: A Review of Theories and Research." *Journal of Personality* 53, 102-149.

Carey, J. C., Fleming, S. D., and Roberts, D. Y. (1989). "The Myers-Briggs Indicator as a Measure of Aspects of Cognitive Style." *Measurement and Evaluation in Counseling and Development* 22, 94-99.

Carland, J. C., and Carland, J. W. (1990). "Cognitive Styles and the Edu-cation of Computer Information Systems Students."*Journal of Research on Computing in Education* 1(23), 114-126.

Carlson, J. G. (1985). "Recent Assessments of the Myers-Briggs Type Indicator." *Journal of Personality Assessment* 49, 356-365.

Carskadon, T. G. (1978). "Uses of the Myers-Briggs Type Indicator in Psychology Courses and Discussion Groups."*Teaching of Psychology* 3 (5), 140-142.

Carskadon, T. G. (1979). "Clinical and Counseling Aspects of the

Myers-Briggs Type Indicator: A Research Review." *Research in Psychological Type* 2, 2-31.

Chave, E. J. (1937). *Personality Development in Children.* Chicago: University of Chicago Press.

Coe, C. K. (1992). "The MBTI: Potential Uses and Misuses in Personnel." *Public Personnel Management* 4 (21), 511-522.

Ellison, R. (1972). *Invisible Man.* New York: Vintage Books.

Hoffman, J. L., and Waters, Keith. (1982). "The Effects of Student Personality on Success With Computer-Assisted Instruction." *Educational Technology* (March), 20-22.

Holsworth, T. E. (1985). "Perceptual Style Correlates for the MBTI." *Journal of Psychological Type 10*, 32-35.

Huckabee, W. (1974). "Introversion-Extraversion and Imagery." *Psychological Reports* 34, 453-454.

Jung, C. G. (1971). *Psychological Types.* (H. G. Bayles, translation revised by R.F.C. Hull). Princeton, NJ: Princeton University Press. (original work published 1921).

Kelly, G. A. (1963). *A Theory of Personality: The Psychology of Personal Constructs.* New York: W. W. Norton.

Kelly, G. A. (1969). *Clinical Psychology and Personality: The Selected Papers of George Kelly.* New York: Wiley.

Levy, N., Murphy, C., and Carlson, R. (1972). "Personality Types Among Negro College Students." *Educational and Psychological Measurement* 32, 641-653.

Mamchur, C. M. (1981). "Determining Cognitive Style by Systematic Observation." *Canadian Journal of Education* 6 (4), 92-104.

Mendelson, G. A. (1965). "The Myers-Briggs Type Indicator." In O. K. Burtos, ed., *The Sixth Mental Measurements Yearbook.* Highland Park, NJ: The Gryphon Press.

Myers, I. B., and McCaulley, M. H. (1985). *Manual: A Guide to the Develop-ment and Use of the Myers-Briggs Type Indicator.* Palo Alto, CA: Consulting Psychologist Press.

Myers, I. B. and Myers, P. B. (1980). *Gifts Differing.* Palo Alto, CA: Consulting Psychologist Press.

Riding, R. J., and Wicks, B. J. (1978). "The Effect of Extraversion and Presentation Order on Learning From Picture-Commentary Sequences by Children." *Educational Review* 30, 255-257.

Scarr, S. (1969). "Social Introversion-Extraversion as a Heritable Response." *Child Development* 40, 823-832.

Smith, A., Irey, R., and McCaulley, M. H. (1973). "Self-Paced Instruction and College Student's Personality." *Engineering Education* 63 (6), 435-440.

Stricker, L. J., and Ross, J. (1963)." Intercorrelations and Reliability of the Myers-Briggs Type Indicator Scales." *Psychological Reports* 12, 287-2932.

Thompson, B., and Borrele, G. M. (1986). "Second Order Factor A Structure of the MBTI: A Construct Validity Assessment." *Measurement and Evaluation in Counseling and Development* 18, 148-153.

Van, B. (1992). "The MBTI: Implications for Retention." *Journal of Developmental Education* 16 (1), 20-25.

7

Cognitive Style of Leveling-Sharpening

> The crucial importance of cognitive style is that it offers a way to examine the processes of perceiving and interacting with the world in a much more articulated manner than was previously possible with unifactor models of intelligence, or even more sophisticated models of separate, developed abilities. It offers a more flexible, and probably a more appropriate/practice scheme for investigating learning success, differences and problems by focusing on task requirements and the possibility with their interacting with various approaches and styles of information processing.
>
> —Shipman and Shipman

Leveling and Sharpening as a cognitive style paradigm was first introduced in 1954 through the work of Holzman and Klein. The underlying principles suggest that all experiences leave significant memory traces from which future information processing by the individual can select for assimilation into forming new ideas and concepts. This memory selection process is rather consistent among individuals, with levelers selecting a great deal from previous memory for interaction with current experiences, and sharpeners selecting very little from memory traces. The concepts associated with various studies of this cognitive style can be found in psychoanalytical foundations.

Klien and associates have utilized the Squares Test, an instrument that was developed at the Menninger Foundation to identify the cognitive style relationship between individual characteristics labeled leveling and sharpening. Fitzgerald and Hong have described the Squares Test in this manner:

There are 14 squares ranging from 1.3 to 13.7 in. in size. The test begins with the five smaller squares presented in ascending order followed by two random orders and then, by dropping the smallest of the five and adding the next largest square after each series of 15 estimates and repeating the procedure, the sequence of 150 projections is completed. At one performance extreme, "sharpeners" are able correctly to differentiate between successive squares (ranking accuracy) and also follow the general increase in size (increment accuracy). At the other extreme, "Levelers" fail to maintain accuracy in ranking the squares and lag behind the trend in increasing size. (1970, 211)

Fitzgerald and Hong (1970) designed a study to examine the Holzman and Klien hypothesis related to the different characteristics attributed to levelers and sharpeners. Using representation learning tasks, they examined the extent to which sharpeners were able to recall from the memory of previous experiences critical elements that were useful for understanding issues and events in the immediacy. It was assumed that levelers would be less likely to assimilate memories related to issues and events at hand. With 96 female students enrolled in a psychology course at the University of Hawaii as subjects, Fitzgerald and Hong designed a study that examined leveling-sharpening characteristics in the context of associative learning tasks. They reported that, "in a paired-associate task in which the intelligibility of the stimulus terms depends on representational memory, sharpeners . . . perform significantly better than levelers. " (213)

The early work of Freud with patients who he concluded practiced repression of previous experiences, that for whatever reason were too threatening to acknowledge, employed principles comparable to leveling and sharpening. To Freud, repression was the act of preventing the interaction of memory traces from previous experiences with present consciousness, in the formation of new ideas that might be too painful to assimilate. Freud later discovered from an experience with his friend and colleague, Wilhelm Fliess, that such selectivity of memory can also serve every-day ego function.

In one of many letters to Fliess, Freud mentioned that he had discovered the essential connection between neuroses and the assumption that individuals must possess a bisexual foundation in order for his current theory to make sense. Fliess was quick to remind Freud that this was an idea that he had advanced years earlier, and that Freud had rejected it at that time. After giving Fliess' claim to the idea some thought, Freud admitted that he had repressed from present consciousness the memory traces of that particular knowledge. Freud concluded that, to allow memory to contribute to his present awareness would have denied him the positive ego reinforcement of having made a new discovery. This incident later contributed to a painful loss of friendship between Freud and Fliess. In 1959, from studies of leveling and sharpening, Gardner and Holzman reported a significant correlation between some aspects of extreme leveling and extreme repression. Almost two decades later in 1976, Samuel Messick, in *Individuality in Learning,* reviewed what was then theorized about the paradigm:

> Leveling versus sharpening concerns reliable individual variations in assimilation in memory. Persons at the leveling extreme tend to blur similar memories and to merge perceived objects or events with similar but not identical events from previous experience; differences in remembered objects tend to be lost or attenuated. Sharpeners at the other extreme, are less prone to confuse similar objects and may even magnify small differences between similar memory traces, thereby exaggerating change and heightening the differences between the present and the past. (p. 18)

In 1962 Gardner and Long introduced a related concept called scanning as a cognitive style. Scanning theories, much like leveling vs. sharpening, are based upon psychoanalytic foundations. From a psychoanalytic perspective, scanning has been associated with theories of projection and defense mechanisms. Scanning refers to the extent to which individuals demonstrate preferences for a detailed purview of an experience to heighten the awareness of observations and events to a sense of vividness. It has been suggested that there are two types, each employing specificity; those who scan with a wide base focus, and those who employ a narrow base. The more extreme scanners do so with an intensity that calls forth heightened attention to differences and details.

Psychoanalytic interpretations of extreme scanners have related their actions to defense mechanisms occasionally employed by obsessively paranoid individuals. The act of scanning under these circumstances possibly serves to heighten the detection of on-coming dangers in an environment that the individual distrusts.

Several approaches to the explanation of role of experience in the acquisition of knowledge define this process in terms of memory traces as in Gestalt views that emphasize perception in the global sense, as opposed to the objective stimulus response constructs of the behaviorists. From the theoretical perspective of the Gestaltists, Wulf (1939) expressed that individual perception interacted with experiences in three organizational modes—*leveling, sharpening, and normalizing.*

Fundamentally, for perceptual modes, it is surmised from the laws of perceptual organization, that information tends to achieve the best possible structure. This fits rather well into Lewin's concept of *Life Space* because he views this construct as relative, in that, it is whatever the experiencing person perceives. Objective reality, or what actually exists (if one believes that this is possible), is irrelevant.

Wulf's perceptual mode leveling modifies information that is fuzzy and unclear. Sharpening is the perceptual manner in which objects and events are particularized and made more distinctive. Normalizing calls forth memory traces of previous experiences, and functions to make the interpretation of the present event conform to the earlier perception.

Wulf's theory conforms to the Laws of Perception that were first proposed by Gestalt Psychologists. Wertheimer identified one particular perceptual occurrence as the *phi phenomenon.* This phenomenon can be demonstrated by two or more lights flashing *alternately* in sequence. They are not perceived as alternating but instead as *moving* lights. This was another example of the perception of the whole as being greater than its individual parts. It is also true, in a human experience as when one plans a social event to which ten people are being invited. Care is taken as to which configuration of ten persons to invite at any given time, because the group always acquires *group characteristics* depending upon *which* persons comprise the group.

Another perceptual Gestalt is termed the *Principle of Proximity,* and theorized by Wertheimer, Koffka, and Köhler. When parents are having difficulty with the safety of an active 24 month old child exploring dangerous areas of the household, some plans for restrictive movement might call for placing a favorite set of toys in a safe area. Here the proximity of the toys would reduce the likelihood that the active child would wander off into unsafe areas. Another aspect of this domain was called the *Principle of Closure* involving visual perception. Here, one tends to perceive a familiar figure as complete when several sections are missing. If the word MOTEL, for example, was displayed on road sign without the middle letter (MO EL), perceptually we would insert the missing letter to complete the word because from earlier experiences configuration had created memory traces. *The Principle of Continuity* suggests that an observed pattern (or experience), has a tendency to be perceived as a continuous pattern once a pattern is established. *The Principle of Similarity* implies that objects or events perceived as similar are usually perceived as related.

Theoretically, there are developmental issues involved in concepts associated with scanning. These theories involve perception, schemata (Piaget), and memory. Bowers studied the various schemes (units of thought) that infants use to determine object permanence. Piaget has theorized a stage of early development called sensorimotor, during which time an infant is unaware of the existence of objects when such objects are beyond their line of sight. This period, according to Piaget can span twenty-four months. It is his view that individuals learn to solve problems through an interaction between our sensory system and our interactions with objects. Controlled experiments with infants in various situations tend to support Piaget's developmental hypothesis.

Studies of infants in various contexts have frequently employed methods designed to examine infant scanning. In one object permanence study, T.G.R. Bower (1971) observed the startle reaction of infants who were placed in a position to scan brightly colored objects that were strategically presented for sensory perception. The study involved infants who were twenty, forty, eighty, and one-hundred days old. A brightly colored ball was placed in front of infants who were propped in a sitting position. When it was apparent that the infant had seen the ball, a screen was placed in position to hide it from view for almost two seconds, three seconds, almost eight seconds, or 15 seconds. Bower surmised that infants who had an awareness of object permanence, during the scanning of the environment, would expect the ball to be present when the screen was removed. Infants who had not reached an understanding of object permanence would be surprised to see the ball, but not surprised if it had disappeared. Bower's results were reported to vary in terms of the age of the infant and the length of time the objects were removed from view.

When the screen was removed after less that 2 seconds, all infants in the study, regardless of age, were surprised when the ball was gone, and none were surprised when the ball was still there. Bowers concluded from this scanning experiment that some awareness of object permanence exists for children as young as twenty days. Piaget theorized that infants would have only a passive awareness of object permanence from 60 to 100 days old, and no awareness from birth to 60 days old. The possibility that methods employed in Bower's testing situation actually measured spatial and temporal orientations related to scanning, rather than the infant's intended intellectual awareness of object permanence was not discussed.

Various infant studies have paired scanning methodologies with startle expressions, while others have used scanning together with other facial expressions, changes in heart beat and breathing variations. In practically all infant studies, sensory modalities related to scanning has been the fundamental approach to measurement.

D. Maurer (1983) also examined the scanning behaviors of infants. In her study, she presented three different features of an object to be scanned by one and two month old subjects. One presentation involved a small square presented inside a slightly larger frame, then the frame was presented alone, followed by the square alone. From a series of trials and observations, Maurer reported:

From the results of these experiments we can evaluate the relationship between infants' scanning and their discriminitive capacity. Newborns and one-month-olds can discriminate between a variety of shapes, but appear not to discriminate between these same shapes when each is framed by a larger square. Starting at 2 months infants demonstrate such discriminations even with framed stimuli. . . . Newborns and 1-month-olds will fixate a small square presented alone but virtually ignore it if it is framed. (447).

Infant reaction to scanning of the human face has been a topic of interest among scholars who study perception in newborns. In terms of cognitive preferences among infants, reports suggest that a significant preference is demonstrated for the human face when other attractive choices are presented. Scholars have differed in their conclusions as to whether this greater interest in the human face is affective or cognitive in nature. With the awareness that affective preferences by definition involve cognition, the questions remain as to whether the infant's preferred interest in the human face—even when scanning opportunities provide attractive alternatives like a brightly colored globe or red square—is due to the "humanness" of the face, or, compared to a square or ball the human face is more complex and interesting (Franz and Miranda, 1975; Ganon and Swartz, 1980; Maurer and Salapatek, 1976).

Studies related to developmental changes in infant perception of the human face has undergone some negative criticism because of the methods employed. The harshest and most frequent complaint is that some investigators use symbolic images as substitutes for real models. Haith, Bergman and Moore (1977) for example, pointed out that studies using drawings or photographs of the human face are not necessarily generalizable to the actual behavior of newborns when they scan human features. This is also true for studies that employ masks. What is missing in some methodologies is the realistic nature of human eyes and multi-dimensional contours of the human face.

The aforementioned scanning studies have important implications for developmental issues. Implications are that the observed scanning behaviors that appear in infancy are in all likelihood precursors to the emergence of cognitive structures that are required for academic performance like decoding complex number concepts, the recognition of word sounds, and negotiating the spatial nature of the left-to-right printed page.

The acquisition of spatial and temporal orientation has been the focus of studies aimed at diagnosing young children with delayed intellectual development. For the purpose of early intervention in reading disabilities, preschool children were the focus of Silver, Hagin and Beecher, who developed an instrument to evaluate scanning capabilities of young children (1978). It is "based on the concept that antecedents to learning failure may be found in the acquisition of spatial and temporal orientation." The scanning instrument is an individually administered test consisting of ten components. After completing a one-day training session, classroom teachers are able to administer the test. The ten sections of this preschool screening test are designed to evaluate (1) visual discrimination of asymmetric figures, (2) immediate recall of asymmetric figures, (3) visual motor copying, (4) ordering rote sequences, (5) elements within the sequence, (6) discrimination between words that vary by one phoneme, (7) articulate specific sounds or words, (8) associate sounds with their visual symbols, (9) locate tactile stimuli to fingers, and (10) develop the oppositional relationship between finger and thumb (as in a pencil grip).

When used as an instrument to provide valuable information to teachers who administer school reading programs, Silver, et al. (1978) caution about the possibility of false-positives due to "the impact of the many factors contributing to beginning to read—the quality and intensity of instruction, family disorganization, motivation, and illness—all of which (the instrument) does not assess." (51)

In general, the precautions mentioned by Silver and colleagues can serve as guidelines for all educators when interpreting results of tests, especially when such results are intended for use as classification.

REFERENCES

Benfari, R. (1966). "The Scanning Control Principal and its Relationship to Affect Manipulation." *Perceptual and Motor Skills* 22, 203-216.

Bower, T. G. R. (1971). "The Object World of the Infant." *Scientific American* 225, 30-38.

Fitzgerald, D., and Hong, H. O. (1970). "Leveling-Sharpening and Representational Learning." *Perpetual and Motor Skills* 30, 211-214.

Frantz, R., and Miranda, S. (1975). "Newborn Infant Attention to form and Contours." *Child Development* 46, 224-228.

Freud, S. (1954). *The Origins of Psycho-analysis: Letters to Wilhelm Fliess, Drafts and Notes: 1887-1902.* New York: Basic Books.

Ganon, E., and Swartz, K. (1980). "Perception of Internal Elements of Compound Figures by One-Month-Olds." *Journal of Experimental Child Psychology* 30, 159-170.

Gardner, R. W. (1953). "Cognitive Styles in Categorizing Behavior." *Journal of Personality* 22, 214-233.

Gardner, R. W. (1961). "Cognitive Controls of Attention Deployment as Determinants of Visual Illusions." *Journal of Abnormal Social Psychology* 62, 120-127.

Gardner, R. W., and Long, R. I. (1960). "Leveling Sharpening and Serial Learning." Journal of *Perceptual and Motor Skills* 10, 179-195.

Gardner, R. W., and Long, R. I. (1962). "Control Defense and Centration

Effect: A Study of Scanning Behavior." *British Journal of Psychology* 53, 129-140.

Gay, P. (1988). *Freud: A Life for Our Time.* New York, NY: W. W. Norton.

Holzman, P. S., and Gardner, R. W. (1959). "Leveling and Repression." *Journal of Abnormal Social Psychology* 59, 151-155.

Holzman, P. S., and Klein, G. S. (1954). "Cognitive System-Principles of Leveling and Sharpening: Individual Differences in Assimilation Effects in Visual Time-Error." *Journal of Psychology* 37, 105-122.

Holzman, P. S., and Rousey, C. (1971). "Disinhibition of Communicated Thought: Generality and Role of Cognitive Style." *Journal of Abnormal Psychology* 77, 263-274.

Israel, N. (1969). "Leveling-Sharpening and Anticipatory Cardiac Response."*Psychosomatic Medicine* 31, 499-509.

Maurer, D. (1983). "The Scanning of Compound Figures by Young Infants." *Journal of Experimental Child Psychology* 35, 437-448.

Maurer, D., and Barrera, M. (1981). "Infants' Perception of Natural and Distorted Arrangements of a Schematic Face." *Child Development* 52, 162-202.

Maurer, D., and Salapatek, P. (1976). "Developmental Changes in the Scanning of Infant Faces." *Child Development* 47, 523-527.

Messick, S. (1976). *Individuality in Learning.* San Francisco, CA: Jossey-Bass.

Haith, M., and Bergman, T., and Moore, M. (1977). "Eye Contact and Face Scanning in Early Infancy." *Science 198*, 835-855.

Piaget, J. (1952). *The Origins of Intelligence in Children.* New York: International University Press.

Romney, D. M., and Bynner, J. M. (1993). *The Structure of Personality Characteristics.* Westport, CT: Praeger.

Santostefano, S. G., and Paley, E. (1964). "Development of Cognitive Controls in Children." *Child Development* 35, 939-949.

Shipman, S., and Shipman, V. C. (1985). "Cognitive Styles: Some Conceptual, Methodological, and Applied Issues." In E. W. Gordon, ed., *Review of Research in Education* (pp. 229-291). Washington, D.C.

Sigel, J. I., Jarman, P. D., and Hanesian, H. (1967). "Styles of Categorization and Their Intellectual and Personality Correlates in Young Children." *Human Development* 10, 1-17.

Silver, A. A., Hagin, R. A., and Beecher, R. (1978). "Scanning, Diagnosis, and Intervention in the Prevention of Reading Disabilities." *Journal of Reading Disabilities* 11(7), 439-445.

Wulf, S. (1938, originally published 1922). "Tendencies and Figural Variations." In W. D. Ellis, ed., *A Source Book of Gestalt Psychology.* New York, NY: Harcourt Brace and World.

8

Conclusion

> If I have a hidden agenda, as a teacher, it is to watch *how* the students learn. I watch and I puzzle over why striking differences in perception so regularly occur. In our discussion, I notice these differences again: some students tell us how they feel about the winds themselves; some ask questions to help them think about how they'll describe an experience they once had in nature and make it into something "meaningful"—they're thinking about the next assignment; some wax philosophical about Didion's ironic stance and some are aware only of the sound of the wind buffeting the windows as we speak, the swish of my skirt, and the way their hearts pound as I give out the assignment.
>
> —Lori Ann Miller

Cognitive style has experienced a great deal of research interest over the past fifty years, but this interest has not been sustained at levels equal to its early years. This interest, as you now know, has encouraged studies of personality, problem-solving behavior, cognition, dysfunctional behaviors, and the general processing of information.

The 1950s work of Adorno and others in *The Authoritarian Personality,* and Rokeach, in *The Open and Closed Mind*, were among selected psychological theories that integrated theories of personality into cognitive preference studies. The work that followed provided hundreds of cognitive style studies that extended through the 1960s. During this period cognitive style researchers attempted to highlight various implications for educators within the context of cognitive style theories.

For example, in a scholarly environment replete with descriptions of African American children and children of Hispanic descent as "culturally deprived," cognitive style theorists suggested that such children were not "deprived" of a culture since they had their own. It was also suggested, that in terms of culture, "culture conflict" and not cultural deprivation might be a more appropriate avenue for studies of group differences in classroom performance.

In this regard, Rosalie Cohen (1969) reported that learners with field dependent, relational, and nonanalytical cognitive styles might not do as well as their counterparts on standardized tests because such tests were oriented toward field independent and analytical conceptual styles. Cohen observed that schooling is organized in a manner that some children come face-to-face with cultural conflict because their conceptual style is incompatible with the academic model employed by the system. This she concludes is cultural conflict and not cultural deprivation.

In the next decade, cognitive style research had earned a respectable place in psychology and education circles, and perhaps the 1970s witnessed the highest level of scholarly activity on the topic. Scholars in various fields of psychology and psychiatry expanded their studies to investigate relationships between cognitive styles and theories that were emerging within the specific context of their disciplines. An important example can be cited from studies concerned with lateralization of the brain. Here, researchers reported that in general the left hemisphere of the brain is more concerned with the processing of analytical information like language, and the right hemisphere specializes more in spatial information that utilize imagery. A great deal of interest in the study of the relationship between the left and right hemispheres of the brain, curriculum design, and pedagogy, extended through the 1970s. Cohen, et al. (1973) reported a significant relationship between field dependence and brain lateralization. They reported that among patients who were treated for epilepsy, those who received intrusive treatment to the right hemisphere of the brain became less field dependent. Patients who were rendered the same type of treatment to the left hemisphere became more field dependent.

During the most active period of the 1970s, the "discussion" sections of cognitive preference studies were raising serious questions about the various labels used to describe cognitive variances and instruments designed to measure specific constructs. Block, Block and Harrington (1974) devoted an entire study to critically analyzing the conceptualization of impulsivity/reflectivity and the common use of the matching familiar figures test to measure the extent to which individuals could be labeled impulsive or reflective. The following year, Kagan and Messer (1975) responded to critical issues articulated in the above referenced work. In 1976, Nathan Kogan organized what was then known about the cognitive styles of young children. His book, *Cognitive Styles in Infancy and Early Childhood* provided an important focus to cognitive style research during that period.

The *Review of Research in Education* was the source of the most comprehensive critical review of cognitive style research to appear in the 1980s. An investigation by Shipman and Shipman (1985) reported a comprehensive review of cognitive style research from its inception. The authors identified many of the lesser known constructs along with the most actively researched ones.

Discussions continued to emerge regarding the relationship between theories of cognitive style, their appropriate application in the classroom, how they are measured, and implications for curriculum development and the structure of the school.

During internal debates and confusion introduced through the use of new and unclearly defined cognitive style labels, other theorists were borrowing from the basic works to create new directions. Some of these "new directions" credited cognitive style researchers, while others embraced the knowledge as their own creativity. Multiple Intelligence (MI) theory was among those approaches that reframed discussions about individual differences in thinking and problem-solving without citing cognitive style as one of its origins. In defining multiple intelligence Howard Gardner proposed the theory that the human organism possessed seven distinct units of mental functioning. He labels these units "intelligences." He also asserted that these separate intelligences have their own specific sets of abilities that can be observed and measured (Gardner, 1983). Since the introduction of the idea, possibly hundreds of articles, book chapters, and similar citations associated with Gardner's concept of intelligence have been published. The basic concept, however, is completely described in the Gardner text (1983); and more recently, the MI theory was framed in the form of scientific research (Gardner and Hatch, 1989).

The theory that multiple factors contribute to what is generally considered intelligence is not new. What is novel about Gardner's proposal is that each factor (as identified by his work) constitutes a separate construct that would qualify as an intelligence. There is sufficient evidence, however, to suggest that the seven areas of human performance described in the MI theory are more realistically cognitive styles. The similarities are so striking that it is surprising how cognitive style theory could have gone unnoticed by Gardner and several others who have written on the subject (Morgan, 1996).

MI theory provoked a tremendous outpouring of articles, dissertations, commercial "how-to" literature, and consultants in quantities that overwhelmed classroom teachers, school district administrators, and educators of gifted and "at-risk" students, and created lucrative markets that have flourished. Finally, in the mid-

1990s, several publications overcame the temerity to publish a critical review of MI theory and link basic MI ideas to cognitive style research of the 1950s.

For various complex reasons, the research community concerned with cognitive styles had not significantly changed its basic approach to work over two decades. Studies of cognitive preference as it related to newly emerging ideas in education like whole language, cooperative learning, individualized education plans, invitational education, and needs of at-risk learners, just to name a few, were absent from cognitive style scholarly activity. In response to this condition, several observers made mention of this condition and B. N. Lewis offered the following assessment:

> At the present time, we have a situation in which different groups of researchers seemed determined to pursue their own pet distinctions in cheerful disregard of one another. There is a focussing versus scanning distinction, which seems to indicate something about the way in which attention is distributed. There is the impulsive versus reflective distinction, which seems to indicate something about the tempo of learning. There is a field dependent versus field independent distinction, the serialist and the holists, and a lot more. . . . There is no shortage of people doing active research on the subject of individual differences. But there seems to be an acute shortage of people who are trying to find out which kinds of individual differences are the most basic and thus most worth incorporating into individualized teaching programs. (1967, 305)

During the 1980s, several psychologists and educators did respond with studies on cognitive style measurement, research, and theory, but in a manner that more confusion than clarity dominated the field. Recognizing this, Alan Miller in, "Cognitive Styles: An Integrated Model," built upon what was known up to that time, while advancing a noteworthy reconceptualization of cognitive style research, theory, and practice. In the above mentioned work, Miller suggested:

> Cognitive styles are potentially useful in education as a means of characterizing stable individual differences that influence the effectiveness of teaching and learning. However, anyone interested in using styles in either research or practice is faced with a literature that is not only disorganized but also dated. Little basic research is being done to clarify the conceptual; and measurement problems that bedevil the field. One way to revive interest in basic research would be to link "traditional" conceptions of cognitive style with the more vigorous field of cognitive psychology. This might result in new ways of conceptualizing individual styles, as well as resolving the problem of the relationships between styles. (1987, 251)

Miller proposed the integration of a model of cognitive processing with cognitive styles from three domains; perception, memory, and thought. This approach, from a psychological perspective, would include the basic theoretical foundations similar to what is described in Chapter 2 of this book. Miller's perception domain would include two levels: one level of pattern recognition (part/whole relations), paired with leveling versus sharpening. Attention (selective attention) is the other level of perception and is paired with field articulation. The memory domain has three levels: representational, organizational, and retrieval. The representational (memory codes) level leads to analytic/analog memory. Organizational memory (conceptual networks) incorporates conceptual/complexity memory, while retrieval (search strategies) includes convergent versus divergent memory. Thought (inductive reasoning) also has three levels with representative cognitive styles: classification (serial versus holistic), anological reasoning (tight versus loose) and judgment (actual versus intuitive).

Cognitive style studies in the 1990s witnessed some important attempts at integrating the more frequently cited cognitive styles into a comprehensive system for identification and measurement. Riding and Cheema (1991), for example, in an introduction to their work toward a systematic integration of various cognitive styles, summed up the state of the art during that time period:

> The cognitive style construct has been elusive; this is partly due to the fact many researchers . . . fail to mention the existence of other types of styles. As a result, like the blind man and the elephant, different theorists have been working with different concepts. . . . Attempts to unite these scattered schools of thought have been extremely rare. (1991, 193)

Riding and Cheema organized the most frequently studied cognitive preference paradigms into an integrated model that differentiated styles from strategies.

> Cognitive style needs to be differentiated from "learning strategy." In the present context a style is considered to be a fairly fixed characteristic of an individual, while strategies are the ways that may be used to cope with situations and tasks. Strategies may vary from time to time, and may be learned and developed. Styles, by contrast are static and are relatively in-built features of the individual. (195-196)

Several scholars have argued that cognitive style labels represented considerable duplication and overlap. Riding and Cheema proposed that various cognitive styles be arranged into two major groups. They have recommended holistic (process information as wholes) at one end of a continuum and analytic (process information in parts) at the other end, both along a vertical axis. Verbalizer (inclined to represent information verbally) versus imagery (tendency to represent information in mental pictures) are at opposing ends along the horizontal axis. In this cluster, field dependence is placed with the holistic thinkers, and field independence with the analytics. Impulsivity is also included among the holists and reflectivity among the analytics. Levelers are placed among the holists and sharpeners are placed with the analytics. Using this theoretical format Riding and others developed the cognitive style analysis (CSA) to measure the individual's status along verbal-imagery and holistic-analytic dimensions (Riding and Cheema 1991).

By the 1990s it was apparent that thinking, problem-solving, and classroom issues like reading competence were dominating cognitive style research. There also appeared to be an emerging interest in returning to some of the theoretical and philosophical foundations of individual differences in cognitive processing. Riding, Glass, and Douglas revisited basic neurophysiological issues and brain function that were discussed in Chapter 2 of this book.

> During thinking and decision making . . . different people process the same information in different ways, using different areas of the brain. . . . This is not to be interpreted as meaning that individuals do not, or cannot, use the whole brain, but rather that they have a habitual tendency to use certain areas in preference of others. . . . The different ways of processing reflect two basic dimensions of cognitive style. It is probable that these styles have an underlying cerebral basis. The styles are likely to be related to cerebral orientation. The specialization of one cerebral hemisphere for verbal function and the other for visio-spatial has been long established. (1993, 268)

Continuing the "back to basics" trend, Riding proceeded to link studies of personality with cognitive style. Riding and others, using his CSA, made attempts to revisit the original psychological roots by infusing studies of personality into current cognitive preference studies.

> The ways in which individuals represent, and think about, the social environment in which they live, and the situations they encounter, are influenced by their cognitive style. This in turn, is related to their personality. However, books on personality . . . do not index either "cognitive styles," or a specific common label such as "field-independence-dependence." (1993, 113)

In a study with school age children, Riding and his associates (1995) reported a significant relationship between cognitive style, personality, and school performance. They suggested that academic performance can be enhanced by structuring learning materials and the manner in which they are presented to accommodate pupils' motivational and behavioral characteristics—which are ultimately shaped by personality traits. It was, after all, Gordon W. Allport's book *Personality: A Psychological Interpretation,* published in 1937, that first mentioned cognitive style.

By 1996, *The Encyclopedia of African-American Education,* a reference work that described significant issues related to education, defined a theoretical framework for understanding cognitive preferences found among African-American learners.

Among the most interesting ideas of the 1990s is a report that identifies creativity as a cognitive style. Corbalan-Berna noted that research in the various domains of creativity seem to lack a theoretical framework on which scholarly agreement can be achieved. To satisfy this absence, Corbalan-Berna provides empirical support for the acceptance of creativity as a cognitive style.

> The investigation studied, from a symbolic point of view, a series of cognitive processes theoretically involved in the cognitive style, "creativity," and found at the initial, central or final stages of information processing. From a semantic point of view, a theoretical interpretation of creativity as an inquiring attitude towards the environment is suggested. Question generation is the key factor which characterizes it. . . . Flexibility, Fluency, Originality, and Developmental Production, were studied as well as ten different cognitive processes, Question generation, Details perception, Metaphor generation, Spatial perception, Memory, Contextual patterning, Attention-Perceptual speed, Stoop effect, Letter search and Reaction time. (1992, 163-164)

Not unlike professionals who are new to any field of human service, beginning teachers often search for a method which they hope will accommodate every learner. Experienced teachers consider it a disadvantage to be limited by a single philosophy or theory of child development that dictates practice. They resist the limitations that accompany commitments to a single teaching method that prescribes a structured approach to work and a specific standardized measuring instrument as an index against which to measure the child's capacity for learning.

As a high school teacher, Mark Sweeting viewed the World War II era as one rich with opportunities to explore an unusually wide range of topics with his students. Topics for exploration and study could included Nazism, Pearl Harbor, the Nurenberg trials, the beginning of the cold war, the only time the atomic bomb was used for the purpose of killing other human beings, and concentration camps for Jews in Germany and Japanese Americans in the United States. Sweeting cited another important reason for exploring this topic with his students.

> One reason is that I teach in Oregon, which along with California and Washington was one of the states most affected by Executive Order 9066 which mandated the internment. Executive Order 9066 signed by President Franklin Roosevelt on Feb. 19, 1942, empowered the Secretary of War to force Japanese Americans (two-thirds of whom were U.S. citizens) on the coast into hastily built prisons in the desert regions of the American West. For the war 's duration,

120,000 innocent and un-accused Japanese Americans were imprisoned. The order is perhaps the single largest collective civil rights violation in post-Civil War America. Even an abbreviated list of the Constitutional rights violated by the executive order is distressing; freedom of speech, freedom from unreasonable search and seizures, the right to be informed of charges, the right to a speedy and public trial, and the right to equal protection under the law.

During the process of seeking appropriate study materials for his students, Mark Sweeting was dismayed at how little information was available from traditional sources.

Desperate, I turned to the district-adopted text book for the class. . . . In looking for information on the internment, I found only two paragraphs conveniently buried at the end of a chapter on the initial stages of World War II. The heading for the paragraph read: "Nation Relocates Japanese Americans." Relocates! I did not expect to see this term still used to describe Executive Order 9066. I doubted whether anyone who had endured the internment would describe it as merely being "relocated."

Following discussions and a creative class dramatization that juxtaposed the act and meaning of "relocate," with what actually happened to the interned Japanese Americans, the students reacted to the chapter heading ("Nation Relocates Japanese Americans") with spontaneous laughter. Students remarked: "Arrest them is more like it." "The authors are just trying to make it sound better, more polite." Mark Sweeting, their teacher, concluded:

As a result of this exercise, I appreciated the power of words. And I became even more aware of how the teaching of history is shaped by the materials we use in our classrooms. American history textbooks, unfortunately, are filled with euphemisms and sanitized language for many indefensible acts. (1996, 9)

We know that youth are continually making meaning from their experiences. Adults are in the most strategic position of control and have the power and influence to manipulate social structures from which youth derive meaning for their lives. Within this context, young people are observers and participants in social institutions that are designed by adults. Through their experiences, they interact with peers and others within these structures and study the laws that govern the meanings for their lives. In a variety of ways, youth are like their country. What their country does finds its way into the fabric of the meanings they make for their own existence. Occasionally we refer to these phenomena as rites of passage.

Events that emerge from domestic and foreign policies continue to unfold during the early growing years of our youth and contribute to how they develop their values. For example, during a ten year period starting in the 1980s, the U.S. government launched a military attack upon a tiny country in the Caribbean called Grenada. Using outdated tourist maps, the U.S. invaders mistakenly bombed a hospital for mental patients and killed and injured people who were housed there. Other civilian casualties occurred but no one knows for certain how many, because reporters were barred from investigating or reporting on the casualties.

Also during the administration of President Ronald Reagan, media reported that the president ordered an air attack on the home of Libya's President Gadhafi. His family and his military forces were the targets. After the raid, media sources also reported that one of Gadhafi's children was killed. In the same time frame one of our military ships "accidentally" shot down one of Libya's passenger planes, killing over one hundred civilians. Our media had created such hate for Libya and Gadhafi that there was very little outcry among U.S. adults regarding this tragic loss of civilian life. This was, however, a meaningful event in the lives of children in the United States because they probably had little trouble identifying with children of the world.

During the presidency of George Bush, the U.S. military invaded another small country—Panama. This act was in violation of our treaty with the Organization of American States and international law as agreed upon through the Geneva Conventions. After the war, the United Nations General Assembly voted overwhelmingly to condemn our invasion of Panama.

The main targets of the destruction were civilians in the most impoverished neighborhoods of the city. The casualties were high and U.S. newspaper and media professionals in Panama were severely restricted to interviewing "official" U.S. military designated informants. One photographer for a foreign reporting service was reported shot and killed by U.S. military for taking pictures of the invasion.

The reporting of 540 civilian casualties by official U.S. information services was ridiculed by international human rights organizations as underreporting. International and Panamanian Human Rights Organizations reported the number killed was 2,500 to 4,000, mostly Black and from the poorest neighborhoods. The poor who survived the war had their homes burned by U.S. military, and were temporarily housed in makeshift cubicles set up in an airplane hangar. While crowded in these unsanitary conditions, many poor families lost track of their children and other relatives, having only word-of-mouth information regarding their life or death fate.

After the invasion, a new Panamanian president who was willing to install a government more amenable to U.S. policy was given the oath of office in U.S. military headquarters. The new president and a terrified Panamanian Congress voted to dismantle all Panamanian military forces and thus relinquish formal claims to the Panama Canal.

Journalists from around the world, including those who had been restricted by the U.S. military during the invasion, went to Panama to interview ordinary citizens, civil rights activists, government officials, children, and adult victims to get the full story of the invasion of that small country.

A media group named *The Empowerment Project* thought that the event was so appalling that they used the information from the fact-finding mission to produce a documentary film called *The U.S. Deception*. This film aired on public broadcast outlets and was made available to schools, colleges, and universities around the world. In the film, bodies of adults and children were shown strewn about the streets, along with completely destroyed sections of poor neighborhoods. Civilians were shown being herded off the streets into concentration camps. More than a dozen mass grave sites were discovered where the U.S. military had dumped hundreds of Panamanian bodies. Unknown to U.S. officials at the time of their interviews by the filmmakers, pictures of U.S. atrocities in Panama were interspersed with each statement of U.S. officials denying the occurrence of brutality, as the very acts of brutality by the U.S. military were being shown.

Practically all major news outlets in the U.S. supported the invasion, and while our children were watching, media suggested to the public that President Bush demonstrated strong leadership and could no longer be considered a "wimp."

Some time later, under the orders of President George Bush, the United States and their allies mounted military action against Iraq to drive their army out of their neighbor's territory. A disagreement between Iraq and Kuwait had been simmering over price-fixing of oil on the world market, as well as Iraq's long standing discontent over geographical boundaries that were originally created by European colonizers many years before.

Iraqi leaders claimed that they had presented their case to the U.S. State Department representative to their country, and the U.S. representative told them that the United States would not interfere if they used military force to settle their disagreements with Kuwait.

When the news media attempted to confirm Iraq's side of the story regarding U.S. tacit approval of their military action, the U.S. representative who was claimed to have met with Saddam Hussein disappeared somewhere in the U.S. government and was not available for confirmation.

After Iraq's invasion of Kuwait, if the Iraqi version of our original policy is true, there appeared to be a change in U.S. policy when the possibility emerged that the world's flow of oil might be interrupted. Ultimately, the U.S. opposed the Iraqi invasion of Kuwait, and organized European and other allies to aid in driving Iraq's military forces out of their neighbor's territory. Dinner table conversations among informed citizens educated children about daily events, and media outlets gave a voice to the outrages of American parents.

> Deep in my Queens neighborhood . . . ugly news had reached me through the twin portals of my TV set and my New York Times subscription. The country was preparing for war ecstatically, whipped on by William Safire (for whom Saddam Hussein was "this generation's Hitler") and George Bush ("Vital issues of principle are at stake"), whose approval rating stood at 89 percent. In the righteousness of the nation's hatred of a man who until recently had been our close petropolitical ally, as in the near total absence of public skepticism about the war, the United States seemed to me as terminally out of touch with reality as Austria had been in 1916, when it managed to celebrate the romantic "heroism" of mechanized slaughter in the trenches. I saw a country dreaming of infinite oil for its hour-long commutes, of glory in the massacre of faceless Iraqis, of eternal exemption from the rules of history. . . . I began to think that the most reasonable thing for a citizen to do might be to enter a monastery and pray for humanity. (J. Franzen, 1996, 35)

This war with its many gruesome graphics, was televised. A reporter for an Atlanta newspaper wrote about a personal experience he had at home while listening to his children's conversation as they observed the televised war that the United States and their European Allies waged against Iraq. He reported that his three-year-old daughter, upon seeing the television version of an actual bombing of civilian targets said, "Fireworks!" She was corrected by her five-year-old brother who remarked, "No, they are bombs!"

During the same period U.S. forces bombed an Iraqi building known to be a shelter for mothers and children because, according to the U.S. military, it was suspected of serving as an Iraqi military communications center. An international investigating team went to Baghdad to investigate the charges but could find no evidence of the U.S. claim. And, our children watched as the bodies of women, children, and the elderly were removed from the rubble. Families around the world watched television pictures of the events in horror. Following massive bombings of Iraqi civilian and military targets, and the surrender of Iraq to the U.S. and their allies, the missing U.S. diplomat reappeared and denied Saddam Hussein's version of their prewar discussion.

Parents and teachers are seldom aware of the need for children to discuss the meanings of such events in relation to childhood thoughts and values. Do we hurt other people because they are different from ourselves? When are such actions right and when are they wrong? Like the five year-old boy who tried to provide a sense of reality for his sister, classrooms need to provide an opportunity for learners to discuss all facets of such events rather than framing information in a manner that justifies cruelty. As adults, we focus too little attention on how these events affect our children because we believe, in part, that such events are unimportant and isolated experiences for children.

At the end of the 1980s during rites of passage when our youth were searching for meaning within the context of family, school, church, and their country it should not surprise us that the behavior of some would be like that of their country. Few would want to enter adulthood as a wimp. Shortly after the period that we were participating in the killing of citizens in foreign countries, the U.S. Justice Department reported that in our own country, between the early 1980s and 1995, the number of U.S. teens who killed their friends, their parents, and strangers, exceeded 26,000. At the end our ten-year war-making period, teenage killing in the U.S. tripled. The Office of Juvenile Justice and Delinquency Prevention reported that, for this same period, starting in the early 1980s, youthful offenders seemed more likely to possess firearms, and were more willing to use them (Ostrow, 1996).

We do not fully understand the impact that a country's killing of people in other parts of the world might have had upon youth during their rites of passage, or how much they dwell upon the fact that their country is the only one in the world that has ever used atomic bombs to kill people. We do know that German youth study the acts of aggression perpetrated by their World War II governmental leaders. Despite the fact that these German atrocities occurred long before their youth were born, Germany's school authorities think it necessary for their youth to confront the egregious behavior of their government.

Educators, for the most part, tend to ignore the role that our country's foreign and domestic policies have upon shaping our national character and establishing relationships between youth and adults in the United States.

> The relations between youth and adults have always been marked by strained generational and ideological struggles, but the new economical and social conditions that children face today, along with a callous indifference to their spiritual and material needs, suggests a qualitatively different attitude on the part of many adults toward American youth—one that indicates that the young have become our lowest national priority. To put it bluntly, American society at present exudes both a deep rooted hostility and chilling indifference toward youth, reinforcing the dismal conditions under which young people are increasingly living. . . . The largest growing population of homeless in this country is children and the average age of such children is nine years. For White,

working class youth . . . can look forward to dead-end jobs, unemployment without the benefit of health care, or perhaps, homelessness. (Giroux, 1996, 31)

Classroom teachers are often caught between the aggressive bravado of an active student and the search for a means to accommodate this aggression within the context of a healthy school climate. Teachers are seldom prepared in the immediacy to satisfy the demands of moments such as these. The more experienced teachers have learned over time that the best approach means employing a calming manner with a conversation that seeks a common ground between teacher and student. Teachers who start by invoking their authority will often find themselves deep into an intractable situation where student and teacher have no face-saving way out. Dilemmas such as these are common occurrences in classrooms throughout our nation. This is especially true when children are flexing those aspects of their character being shaped by their country.

Children, their teachers, and other advocates need a voice through which to express their consciousness on critical issues. There tends to be a systematic effective social system that denies this access to selected groups. Social institutions in the United States manage and conduct the majority of their business thorough an extensive use of discourse. For them, the control of this discourse is essential to their power, status, and influence. Controlling discourse is a common practice among colleges and universities, public and private schools, political parties, libraries, departments of government, and funding institutions, just to name a few. The goals and missions of these institutions are shaped through conversations between individuals at various levels of power, status, and influence. The ongoing behavior of these institutions—as dictated primarily by those in positions of power, status, and influence—is reflected in discourse among and between themselves and their counterparts in other institutions.

These institutional interactions create in-groups and out-groups. The in-group understands and participates in how discussions must be framed in order to be accepted and considered. The out-group either does not understand or accept the framing of discourse around particular issues or events. Out-group members are not permitted to participate in shaping national events or issues unless they learn, accept, and participate in the rules governing discourse as defined by the in-group. The remainder of this chapter will discuss how discourse is framed to maintain levels of power, status, and influence away from those who do not ascribe to the discourse that serves to maintain a status quo on class, race, and gender issues in the United States.

The framing of discourse in schooling has been articulated by several philosophers in education. Michael Apple in his book, *Ideology and Curriculum,* suggests that schooling in the United States is designed to get students to accept prevailing thought and dominant values. Jules Henry (1965) proposed that because of predetermined attitudes that dominate the curriculum, neither students nor teachers can engage in discourse that challenges hegemonic social and intellectual structures. There is a continuing reinforcement among students throughout their lives, so as adults, the same values are reinforced by them through the institutions where they are employed. The Black writer, Ralph Ellison (1972) pointed out in his novel *Invisible Man* that hegemonic discourse systematically dismisses the existence of racial issues when the mere acknowledgment poses a threat to White male power structures. Mary Roth Walsh brought professional women's issues to our attention in a similar vein (1977).

Peter McLaren (1994, 1995) has identified "Critical Pedagogy" as an essential feature of the relationship between teachers and their pupils. Within this context, it is the teacher's professional responsibility to provide an atmosphere within which pupils can experience a social consciousness leading to a clarification of personal and group values. McLaren has also provided a persistent voice to the role of critical theory in formulating a pathway for "self-empowerment and social transformation" for teachers and students.

The most common limits placed upon the voices of teachers and students in matters that are essential, is achieved through the framing of discourse by those in control. The manner in which discussions are framed can act as a screen to truncate the content. The framing of discussions is often a rite that establishes agendas in a broad sense, but more important, the act of framing leads to apriori characterizations of phenomena and ultimately controls how issues and events are investigated, acted upon, and recorded. This approach leads to understandings among participants about how things should be valued, the direction of social thought and discourse, and common agreement on permissible conclusions. One of the earliest pre-1960s referents is the use of the word tolerance to describe White characteristics that are free of racial bias. Such a characteristic, it was surmised, enable Whites to be more indulgent, patient, and forbearing, toward African Americans. In this context, African Americans would, a priori, possess qualities that would call forth indulgence, patience and forbearance on the part of Whites. In other words, the pathway toward racial equality in the United States is to foster attitudes among Whites that tolerate African Americans.

This term has been resurrected by the Center for Racial Justice, an effective and well-meaning organization in Alabama that has successfully litigated cases against persons guilty of racial hate crimes. This organization publishes a journal that is free to classroom teachers titled *Teaching Tolerance.* Thus, unwittingly, framing the racial equality question in terms Black dependency and White superiority.

We also observe media commonly referring to "minorities and women" in writing and oral discourse. This approach serves to ignore gender differences within minorities and creates two groups—minority males and minority women in one—and White women in the other. This novel framing of discourse concerning gender provides a cleavage between minority women and White women and substantially reduces the power of all women in numbers. A modest change in rephrasing the discourse to "women and minority males" would place this referent in its proper semantic perspective.

As another example, the current construct labeled Affirmative Action, was introduced into the lexicon of social policy and quickly became a concept in public discourse to mean unearned advantages for minority males and women. In reality, the legislation and public policy that brought about affirmative action as practiced, has been with us for many years. For example, following World War II, affirmative action was introduced to civil service employment by various federal, state, and municipal governments to grant special privileges to veterans of the war.

One common affirmative action for these veterans was to grant them a number of "points" to be added to their civil service test score, and/or place them at the top of the list for employment in a specified job. In addition, they were granted government-backed mortgages and free college tuition. These actions were legislated, and therefore legal, and in most cases deserved by the recipients. Intended primarily for White males, these special accommodations aided relatively few minority males and women who had also served in World War II. For veterans of the war, this affirmative action was viewed as their right. When special accommodations were legislated for minority males and women for past discrimination in the work place, media framed the discussion as a privilege. This model successfully diverts attention away from persons to whom affirmative action has historically advantaged—as in the case of World War II veterans—and framed it in a context that implies unearned advantages for today's minority males and women.

During the 1990s a major issue affecting all citizens was crime, and discussions were framed in the media, academic institutions, and governmental agencies by the majority who directed policies from their dominant policy-making positions. As a result, unlawful activity in the African American community was framed as Black on Black crime, and this gave rise to another example of reductionism that emanates from the framing of the discussion. In this particular example, crimes perpetrated against Whites by Whites were never framed as White on White crime. This selective framing suggested that Blacks committing crimes against other Blacks created a race problem, while Whites committing crimes against other Whites represent a social problem for the nation.

Following the period of the popularization of the Black on Black crime chant by journalists and others, institutions in the Black community like churches, social agencies and schools, mounted programs, projects, and marches, designed to "reduce" Black on Black crime. Essentially, the Black community selected-in to the framing that was created by popular media. Such an acceptance suggested to African American children that crime was a social problem created primarily by people with whom they identified. Ultimately it was accepted as their problem and not a problem of their country that affected both Blacks and Whites equally—as perpetrators and victims. How these discussions were framed was important, but who framed the discussion was an equally important question.

During the 1980s and 90s, national media reported with great frequency on the violence between Blacks and Whites in South Africa. As Black South Africans pursued voting rights and power-sharing with White South Africans, Blacks and Whites formed coalitions within and between groups. All factions, at some time during the confrontations, were reported to have committed violent acts against others. When Black factions committed violent acts against Black individuals, journalists framed their reporting, as Black on Black violence.

Shortly following this same period, Yugoslavia, as a nation made up of multiethnic and multireligious groups, was crumbling. This tumultuous process involved violent acts of destruction and murder between Serbians, Croatians, and smaller factions of other groups. In a country that is centuries old, and made up of various ethnic and religious groups, the Serbians, who are Christians, were intent upon securing territory for people like themselves. Another Christian group, the Croatians were involved in violent acts against the Serbians who for many years were friendly neighbors, but who were at that time considered the enemy to be attacked and killed. These two White Christian groups committed atrocities against each other's families and children, and in some cases, forced people to abandon their homes.

Violence between various ethnic groups in Yugoslavia reached such an egregious level that one group set up what appeared to be a concentration camp, and the world was outraged at the possibility that a new holocaust was emerging. The same year, independent observers discovered what they suspected were mass graves. These events, however, were never framed as White on White violence, or even Christian on Christian violence by media or scholarly institutions where such events are discussed. Here, the framing of the discourse implied that Whites committing violence against other Whites was a problem for humanity—while Blacks committing violence against other Blacks was a problem for Blacks.

There is persistent and systemic rhetoric concerning something called "reverse discrimination." The implications here include the notions that only Whites (primarily White males) are bestowed with the power to discriminate, and if Blacks choose to discriminate, it is merely the reverse of what Whites do.

This practice of framing discussions so as to place selected groups outside the mainstream of intellectual discourse is generally ignored; but it is an effective form of maintaining power and control. This reductionist activity takes place in media and scholarly institutions and is one of the remaining barriers that undermines efforts by some writers, journalists, and intellectuals who consciously strive to create a dialogue that includes minority male's and women's issues within the mainstream of general discourse.

Selective framing also serves to perpetuate attitudes and styles of discourse that tend to marginalize African American people and issues that directly affect all of our lives. This framing cuts across all groups when it relates to gender, because all women are victims of the effects of discourse control. This approach to defining ideas has taken on a life of its own to the extent that women and African American, Hispanic, and Asian males are encouraged to participate in their own victimization. And we are all responsible.

In this age of computer access, teachers need not limit the inquiry by themselves and their students to traditional textbooks and mainstream media. As mentioned earlier, Mark Sweeting found it necessary to go beyond the school's approved textbook in order to obtain a fair review of the plight of Japanese Americans during the WW II era. A previously excellent source of information was public media like National Public Radio (NPR), and Public Television. During the early 1990s these outlets were threatened by national and local governments to reduce funding if they continued to explore subjects that were not mainstream. There coverage of events has been muted since that time but other outlets are available to teachers and students.

For educators who wish a more critical examination for their students, there are computerized library services that can be accessed by subject and author for biographies, newspaper reporting, major speeches, and scholarly articles. Abstracts are also available for practically all scholarly works. School librarians and media specialists should be consulted for identification and access to these sources.

An Atlanta social studies teacher led her students into a study of the downing of passenger airplanes that were suspected of being terrorist acts sponsored by governments. The students were motivated by the tragic circumstances revealed in an article in their local newspaper about Syracuse University students killed in an airplane that crashed in Scotland. Evidence was presented by investigators that a bomb planted in luggage on board was responsible for the downing of the airliner. In follow-up newspaper stories it was reported that evidence led the investigators to conclude that the perpetrators were probably agents sponsored by the government of Libya.

As the students expanded their studies to include similar incidences they realized that this was a problem for humanity and not limited solely to acts against the U.S. Their review of newspaper and magazine stories gave them access to a wider array of accounts—some obscured in back pages of local media or parts of related events. They discovered that the Libyan government was thought to be responsible for a variety of terrorist acts in various parts of the world.

Students also learned that a U. S. warship in the Persian Gulf shot down an Iranian passenger airplane killing 290 people. The U.S. government reported that it was an accident because the Iranian A-300 Airbus was mistaken for a military airplane. U.S. officials reported that several warnings were broadcast to the airplane with no response.

After a year-long investigation by the International Civil Aviation Organization (ICAO), it was revealed that the attacking warship, the USS Vincennes, broadcast the warning on a radio frequency that was not available to the Iranian airbus. It appeared that another ship in the area, the USS Sides, did broadcast a warning on the Iranian airbus' frequency—and this gave the Iranian passenger plane only 40 seconds to respond. This report was made public by the Reuters News Service and reported out of Montreal, Canada.

While students concluded that this air disaster could have been attributed to an accident on the part of the USS Vincennes' crew, a more recent report by the Intelligence Oversight Board indicated that the CIA supported terrorist activities in Guatemala, and that human rights violations, executions, and torture, were intentionally perpetrated. President Clinton ordered an inquiry in 1995 when it was suspected that in the 1990s, those working for the CIA in Guatemala were guilty of terrorist acts that included the execution of a rebel leader and the killing of more than 100,000 Guatemalan civilians. In 1996, students in Atlanta read an editorial in their local newspaper criticizing the report issued by the president's Intelligence Oversight Board of the White House for providing too few details in their effort to avoid the U.S. being paired with other nations guilty of terrorism.

It is also true, educational professionals allow important race, gender, and social class issues to go under-reported and occasionally distorted by the framers of the debate on national education issues. For example, there has been much ado about the National Educational

Goals disseminated by the National Governor's Association in 1990. This was followed by a missive from the office of the President through the U.S. Department of Education labeled America 2000. Despite the fact that more than twenty years of studies have identified gender bias as a major problem in all grades, providing equitable treatment for girls remains unmentioned in these widely read documents, as well as other materials that are referenced by professionals who direct national discourse on educational policy.

We know, for example, that when higher education scholarships are offered based on SAT scores, boys are more likely than girls to receive them. However, of the boys and girls receiving the same SAT score, girls are more likely to outperform their male counterparts in post-secondary school achievement. It is also true that even when girls are highly competent in math, they are less likely than boys to pursue scientific careers.

How is it possible that such knowledge has not found its way into current training of secondary school counselors, or on the agendas of elite panels that are busy planning the future direction of education in our country? The work of bell hooks (1994) suggests that teachers at all levels should be more involved with students in what she calls "engaged pedagogy." In her view, teachers need to be involved in the lives of students beyond the classroom and constantly promote a critical consciousness that extends to creative dialogue about such things as knowledge, work, careers, and public policy.

At state and national levels educators also need a critical consciousness in examining public and professional policy issues. It is known that 20% of our nation's children are raised in poverty, and their mothers have seldom had prenatal care or adequate nutrition. In the 1990s, framers of educational goals for the year 2000 were actively introducing legislation designed to reduce aid to the poor, and ultimately placing full burden of financing aid-to-poor-families programs on the states through federal block-grants.

An understanding of issues related to the framing of discourse is essential to educators and other human service providers whose goals include empowerment of their client(s). Empowerment has become common rhetoric among us, but too few who attempt this process actually understand how it is achieved. Occasionally, we are led to believe that opportunities are achieved for particular individuals or groups based on their previous victimization. A careful assessment of such opportunities will often reveal that programs designed for victims of past wrongs are actually intended to benefit others. It is not as important to keep track of programs as it is to understand how programs and opportunities reduce restrictions that are kept in place through the control of how issues are framed in institutions and the general media.

One would expect that the general media with their vast resources of reporters and informed sources would provide up-to-date valid and reliable assessments of critical issues confronting our schools. Unfortunately, information for too many newspaper and TV news stories is drawn from the same group of "experts" who remain on the reporter's *Rolodex* file because their points of view are predictable.

When modest levels of empowerment do occur in the present social structures in the United States, it is restricted to various levels of status within the victimized group(s). In the present circumstances of nationally controlled discourse, empowerment cannot occur beyond the social boundaries of victimized groups. The role of educators has to start in the early grades to expand the number of ways that students can confront issues from any perspective they are able to identify and define.

Such a critical consciousness should provide a continual critique of our own work. In the department of Early Childhood Education at the institution where I work, I pointed out to the teaching faculty that a primary text being used referred to African Americans solely within the context of poverty and single parent families. This restrictively framed image of Black families could set in motion a series of expectations that will negatively frame university students' approach to work when they become teachers.

The framers of media and institutional discourse control the marketplace and the academy. Until profitability and media ratings respond to the current shaping of discourse that separates affected groups from the forum, resources and policy will be directed toward leaving things as they are, and barriers to inclusive discourse will not be lowered. This will continue to obscure potentials for national dialogue about the social and political context that articulate issues of race, gender, and social class.

From personalized experiences all children share the behaviors of their country, their family and their neighborhood. These behaviors maintain a critical role in shaping their values as they mature into adulthood. The cliché that one cannot go home again is only partially true because our country, our neighborhood, and our family will always remain a part of who we are.

REFERENCES

Adorno, T. W., Frankel-Brunswik, E., Levinson, D. J., and Sanford, R.N. (1950). *The Authoritarian Personality*. New York: Harper and Row.

Allport, G. W. (1936). *Personality: A Psychological Interpretation*

New York, NY: Henry Holt and Company.
Ames, C. (1992). "Classrooms: Goals, Structures and Student Motivation." *Journal of Educational Psychology* 84 , 261-271.
Apple, M. (1979). *Ideology and Curriculum*. New York: Routledge and Kegan.
Apple, M. (1992). "Education, Culture, and Class Power: Basil Bernstein and the Neo-Marxist Sociology of Education." *Educational Theory* 42 (2), 127-145.
Apple, M. (1972). "Community, Knowledge, and the Structures of Disciplines." *The Educational Forum* 37, 75-82.
Ashton, P. (1991). "Alternate Approaches to Teacher Education." *Journal of Teacher Education* 42 (2) 82.
Bartky, S. (1990). "Femininity and Domination: Studies in the Phenomenology of Oppression." New York: Routledge.
Berliner, D., and Biddle, B. (1995). *The Manufactured Crisis: Myth Fraud and the Attack on America's Schools.* New York: Addison-Wesley.
Block, J., Block, J. H., and Harrington, D. M. (1974). "Some Misgivings About the Matching Familiar Figures Test as a Measure of Reflection-Impulsivity." *Developmental Psychology* 10 (5), 611-632.
Bracey, G. (1996). "International Comparisons and the Condition of American Youth." *Educational Researcher* 25 (1), 5-11.
Brantlinger, E. (1993). "The Politics of Social Class in Secondary School: Views of Affluent and Impoverished Youth." New York: Teachers College Press.
Brown, A. L. (1995). "The Advancement of Learning." *Educational Researcher* 23 (8), 4-12.
Cohen, B. D., Berent, S., and Silverman, J. (1973). "Field-dependence and Lateralization of Function in the Human Brain." *Archives of General Psychiatry* 28, 165-167.
Cohen, R. (1969). "Conceptual Styles, Culture Conflict, and Nonverbal Tests of Intelligence." *American Anthropologist* 71, 828-856.
Corbalen-Berna, F. J. (1992). "Creativity as a Cognitive Style: Summary Report on an Empirical Investigation." *The Journal of Creative Behavior* 26 (3), 163-164.
Fairclough, N. (1985). *Language and Power.* London: Longman.
Falk, R. A., Kolko, G., and Liftin, R. J. (1971). *Crimes of War.* New York: Random House.
Franzen, J. (1996). "Perchance to Dream." *Harpers* (April, 1996), 292.
Gardner, H. (1983). *Frames of Mind: The Theory of Multiple Intelligence.* New York: Basic Books.
Gardner, H. (1987). "The Theory of Multiple Intelligence." *Annals Of Dyslexia* 37, 19-35.
Gardner, H., and Hatch, T. (1989). "Multiple Intelligences Go to School: Educational Implications of the Theory of Multiple

Intelligences." *Educational Researcher* 18 (8), 4-10.

Gelles, R. (1978). "Violence Towards Children in the United States." *American Journal of Orthopsychiatry* 48, 590-592.

Gewirtz, J. L. (1972). *Attachment and Dependency.* New York: Halstead Press.

Gibson, J. J. (1966). *The Senses Considered as Perceptual Systems.* Boston: Houghton Mifflin.

Giroux, H. A. (1996). "Hollywood, Race, and the Demonization of Youth: The Kids Are Not Alright." *Educational Researcher* 25 (2), 31-35.

Graves, S.B., Gargiulo, R. M., and Sluder, L. C. (1996). *Young Children: An Introduction to Early Childhood Education.* St. Paul, MN: West Publishing Company.

Henry, J. (1965). *Culture Against Man.* New York: Vintage Books.

hooks, b. (1989). *Talking Back.* Boston: South End Press.

hooks, b. (1994). *Teaching to Transgress: Education as the Practice of Freedom.* New York: Routledge.

Kagan, J., and Messer, S. G. A. (1975). A Reply to "Some Misgivings About the Matching Familiar Figures Test as a Measure of Reflection-Impulsivity." *Developmental Psychology* 11, 244-248.

Kelman, H. C., and Hamilton, W. L. (1989). "Crimes of Obedience: Toward a Social Psychology of Authority and Responsibility." New Haven, CT: Yale University Press.

Knapp. M. S., and Shields, P. W. (1991). *Better Schooling for the Children of Poverty: Alternatives to Conventional Wisdom.* Berkeley, CA: McCutchan.

Kogan, N. (1976). *Cognitive Styles in Infancy and Early Childhood.* Hillside, NJ: Lawrence Erlbaum.

Kozol, J. (1995). *Amazing Grace: The Lives of Children and the Conscience of a Nation.* New York: Crown Publishers.

Lather, P. (1991). *Getting Smart: Feminist Research and Pedagogy With/In the Postmodern.* New York: Routledge.

Lewis, B. N. (1967). "Commentary: Avoidance of Aptitude Treatment Trivialities." In S. Messick ed., *Individuality in Learning* 301-308. San Francisco, CA: Jossey-Bass.

Lifton, R. J. (1970). *History and Human Survival.* New York: Random House.

Lifton, R. J., and Markusen, E. (1988). *The Genocidal Mentality.* New York: Basic Books.

Luke, C., and Gore, J. (1992). *Feminism and Critical Pedagogy.* New York: Routledge.

Matthews, D. (1988). "Gardner's Multiple Intelligence Theory: An Evaluation of Relevant Research Literature and a Consideration of its Application to Gifted Education." *Roeper Review* 11, 100-104.

May, R. (1972). *Power and Innocence: A Search for the Sources of Violence.* New York: Norton.

McCaslin, M., and Good, T. (1992). "Compliant Cognition: The Misalliance of Management and Instructional Goals in Current School Reform." Educational Researcher 21 (3), 4-17.

McCaslin, M., and Good, T. (1996). *Listening in Classrooms.* New York: Harper Collins.

McGilly, K. (1995). *Classroom Lessons: Integrating Cognitive Theory and Classroom Practice.* Boston, MA: MIT Press.

McLaren, P., and Leonard, P. (1993). *Paolo Freire: A Critical Encounter.* London: Routledge.

McLaren, P. (1994). *Life in Schools: An Introduction to Critical Pedagogy in the Foundations of Education.* White Plains, NY: Longman.

McLaren, P. (1995). *Critical Pedagogy and Predatory Culture: Oppositional Politics in a Postmodern Era.* New York: Routledge.

McLaren, P. L., and Giarelli, J. M. (1995). *Critical Theory and Educational Research.* New York: State University of New York.

Miller, A. (1987). "Cognitive styles: An Integrated Model." *Educational Psychology* 7 (4), 251-268.

Miller, L. A. (1989). "Who Knows How the Wind Blows: Cognitive Styles Inside (and Outside) the Classroom." *Writing On The Edge,* 44-49.

Morgan, H. (1996). "An Analysis of Gardner's Theory of Multiple Intelligence." *Roeper Review* 18 (4), 263-269.

Ostrow, R. J. (1996). *Justice Department Report: Teenage Killers Triple in 10 Years.* The Atlanta Journal/Constitution (April) 8.

Peterson, P. (1996). "Will America Grow Up Before it Grows Old?" Atlantic Monthly 277, 55-86.

Plucker, J. A., Callahan, C. M., and Tomchin, E. M. (1996). "Wherefore Art Thou, Multiple Intelligences? Alternative Assessments for Identifying Talent in Ethnically Diverse and Low Income Students." *Gifted Child Quarterly* 40 (2), 81-92.

Rees, H., and Lipsitt, L. (1980). *Advances in Child Development and Behavior.* New York: NY Academic Press.

Riding, R. J. (1991). *Cognitive Style Analysis Users Manual.* Birmingham, England: Learning and Training Technology.

Riding, R., and Cheema, I. (1991). "Cognitive Styles—An Overview and Integration." *Educational Psychology* 11 (3 and 4), 193-215.

Riding, R., Burton, D., Rees, G., and Sharratt, M. (1995). "Cognitive Style and Personality in 12-year-old Children." *British Journal of Educational Psychology* 65, 113-124.

Riding, R. J., Glass, A., and Douglas, G. (1993). "Individual Differences in Thinking: Cognitive and Neurophsiological Perspectives." *EducationalPsychology* 13 (3 and 4), 267-279.

Riding, R. J., and Mathias, D. (1991). "Cognitive Style and Preferred

Learning Mode, Reading Attainment and Cognitive Ability in 11-Year-Old Children." *Educational Psychology* 11, 383-395.

Romney, D. M., and Bynner, J. M. (1993). *The Structure of Personality Characteristics*. Westport, CT: Praeger.

Sanford, N., and Comstock, C. (1971). *Sanctions for Evil*. San Francisco: Jossey-Bass.

Sharan, S. (1980). "Cooperative Learning in Small Groups: Recent Methods and Effects of Achievement, Attitudes, and Ethnic Relations." *Review of Educational Research* 50, 241-272.

Shipman, S., and Shipman, V. C. (1985). "Cognitive Styles: Some Conceptual, Methodological, and Applied Issues." In E. W. Gordon, ed., *Review of Research in Education*, vol. 12, 229-291. Washington, DC: American Educational Research Association.

Stoddart, T. (1993). "Who is Prepared to Teach in Urban Schools?" *Education and Urban Society* 26 (1), 29-48.

Sweeting, M. (1996). "The Power of Words: A Lesson on the Japanese-American Internment." *Rethinking Schools* 11 (1), 9.

Walsh, M. R. (1977). *Doctors Wanted: No Women Need Apply*. New Haven, CT: Yale Press.

Selected Bibliography

Achenbach, T. M., and Weisz, J. R. (1975). "Impulsivity-Reflectivity and Cognitive Development in Preschoolers: A Longitudinal Analysis of Developmental and Trait Variance." *Developmental Psychology* 11, 413-414.

Adevai, G., Silverman, A. J., and McGough, W. E. (1970). "Ethnic Differences in Perceptual Testing." *International Journal of Social Psychiatry* 16, 237-239.

Adorno, T. W., Frankel-Brunswik, E., Levinson, D. J., and Sanford, R. N. (1950). *The Authoritarian Personality.* New York: Harper and Row.

Anderson, J. (1988). "Cognitive Styles and Multicultural Populations." *Journal of Teacher Education* (January-February), 2-9.

Annett, M. (1959). "The Classification of Instances of Our Common Class Concepts by Children and Adults." *British Journal of Educational Psychology* 29, 223-236.

Appel, L. E., Cooper, R. G., McCarrell, N., Sims-Knight, J., Yussen, S. R., and Flavell, J. H. (1972). "The Development of the Distinction Between Perceiving and Memorizing." *Child Development* 43, 1365-1381.

Aries, P. (1962). *Centuries of Childhood.* New York: Vintage.

Aronfreed, J. (1968). *Conduct and Conscience: The Socialization of Internalized Control Over Behavior.* New York: Academic Press.

Asch, S. E., and Witkin, H. A. (1948). "Studies in Space Orientation. I. Perception of the Upright With Displaced Visual Fields." *Journal of Experimental Psychology* 38, 325-337.

Ault, R. L., Crawford, D. E., and Jeffrey, W. E. (1972). "Visual Scanning Strategies of Reflective, Impulsive, Fast-Accurate and Slow-Inaccurate Children on the Matching Familiar Figures Test."

Child Development 43, 1412-1417.

Ault, R. L., Mitchell, C., and Hartmann, D. P. (1976). "Some Methodological Problems in Reflection-Impulsivity Research." *Child Development* 47, 227-231.

Baird, R. R., and Bee, H. L. (1969). "Modification of Conceptual Styles Preference by Differential Reinforcement. *Child Development* 40, 903-910.

Baltes, P. B., and Reinert, G. (1969). "Cohort Effects in Cognitive Development of Children as Revealed by Cross-Sectional Sequences." *Developmental Psychology* 1, 169-177.

Barclay, A., and Cusumano, D. R. (1967). "Father Absence, Cross-Sex Identity, and Field-Dependent Behavior in Male Adolescents." *Child Development* 38, 243-250.

Bargar, R. R., and Hoover, R. L. (1984). "Psychological Type and the Matching of Cognitive Styles." *Theory Into Practice* 23 (1), 56-63.

Barrett, G. V., and Thornton, C. L. (1967). "Cognitive Style Difference Between Engineers and College Students." *Perceptual and Motor Skills* 25, 789-793.

Beard, R. M. (1969). *An Outline of Piaget's Developmental Psychology For Students and Teachers.* New York: Basic Books.

Beech, R. P., and Schoeppe, A., (1974). "Development of Value Systems in Adolescents." *Developmental Psychology* 10, 644-656.

Bergman, H., and Engelbrekston, K. (1973). "An Examination of Factor Structure of Rod-&-Frame Test and Embedded-Figures Test." *Perceptual and Motor Skills* 37, 939-947.

Berry, J. W. (1971). "Ecological and Cultural Factors in Spatial Perceptual Development." *Canadian Journal of Behavioral Science* 3, 324-336.

Berry, J. W. (1976). *Human Ecology and Cognitive Style: Comparative Studies in Cultural and Psychological Adaptation.* New York: Wiley.

Bertini, M., Pazzamiglio, L., and Wapner, S. (1986). *Field Dependence in Psychological Theory, Research, and Application.* Hillside, NJ: Lawrence Erlbaum.

Bettleheim, B. (1969). *The Children of the Dream.* New York: MacMillan.

Bigelow, B. J. (1977). "Children's Friendship Expectations: A Cognitive Developmental Study." *Child Development* 48, 246-253.

Blake, R. R., and Ramsey, G. V. (1951). *Perception: An Approach to Personality.* New York: Ronald Press.

Blau, Z. S. (1981). *Black Children/White Children.* New York: Free Press.

Block, J., Block, J. H., and Harrington, D. (1974). "Some Misgivings About the Matching Familiar Figures Test as a Measure of Reflection-Impulsivity." *Developmental Psychology* 10, 611-632.

Bloom, L., Rocissano, L., and Hood, L. (1976). "Adult-Child Discourse: Developmental Interaction Between Information-Processing and Liguistic Knowledge." *Cognitive Psychology* 8, 521-552.

Bloomberg, M. (1971). "Creativity as Related to Field Independence and Mobility." *Journal of Genetic Psychology* 118, 3-12.

Bock, R. D., and Kolakowski, D. (1973). "Further Evidence of Sex-Linked Major Gene Influence on Human Spatial Visualizing Ability." *American Journal of Human Genetics* 25, 1-14.

Brazelton, T. B. (1972). "Implications of Infant Development Among the Mayan Indians of Mexico." *Human Development* 15, 9-11.

Brinkman, E. H. (1966). "Programmed Instruction as a Technique for Improving Spatial Visualization." *Journal of Applied Psychology* 50, 179-184.

Brody, L. R. (1985). "Gender Differences in Emotional Development: A Review of Theories and Research." *Journal of Personality* 53, 102-149.

Brosgole, L., and Cristal, R. M. (1967). "The Role of Phenomenal Displacement on the Perception of the Visual Upright." *Perception and Psychophysics* 2, 179-188.

Broughton, J. (1978). "Development of Concepts of Self, Mind, Reality, and Knowledge." *New Directions for Child Development* 1, 75-100.

Brown, C. (1965). *Manchild in the Promised Land.* New York: New American Library.

Brumby, M. N. (1982). "Consistent Differences in Cognitive Styles Shown for Qualitative Biological Problem-solving." *British Journal of Educational Psychology* 52, 244-257.

Bruner, J. (1964). "The Course of Cognitive Growth." *American Psychologist* 27, 687-708.

Bucky, S. F., and Banta, T. J. (1972). Racial Factors in Test Performance. *Developmental Psychology* 6, 7-134.

Busch, J. C., and DeRidder, L. M. (1973). "Conformity in Preschool Disadvantaged Children as Related to Field-Dependence, Sex, and Verbal Reinforcement." *Psychological Reports* 32, 667-673.

Busse, T. V. (1968). "Establishment of the Flexible Thinking Factor in Fifth Grade Boys." *Journal of Psychology* 69, 93-100.

Cavallaro, S. A., and Porter, R. H. (1980). "Peer Performance of At Risk and Normally Developing Children in Preschool Mainstream Classrooms." *American Journal of Mental Deficiency* 84, 357-366.

Cegalis, J. A., and Leen, D. (1977). "Individual Differences in Responses to Induced Perceptual Conflict." *Perceptual and Motor Skills* 44, 991-998.

Claeys, W., and DeBoeck, P. (1976). "The Influence of Some Parental Characteristics on Children's Primary Abilities and Field Independence: A Study of Adopted Children." *Child Development* 47, 842-845.

Clark, K. B., and Clark, M. P. (1939). "The Development of Consciousness of Self and the Emergence of Racial Identity in Negro Preschool Children." *Journal of Social Psychology* 10, 591-599.

Coates, S. (1972). *Preschool Embedded Figures Test.* Palo Alto, CA: Consulting Psychologists Press.

Coates, S. (1974). "Sex Differences in Field Dependence-Independence Between the Ages of 3 and 6." *Perceptual and Motor Skills* 39, 1307-1310.

Coates, S. (1974). "Sex Differences in Field Independence Among Preschool Children. In R. C. Friedman, R. M. Richard, and R. L. Van de Wiele, eds., *Sex Differences in Behavior* 259-274. New York: Wiley.

Coates, S. (1975). "Field Independence and Intellectual Functioning in Preschool Children." *Perceptual and Motor Skills* 41, 252-254.

Coates, S., Lord, M., and Jakabovic, E. (1975). "Field Dependence-Independence, Social-Nonsocial Play and Sex Differences in Preschool Children." *Perceptual and Motor Skills* 40, 195-202.

Cohen, L. B., and Strauss, M. S. (1979). "Concept Acquisition in the Human Infant." *ChildDevelopment* 50, 419-424.

Coop, R. H., and Brown, L.D. (1970). "The Effects of Teaching Method and Cognitive Style on Categories of Achievement." *Journal of Educational Psychology* 61, 400-405.

Cooper, R. H., and Sigel, I. E. (1970). "Cognitive Style Implications for Learning and Instruction." *Psychology in the Schools* 8 (2), 152-161.

Coopersmith, S. (1967). *The Antecedents of Self-Esteem.* San Francisco: W. H. Freeman.

Corah, N. L. (1965). "Differentiation in Children and Their Parents." *Journal of Personality* 33, 300-308.

Corbalen-Berna, F. J. (1992). "Creativity as a Cognitive Style: Summary Report on an Empirical Investigation." *The Journal of Creative Behavior* 26 (3), 163-164.

Damon, W. (1977). *The Social World of the Child.* San Francisco: Josey Bass.

Davidson, K. S., and Sarason, S. B. (1961). "Text Anxiety and Classroom Observations." *Child Development* 32, 199-210.

Davis, A. J. (1971). "Cognitive Styles: Methodological and Developmental Considerations." *Child Development* 42, 1447-1459.

Davis, A. J., and Lange, G. (1973). "Parent-Child Communication and the Development of Categorization Styles in Preschool Children." *Child Development* 44, 624-629.

Dengerink, H. A., O'Leary, M. R., and Kasner, K. H. (1975). "Individual Differences in Aggressive Responses to Attack: Internal-External Locus of Control and Field Dependence-Independence." *Journal of Research in Personality* 9, 191-199.

Denhan, S. (1986). "Social Cognition, Prosocial Behavior, and Emotion in Preschoolers: Contextual Validation." *Child Development* 57,

194-201.

Denney, D. R. (1971). "The Assessment of Differences in Conceptual Style." *Child Study Journal* 1, 142-155.

Denney, D. R. (1972). "Modeling Effects Upon Conceptual Style and Cognitive Tempo." *Child Development* 43, 105-119.

Dershowitz, Z. (1971). "Jewish Subculture Patterns and Psychological Differentiation." *International Journal of Psychology* 6, 223-231.

Douglas, G., and Riding, R. J. (1993). "The Effect of Pupil Cognitive Style and Position of Prose Passage Title on Recall." *Educational Psychology* 13, 285-293.

Drake, D. M. (1970). "Perceptual Correlates of Impulsive and Reflective Behavior." *Developmental Psychology* 2, 202-214.

Dreyer, A. S., Dreyer, C. A., and Nebelkopf, E. B. (1971). "Portable Rod-& Frame Test as a Measure of Cognitive Style in Kindergarten Children." *Perceptual and Motor Skills* 33, 775-781.

Dreyer, A. S., McIntire, W. G., and Dreyer, C. A. (1973). "Sociometric Status and Cognitive Style in Kindergarten Children." *Perceptual and Motor Skills* 37, 407-412.

Dumsha, T. C., Minard, J., and McWilliams, J. (1973). "Comparison of Two Self-Administered Field Dependency Measures." *Perceptual and Motor Skills* 36, 252-254.

Dunn, J. (1983). "Sibling Relations in Early Childhood." *Child Development* 54, 787-811.

Dunphy, D. C. (1963). "The Social Structure of Urban Adolescent Peer Groups." *Sociometry* 26, 230-246.

DuPreez, P. D. (1967). "Field Dependence and Accuracy of Comparison of Time Intervals." *Perceptual and Motor Skills* 24, 467-472.

Dyk, R. B. (1969). "An Exploratory Study of Mother-Child Interaction in Infancy as Related to the Development of Differentiation." *Journal of the American Academy of Child Psychiatry* 8, 657-691.

Dyk, R. B., and Witkin, H. A. (1965). "Family Experiences Related to the Development of Differentiation in Children." *Child Development* 30, 21-55.

Ebenholtz, S. M., and Benzschawel, T. L. (1977). "The Rod and Frame Effect and Induced Head Tilt as a Function of Observation Distance."*Perception and Psychophysics* 22, 491-496.

Ekstrom, R. B. (1976). "Teacher Aptitudes, Knowledge Attitudes, and Cognitive Style as Predictions of Teacher Behavior." *Journal of Teacher Education* 27 (4), 329-331.

Elkind, D. (1967). "Egocentrism in Adolescence." *Child Development* 38, 1025-1034.

Eron, L. (1980). "Prescription for Reeducation of Aggression." *American Psychologist* 35, 244-252.

Escalona, S. K. (1968). *The Roots of Individuality: Normal Patterns of Development in Infancy*. Chicago: Aldine.

Eska, B., and Black, K. N. (1971). "Conceptual Tempo in Young Grade School Children." *Child Development* 42, 505-516.

Farham-Diggory, S., and Gregg, L. W. (1975). "Color, Form, and Function as Dimensions of Natural Classification: Developmental Changes in Eye Movements, Reaction Time, and Response Strategies." *Child Development* 46, 101-114.

Farley, F. H. (1974). "Field Dependence and Approval Motivation." *Journal of General Psychology* 91, 153-154.

Feffer, M. (1959). "The Cognitive Implications of Role-Taking Behavior." *Journal of Personality* 27, 152-168.

Feldman, A., and Acredola, L. (1979). "The Effect of Active Versus Passive Exploration on Memory for Spatial Location in Children." *Child Development* 50, 698-704.

Field, D. (1981). "Can Preschool Children Really Learn to Conserve?" *Child Development* 52, 326-334.

Field, T., and Fogel, A. (1982). *Emotions and Early Interaction.* Hillsdale, NJ: Erlbaum.

Finley, G. E., and Solla, J. (1975). "Birth Order and Field Dependence-Independence: A Failure to Replicate." *Journal of Genetic Psychology* 126, 305-306.

Fischer, K. W. (1981). "Cognitive Development." *New Directions for Child Development* (12), San Francisco: Josey-Bass.

Franzen, J. (1996). "Perchance to Dream." *Harper's Magazine* (April), 35-54.

Fuqua, R. W., Bartsch, T. W., and Phye, G. D. (1975). "An Investigation of the Relationship Between Cognitive Tempo and Creativity in Pre-School-Age Children." *Child Development* 46, 779-782.

Furstenberg, E. F. (1985). "Sociological Ventures In Child Development." *Child Development* 56, 281-288.

Gaines, R. W. (1975). "Developmental Perception and Cognitive Styles: From Young Children to Master Artists." *Perceptual and Motor Skills* 40, 983-998.

Gardner, R. W., Holzman, P. S., Klein, G. S., Linton, H. B., and Spence, D. P. (1959). "Cognitive Control: A Study of Individual Consistencies in Cognitive Behavior." *Psychological Issues* 1, (Monograph 4).

Gibson, J. J., and Gibson, E. J. (1955). "Perceptual Learning: Differentiation or Enrichment?" *Psychological Review* 62, 32-41.

Gillies, J., and Bauer, R. (1971). "Cognitive Style and Perception of Success and Failure." *Perceptual and Motor Skills* 33, 839-842.

Giroux, H. A. (1996). "Hollywood, Race, and the Demonization of Youth: The Kids Are Not Allright." *Educational Researcher* 25 (2), 31-35.

Goldstein, A. G., and Chance, J. E. (1965). "Effects of Practice on Sex-Related Differences in Performance on Embedded Figures." *Psycho-*

nomic Science 3, 361-362.

Goodenough, D. R. (1976). "The Role of Individual Differences in Field Dependence as a Factor in Learning and Memory." *Psychological Bulletin* 83, 675-694.

Greene, L. R. (1979). "Psychological Differentiation and Social Structure." *Journal of Social Psychology* 109, 79-85.

Greenleaf, P. (1978). *Children Through the Ages: A History of Childhood.* New York: Barnes & Noble.

Grieve, T. D., and Davis, J. K. (1971). "The Relationship of Cognitive Style and Method of Instruction to Performance in Ninth Grade Geography." *Journal of Educational Research* 65 (3), 137-141.

Guardo, C., and Bohan, J. B. (1971). "The Development of a Sense of Self-Identity in Children." *Child Development* 1909-1921.

Haronian, F., and Sugerman, A. A. (1967). "Fixed and Mobile Field Independence: Review of Studies Relevant to Werner's Dimension." *Psychological Reports* 21, 41-57.

Harrison, A., and Nadelman, L. (1972). "Conceptual Tempo and Inhibition of Movement in Black Preschool Children." *Child Development* 43, 657-668.

Hartlage, L. C. (1970). "Sex-Linked Inheritance of Spatial Ability." *Perceptual and Motor Skills* 31, 610.

Hess, R. D., and Shipman, V. C. (1965). "Early Experience and the Socialization of Cognitive Modes in Children." *Child Development* 36, 869-886.

Hoppe, C. M., Kagan, S. M., and Zahn, G. L. (1977). "Conflict Resolution Among Field-Independent and Field-Dependent Anglo-American and Mexican-American Children and Their Mothers." *Developmental Psychology* 13, 591-598.

Hucvka, M. W. (1974). "Introversion-Extraversion and Imagery." *Psychological Reports* 34, 453-454.

Hyman, P. K., Goodenough, D. R., and Witkin, H. A. (1975). "Psychological Differentiation as a Factor in Conflict Resolution." *Journal of Personality and Social Psychology* 32 (4), 730-736.

Inhelder, B., and Piaget, J. (1958). *The Growth of Logical Thinking From Childhood to Adolescence.* New York: Basic Books.

Jones-Wilson, F. C., Asbury, C. A., Okazawa-Rey, M., Anderson, D. K., Jacobs, M. S., and Fultz, M. (1996). *Encyclopedia of African-American Education.* Westport, CT: Greenwood Press.

Joughin, G. (1992). "Cognitive Style and Adult Learning Principles." *International Journal of Lifelong Learning* 1(1), 3-14.

Kagan, J. (1965). "Individual Differences in the Resolution of Response Uncertainty." *Journal of Personality and Social Psychology* 2, 154-160.

Kagan, J. (1966). "Developmental Studies of Reflection and Analysis." In A. H. Kidd and J. L. Rivoire, eds., *Perceptual Development in*

Children. New York: International Universities Press.

Kagan, J., and Kogan, N. (1970). "Individual Variation in Cognitive Processes." In P. Mussen, ed., *Carmichael's Manual of Child Psychology.* Vol. 1. New York: Wiley.

Kagan, J., and Messer, S. G. (1975). "A Reply to Some Misgivings About the Matching Familiar Figures Test as a Measure of Reflection Impulsivity." *Developmental Psychology* 11, 2445-2448.

Kagan, J., Moss, H. A., and Sigel, I. E. (1963). "Psychological Significance of Styles and Conceptualization." In J. C. Wright and J. Kagan, eds., *Basic Cognitive Processes in Children.* Monographs of the Society for Research in Child Development 28, (2, Serial No. 86), 73-112.

Kagan, J., Rosman, B. L., Day, D., Albert, J., and Phillips, W. (1964). "Information Processing in the Child: Significance of Analytic and Reflective Attitudes." *Psychological Monographs* 78 (1, Whole No. 578).

Kagan, S. (1974). "Field Dependence and Conformity of Rural Mexican and Urban Anglo-American Children." *Child Development* 45, 765-771.

Kagan, S., and Zahn, G. L. (1975). "Field Dependence and the School Achievement Gap Between Anglo-American and Mexican-American Children." *Journal of Educational Psychology* 67, 643-650.

Kagan, S., Zahn, G. L., and Gealy, J. (1977). "Competition and School Achievement Among Anglo-American Children." *Journal of Educational Psychology* 69, 432-441.

Kane, M., and Kane, D. (1990). "Right or Left: Which is the Right Cognitive Style for Quality Teaching?" *American Secondary Education* 18 (3), 12-16.

Karp, S. A., and Konstadt, N. L. (1963). *Manual for the Children's Embedded Figures Test.* Brooklyn: Cognitive Tests.

Karp, S. A., Kissing, B., and Husrmyer, F. E. (1970). "Field Dependence as a Predictor of Alcoholic Therapy Dropouts." *Journal of Nervous and Mental Disease* 15, 433-442.

Katz, J. M. (1971). "Reflection-Impulsivity and Color-Form Sorting." *Child Development* 42, 745-754.

Katz, J. M. (1972). "Cognitive Tempo and Discrimination Skill on Color-Form Sorting Tasks." *Perceptual and Motor Skills* 35, 359-362.

Kennedy, K., and Kates, S. L. (1964). "Conceptual Sorting and Personality Adjustment in Children." *Journal of Abnormal and Social Psychology* 68, 211-214.

Klein, G. S. (1970). *Perception, Motives, and Personality.* New York: Knopf.

Klein, G. S., and Schlesinger, H. J. (1949). "Where is the Perceiver in Perceptual Theory?" *Journal of Personality* 18, 32-47.

Klepper, I. L. (1969). "Induction of Field-Dependence Changes by

Body Attention Procedures." *Perceptual and Motor Skills* 29, 139-145.

Kogan, N. (1971). "Educational Implications of Cognitive Styles." In G. S. Lesser, ed., *Psychology and Educational Practice.* Glenview, IL: Scott, Foresman.

Kogan, N. (1973). "Creativity and Cognitive Style: A Life Span Perspective." In P. Baltes and K. W. Schaie, eds., *Life Span Developmental Psychology: Personality and Socialization.* New York: Academic Press.

Kogan, N. (1976). "Sex Differences in Creativity and Cognitive Styles." In S. Messick, ed., *Individuality in Learning: Cognitive Styles and Creativity for Human Development."* San Francisco: Jossey-Bass.

Kolodany, A. (1991). "Colleges Must Recognize Students' Cognitive Styles." *The Chronicle of Higher Education* (Feb.) 6.

Konstadt, N., and Forman, E. (1965). "Field Dependence and External Directedness." *Journal of Personality and Social Psychology* 1, 490-493.

Krippner, S., and Brown, D. P. (1973). "Field Independence/Dependence and Electrosone 50 Induced States of Consciousness." *Journal of Clinical Psychology* 29, 316-319.

Lee, L. C., Kagan, J., and Rabson, A. (1963). "The Influence of Preference for Analytic Categorization Upon Concept Acquisition." *Child Development* 35, 433-442.

Lefever, M. M., and Ehri, L. C. (1976). "The Relationship Between Field Independence and Science Disambiguation Ability." *Journal of Psycholinguistic Research* 5, 99-106.

Leithwood, K. A., and Fowler, W. (1971). "Complex Motor Learning in Four-Year-Olds." *Child Development* 42, 781-792.

Lesser, G. S. (1971). *Psychology and Educational Practice.* Glenview, IL: Scott Foresman & Company.

Lewis, M., Rausch, M., Goldberg, S., and Dodd, C. (1968). "Error, Response Time, and IQ: Sex Differences in the Cognitive Style of Preschool Children." *Perceptual and Motor Skills* 26, 563-568.

Lynn, D. B. (1969). "Curvilinear Relation Between Cognitive Functioning and Distance of Child From Parent of the Same Sex." *Psychological Review* 76, 236-240.

Maccoby, E. E. (1966). "Sex Differences in Intellectual Functioning." In E. E. Maccoby, ed., *The Development of Sex Differences.* Stanford, CA: Stanford University Press.

Maccoby, E. E., and Jacklin, C. N. (1974). *The Psychology of Sex Differences.* Stanford, CA: Stanford University Press.

MacEachron, A. E., and Gruenfeld, L. W. (1978). "The Effects of Family Authority Structure and Socioeconomic Status on Field Independence." *Journal of Social Psychology* 104, 49-56.

Massari, D., and Massari, J. A. (1973). "Sex Differences in the Relationship of Cognitive Style and Intellectual Functioning in Disadvantaged Preschool Children." *Journal of Genetic Psychology* 122, 175-181.

McLaren, P. (1993). *Schooling as a Ritual Performance: Towards a Political Economy of Education Symbols & Gestures.* New York: Routledge.

Meichenbaum, D. H., and Goodman, J. (1969). "Reflection-Impulsivity and Verbal Control of Motor Behavior." *Child Development* 40, 785-797.

Messer, S. (1970). "The Effect of Anxiety Over Intellectual Performance on Reflection-Impulsivity in Children." *Child Development* 41, 723-735.

Messick, S., and Damarin, F. (1964). "Cognitive Styles and Memory for Faces." *Journal of Abnormal and Social Psychology* 69, 313-318.

Messick, S., and Kogan, N. (1963). "Differentiation and Compartmentalization in Object Sorting Measures of Categorizing Styles." *Perceptual and Motor Skills* 16, 47-51.

Messick, S., and Kogan, N. (1965). "Category Width and Quantitative Aptitude."*Perceptual and Motor Skills* 20, 493-497.

Miller, A. (1987). "Cognitive Styles: An Integrated Model." *Educational Psychology* 7, 251-268.

Munroe, R. H., and Munroe, R. L. (1971). "Effect of Environmental Experience on Spatial Ability in an East African Society." *Journal of Social Psychology* 83, 15-22.

Nedd, A. N. B., and Gruenfeld, L. W. (1976). "Field Dependence-Independence and Social Traditionalism: A Comparison of Ethnic Subcultures of Trinidad." *International Journal of Psychology* 11, 23-41.

Nedd, A. N. B., and Schwartz, H. (1977). "A Cross-Cultural Investigation of the Relative Importance of Child Rearing and Socioeconomic Antecedents of Field-Dependence-Independence." *Journal of Psychology* 96, 63-70.

Nelson, K. (1973). "Structure and Strategy in Learning to Talk." *Monographs of the Society for Research in Child Development* 38, (1-2, Serial No. 149).

Nerlove, S. B., Munroe, R. H., and Munroe, R. L. (1971). "Effect of Environmental Experience on Spatial Ability: A Replication." *Journal of Social Psychology* 84, 3-10.

Nurmi, J. E., Onatsu, T., and Haavisto, T. (1995). "Underachievers' Cognitive and Behavioral Strategies-Self Handicapping at School." *Contemporary Educational Psychology* 20, 188-200.

Odom, R. D., McIntyre, C. W., and Neale, G. S. (1971). "The Influence of Cognitive Style on Perceptual Learning." *Child Development* 42, 883-891.

Ohnmacht, F. W. (1967). "Factorial Invariance of the Teacher Characteristics Schedule and Measure of Two Cognitive Styles." *Journal of Psychology* 69, 193-199.

Okonji, M. O., and Olagbaiye, O. O. (1975). "Field Dependence and the Coordination of Perspectives." *Developmental Psychology* 11, 520.

Olesker, W. (1978). "Cognition and the Separation-Individuation Process: A Study of Three Boys at Nursery School." *Psychoanalysis and Contemporary Thought* 1, 237-268.

Oltman, P. K. (1968). "A Portable Rod-&-Frame Apparatus." *Perceptual and Motor Skills* 26, 503-506.

Parente, J. A., and O'Malley, J. J. (1975). "Training in Musical Rhythm and Field Dependence of Children." *Perceptual and Motor Skills* 40, 392-394.

Piaget, J. (1950). *The Psychology of Intelligence.* New York: Harcourt Brace.

Piaget, J. (1952). *The Language and Thought of the Child.* London: Routledge and Kegan Paul.

Piaget, J. (1953). *Logic and Psychology.* New York: Basic Books.

Piaget, J. (1954). *The Construction of Reality in the Child.* New York: Basic Books.

Piaget, J. (1969). *The Mechanisms of Perception.* New York: Basic Books.

Powers, J. E., and Lis, D. J. (1977). "Field Dependence-Independence and Performance With the Passive Transformation." *Perceptual and Motor Skills* 45, 759-765.

Ramirez, M., and Price-Williams, D. (1974). "Cognitive Styles in Children: Two Mexican Communities." *Interamerican Journal of Psychology* 8, 93-101.

Ramirez, M., and Price-Williams, D. (1974). "Cognitive Styles of Children of Three Ethnic Groups in the United States." *Journal of Cross-Cultural Psychology* 5, 212-219.

Reali, N., and Hall, V. (1970). "Effect of Success and Failure on the Reflective and Impulsive Child." *Developmental Psychology* 3, 402.

Riding, R. J., and Cheema, I. (1991). "Cognitive Styles—An Overview and Integration." *Educational Psychology* 11, 193-215.

Rokeach, M. (1960). *The Open and Closed Mind.* New York: Basic Books.

Roodin, P. A., Broughton, A., and Vaught, G. M. (1974). "Effects of Birth Order, Sex, and Family Size on Field Dependence and Locus of Control." *Perceptual and Motor Skills* 39, 671-676.

Russakoff, L. M., Fontana, A. F., Dowds, B. N., and Harris, M. (1976). "Psychological Differentiation and Psychotherapy." *Journal of Nervous and Mental Disease* 163, 329-333.

Salome, R. A., and Reeves, D. (1972). "Two Pilot Investigations of Perceptual Training of Four-and Five-Year-Old Kindergarten Children." *Studies in Art Education 13*, 3-10.

Salt, E. (1971). *The Cognitive Bases of Human Learning.* Homewood, IL: Dorsey.

Sanders, M., Scholz, J. P., and Kagan, S. (1976). "Three Social Motives and Field Independence-Dependence in Anglo American and Mexican American Children." *Journal of Cross-Cultural Psychology* 7, 451-462.

Santostefano, S. G. (1964). "A Developmental Study of the Cognitive Control Leveling-Sharpening." *Merrill-Palmer Quarterly* 10, 343-360.

Saracho, O. N. (1983). "Relationship Between Cognitive Style and Teachers' Perceptions of Young Children's Academic Competence." *Journal of Experimental Education* 51 (4), 184-189.

Saracho, O. N., and Dayton, C. M. (1980). "Relationship of Teachers' Cognitive Styles to Pupils' Academic Achievement Gains." *Journal of Educational Psychology* 72 (4), 544-549.

Schleifer, M., and Douglas, V. I. (1973). "Moral Judgments, Behavior, and Cognitive Style in Young Children." *Canadian Journal of Behavioral Science* 5, 133-144.

Shipman, S., and Shipman, V. C. (1985). "Cognitive Styles: Some Conceptual, Methodological, and Applied Issues." In E. W. Gordon, ed., *Review of Research in Education,* 229-291. Washington, DC: American Educational Research Association.

Siegler, R. S. (1978). *Children's Thinking: What Develops?* Hillsdale, NJ: Erlbaum.

Sigel, I. E., and Olmsted, P. (1970). "Modification of Cognitive Skills Among Lower-Class Black Children." In J. Hellmuth, ed., *The Disadvantaged Child,* Vol. 3. New York: Brunner-Mazel.

Signell, K. A. (1966). "Cognitive Complexity in Person Perception and Nation Perception: A Developmental Approach." *Journal of Personality* 34, 517-537.

Singer, S. S., and Weller, L. "Classification Patterns of Underprivileged Children in Israel." *Child Development* 42, 581-594.

Solar, D., Davenport, G., and Bruehl, D. (1969). "Social Compliance as a Function of Field Dependence." *Perceptual and Motor Skills* 29, 299-306.

Stafford, R. E. (1961). "Sex Differences in Spatial Visualization as Evidence of Sex-Linked Inheritance." *Perceptual and Motor Skills* 13, 428.

Stanes, D. (1973). "Analytic Responses to Conceptual Style Test as a Function of Instructions." *Child Development* 44, 389-391.

Stanes, D., and Gordon, A. (1973). "Relationships Between Conceptual Style Test and Children's Embedded Figures Test." *Journal of Per-*

sonality 41, 185-191.

Stone, M. K. (1976). "The Role of Cognitive Style in Teaching and Learning." *Journal of Teacher Education* 27, 332-334.

Taylor, L. J., and Skanes, G. R. (1976). "Cognitive Abilities in Inuit and White Children From Similar Environments." *Canadian Journal of Behavioral Science* 8, 1-8.

Templeton, W. B. (1973). "The Role of Gravitational Cues in the Judgment of Visual Orientation." *Perception and Psychophysics* 14, 451-457.

Thurstone, L. L. (1944). *A Factorial Study of Perception.* Chicago: University of Chicago Press.

Tobacyk, J. J., Broughton, A., and Vaught, G. M. (1975). "The Effects of Congruence-Incongruence Between Locus of Control and Field Dependence on Personality Functioning." *Journal of Consulting and Clinical Psychology* 43, 81-85.

Tyler, L. E. (1965). *The Psychology of Human Differences.* 3rd ed., New York: Appleton-Century-Crofts.

Van Leeuwen, M. S. (1978). "A Cross-Cultural Examination of Psychological Differentiation in Males and Females." *International Journal of Psychology* 13, 87-122.

Vaught, G. M., Pittman, M. D., and Roodin, P. A. (1975). "Developmental Curves for the Portable Rod-and-Frame Test." *Bulletin of the Psychonomic Society* 5, 151-152.

Vernon, P. E. (1965). "Ability Factors and Environmental Influences." *American Psychologist* 20, 723-733.

Vernon, P. E. (1972). "The Distinctiveness of Field Independence." *Journal of Personality* 40, 366-391.

Vernon, P. E. (1973). "Multivariate Approaches to the Study of Cognitive Styles." In J. R. Royce, ed., *Multivariate Analysis and Psychological Theory.* New York: Academic Press.

Waber, D. P. (1976). "Sex Differences in Cognition: A Function of Maturation Rate?" *Science* 192, 572-574.

Waber, D. P. (1977). "Biological Substrates of Field Dependence: Implications of the Sex Difference." *Psychological Bulletin* 84, 1076-1087.

Waber, D. P. (1977). "Sex Differences in Mental Abilities, Hemispheric Lateralization and Rate of Physical Growth at Adolescence." *Developmental Psychology* 13, 29-38.

Wachtel, P. L. (1968). "Style and Capacity in Analytic Functioning." *Journal of Personality* 36, 202-212.

Wachtel, P. L. (1972). "Field Dependence and Psychological Differentiation: Reexamination." *Perceptual and Motor Skills* 35, 179-189.

Wallach, M. A., and Kogan, N. (1965). *Modes of Thinking in Young Children.* New York: Holt, Rinehart and Winston.

Ward, W. C. (1968). "Reflection-Impulsivity in Kindergarten Children." *Child Development* 39, 867-874.

Weiner, M. (1955). "The Effects of Differently Structured Visual Fields on the Perception of Verticality." *American Journal of Psychology* 68, 291-293.

Weisz, J. R., O'Neill, P., and O'Neill, P. C. (1975). "Field Dependence-Independence on the Children's Embedded Figures Test: Cognitive Style or Cognitive Level?" *Developmental Psychology* 11, 539-540.

Weller, L., and Sharan, S. (1971). "Articulation of the Body Concept Among First-Grade Israeli Children." *Child Development* 42, 1553 - 1559.

Wendt, R. A., and Burwell, E. (1964). "Test Performance of Jewish Day-School-Students." *Journal of Genetic Psychology* 105, 99-103.

Werner, E. (1979). *Cross-Cultural Child Development.* Monteray, CA: Brooks-Cole.

Wertheimer, M. (1945). *Productive Thinking.* New York: Harper.

Whorf, B. (1956). *Language, Thought and Reality.* New York: Wiley.

Whiting, B. B., and Whiting, J. W. M. (1975). *Children of Six Cultures: A Psychological Analysis.* Cambridge, MA: Harvard University Press.

Willemsen, E., Buchholz, A., Budrow, M. S., and Geannacopulos, N. (1973). "Relationship Between Witkin's Rod-and-Frame Task and Piaget's Waterline Task for College Women." *Perceptual and Motor Skills* 36, 958.

Wilson, E. (1975). *Sociobiology.* New York: Wiley.

Wilson, R. S., and Harping, E. B. (1972). "Mental and Motor Development in Infant Twins." *Developmental Psychology* 7, 277-287.

Witkin, H. A. (1964). "Origins of Cognitive Style." In C. Scheerer, ed., *Cognition: Theory, Research, Promise,* 172-205. New York: Harper and Row.

Witkin, H. A. (1965). "Psychological Differentiation and Forms of Pathology." *Journal of Abnormal Psychology* 70, 317-336.

Witkin, H. A. (1973). *The Role of Cognitive Style in Academic Performance and in Teacher-Student Relations.* (RB-73-11). Princeton, NJ: Educational Testing Service.

Witkin, H. A. (1978). *Cognitive Styles in Personal and Cultural Adaptation. The 1977 Heinz Werner Lectures.* Worcester, MA: Clark University Press.

Witkin, H. A., and Asch, S. E. (1948). "Studies in Space Orientation. III. Perception of the Upright in the Absence of a Visual Field." *Journal of Experimental Psychology* 38, 603-614.

Witkin, H. A., and Asch, S. E. (1948). "Studies in Space Orientation IV. Further Experiments on Perception of the Upright With Displaced Visual Fields." *Journal of Experimental Psychology* 38, 762-782.

Witkin, H. A., and Berry, J. W. (1975). "Psychological Differentiation in Cross-Cultural Perspective." *Journal of Cross-Cultural Psychology* 6, 4-87.

Witkin, H. A., Dyk, R. B., Faterson, H. F., Goodenough, D. R., and Karp, S. A. (1962). *Psychological Differentiation.* New York: Wiley.

Witkin, H. A., and Goodenough, D. R. (1977). "Field Dependence and Interpersonal Behavior." *Psychological Bulletin* 84, 661-689.

Witkin, H. A., Goodenough, D. R., and Karp, S. A. (1967). "Stability of Cognitive Style From Childhood to Young Adulthood." *Journal of Personality and Social Psychology* 7, 291-300.

Witkin, H. A., Lewis, H. B., Hertzman, M., Machover, K., Meissner, P. B., and Wapner, S. (1954). *Personality Through Perception.* New York: Harper. (Reprinted: Westport, CT: Greenwood Press, 1972.)

Witkin, H. A., Moore, C. A., Goodenough, D. R., and Cox, P. W. (1977). "Field-Dependent and Field-Independent Cognitive Styles and Their Educational Implications." *Review of Educational Research* 47, 1-64.

Witkin, H. A., Moore, C. A., Oltman, P. K., Goodenough, D. R., Friedman, F., Owen, D., and Raskin, E. (1977). "The Role of the Field-Dependent and Field-Independent Cognitive Styles in Academic Evolution: A Longitudinal Study." *Journal of Educational Psychology* 69, 197-211.

Witkin, H. A., Oltman, P. K., Raskin, E., and Karp, S. A. (1971). *A Manual for the Children's Embedded Figures Test.* Palo Alto, CA: Consulting Psychologists Press.

Witkin, H. A., Price-Williams, D., Bertini, M., Christiansen, B., Oltman, P. K., Ramirez, M., and Van Meel, J. (1974). "Social Conformity and Psychological Differentiation." *International Journal of Psychology* 9, 11-29.

Wolitzky, D. L. (1973). "Cognitive Controls and Person Perception." *Perceptual and Motor Skills* 36, 619-623.

Wright, J. C. (1972). *Technical Report on the Kansas Reflection-Impulsivity Scale for Preschoolers (KRISP).* Lawrence, KS: Kansas Center for Research in Early Childhood Education.

Yando, R. M., and Kagan, J. (1970). "The Effect of Task Complexity on Reflection-Impulsivity." *Cognitive Psychology* 1, 192-200.

Yussen, S. R., and Berman, L. (1981). "Memory Predictions for Recall and Recognition in First, Third, and Fifth Grade Children." *Developmental Psychology* 17, 224-229.

Zabrucky, K., and Ratner, H. H. (1986). "Children's Comprehension Monitoring and Recall of Inconsistent Stories." *Child Development* 57, 1401-1418.

Zajonic, R. B., and Marcus, G. B. (1975). "Birth Order and Intellectual Development." *Psychological Review* 82, 74-78.

Zelniker, T., Jeffrey, W. E., Ault, R., and Parsons, J. (1972). "Analysis and Modification of Search Strategies of Impulsive and Reflective Children on the Matching Familiar Figures Tests." *Child Development* 43, 321-335.

Zigler, E., and Butterfield, E. C. (1968). "Motivational Aspects of Changes in IQ Test Performance of Culturally Deprived Nursery School Children." *Child Development* 39, 1-14.

Index

About the Author

HARRY MORGAN is Professor of Early Childhood Education at The State University of West Georgia in Carrollton. He is the author of *Historical Perspectives on the Education of Black Children* (Praeger, 1995).

ISBN 0-275-95684-9

90000>

EAN

9 780275 956844

HARDCOVER BAR CODE